Psychological concepts
in the classroom

Psychological concepts

in the classroom

RICHARD H. COOP
KINNARD WHITE

The University of North Carolina at Chapel Hill

HARPER & ROW, Publishers

New York, Evanston, San Francisco, London

14148

Sponsoring Editor: Lane Akers
Project Editor: Alice M. Solomon
Designer: Frances Torbert Tilley
Production Supervisor: Valerie Klima

We gratefully acknowledge the use of material from the following sources: Pages 30–31: Quote from Amitai Etzioni, *A Comparative Analysis of Complex Organizations* (New York: 1961), p. 10, by permission of Macmillan. Page 34: Quote from Jean Dresden Grambs, "The Neighborhood School Revisited: A Sociological Journey," in James R. Raths and Jean Dresden Grambs (eds.), *Society and Education* (Englewood Cliffs, N.J., 1965), pp. 260–269, by permission of Prentice-Hall. Pages 42–83: Portions of this chapter have been adapted from the chapter "Teacher Expectations," in Thomas L. Good and Jere E. Brophy, *Looking in Classrooms* (New York, 1972), by permission of Harper & Row and the authors. Pages 84–118: Barbara H. Wasik expresses her thanks to Jay Birnbrauer and Chris Ferguson, who responded to many successive approximations of this chapter; to Frieda F. Brown, Jeanne Mason, and Kathy Perkerson; and to the many teachers in North Carolina who have worked with her over the past five years. Pages 134–135: Quote from V. C. Crandall, et al., "Children's Beliefs in Their Own Control of Reinforcement in Intellectual–Academic Achievement Situations," *Child Development*, 33 (1965), pp. 91–109, by permission of the Society for Research in Child Development and V. C. Crandall. Pages 139: Quote from P. Gurin, et al., "Internal-External Control in the Motivational Dynamics of Negro Youth," *Journal of Social Issues*, 25 (1969), pp. 29–53, by permission of the Society for the Psychological Study of Social Issues. Pages 160, 161–162, and 168: Table "Principle–Instructional Guide" (pp. 328–329), Excerpt "Intermediate School Children ... coldlands" ... "To get students ... existing interests" (pp. 330–331) from *Learning and Human Abilities*, 3rd edition, by Herbert J. Klausmeier and Richard E. Ripple. Copyright © 1971 by Herbert J. Klausmeier and Richard E. Ripple. By permission of Harper & Row, Publishers, Inc. Pages 233, 236, 240, 242, 243, and 245: Figures 8-3–8-8 reprinted by permission of Mary N. Meeker. Page 252: Figure 9-1 reprinted by permission of Irving E. Sigel. Page 254: Figure 9-2 reprinted by permission of Herman A. Witkin.

Psychological Concepts in the Classroom

Library of Congress Cataloging in Publication Data

Coop, Richard H
    Psychological concepts in the classroom.
    Includes bibliographical references.
    1. Educational psychology—Addresses, essays, lectures. I. White, Kinnard, joint author. II. Title.
LB1055.C65   370.15   73-13298
ISBN 0-06-041347-6

TO OUR PARENTS

Mr. and Mrs. Paul Coop

Mr. and Mrs. Paul White

and

TO OUR FAMILIES

Sharon, Kristy, and Kelli

Joan, Kimberly, Doug, Eric, and Jonathan

Contents

Preface

format derived from variety of teaching experiences

This is a book born of frustration. The editors of this volume have taught undergraduate educational psychology in four different universities during the past nine years. These schools have ranged from the so-called emerging state universities with their teachers college heritage to the large universities. In each instance we were frustrated in our search for textbooks or books of readings in educational psychology that validly presented the content area at a level of sophistication appropriate to our students.

The textbooks frequently told our students more than they wanted to know about certain topics (we suspect these were the topics in which the textbook authors did their own research) and skimmed over other areas. Additionally, the textbooks frequently presented the material in such a fashion that it was difficult for our students to integrate it into their own educational backgrounds or apply it to the teaching or student-teaching situations they were experiencing in the real world of public schools.

Books of readings were somewhat better in that the authors of the articles were writing in their own area of specialization, but most of these articles were taken directly from the research journals in which they first appeared and were not edited for the introductory student. Since writers who wish to publish articles in scholarly journals must write for their colleagues (the editors and referees who determine which articles are chosen for publication), rarely are these articles, in their original form, appropriate for undergraduate readers. We also found that most books of readings lacked a unifying theme that provided the reader with a sense of continuity as he progressed from article to article.

written by con-
tent specialists
expressly for
introductory
students

It is our belief that this frustration has given rise to a unique book. First, this book is unique in that each chapter was written expressly for the introductory educational psychology student by a recognized teacher–researcher who specializes in the area of content presented in the chapter. This feature of the book makes it unlike the books of readings that were written for the authors' colleagues. At the same time, however, we were able to avoid the problems of the traditional textbooks that depend on the knowledge of one or two persons to adequately present the broad field of educational psychology.

organized around
scenarios and
case studies

contains
field-related
activities

adaptable to
competency-based
curriculum

Second, by organizing the chapters of this book around a set of scenarios that describe three broad types of schools in American society and six case studies of students from these schools, we have provided a framework for applying psychological concepts to life in classrooms. This organizational framework, together with the suggested field-related activities included at the end of each chapter, provides continuity for the different chapters and also permits the instructor to easily adapt the materials to a competency-based teacher education curriculum.

We would like to express our appreciation to one of our colleagues, Dr. Gary B. Stuck, for his valuable counsel throughout the development of this book and to Carla Shuford and Zena Harvley for their contributions as typist and proofreader, respectively. We also owe a special note of gratitude to Lane Akers, our editor, who alternately pushed and pulled us through our first experiences as editors.

Richard H. Coop
Kinnard White

1 · Psychological concepts in the classroom: An introduction

RICHARD H. COOP
KINNARD WHITE
University of North Carolina at Chapel Hill

You are about to read a unique book in educational psychology. This book incorporates the expertise of a textbook with the topical relevance of a book of readings; yet it is neither of these. This is a book of original essays written especially for you, the classroom teacher or teacher-to-be. Each essay is about a topic in educational psychology judged to be particularly important to the ongoing operation of the classroom.

As you read the essays in this book, you will learn about some of the most recent and important principles and concepts in educational psychology. At the same time you will be shown how you can apply these principles and concepts to increase your understanding of actual classroom operation and your ability to deal effectively with the events that you will face in the classroom. The writers of each essay describe the principles and concepts on which the topic is based and then demonstrate for you how these principles and concepts can be applied to actual classroom situations. Of course, you should be able to think of other ways to apply these principles and concepts to the particular situations in which you find yourself. Certainly, as a result of reading and studying these essays, you should be able to analyze teaching situations and to suggest courses of action that will make you a more competent teacher.

This book is also unique in that we have developed three scenarios, built around representative schools in different community settings, to illustrate the application of the principles and concepts discussed in each of the essays. Each writer, after describing the fundamental concepts on which the topic of his essay is based, discusses the present state of affairs within that particular area and uses these three scenarios to make specific applications to classroom situations. To do this, the writers engaged in what has been called left-handedness in their thinking about the principles and concepts (Bruner, 1966). That is, they generated creative hypotheses and suggested the implications of these hypotheses for classroom practice—implications that are only tentatively suggested by available research evidence. Consequently, many of the writers' suggested applications are based on expert opinion and are not directly tied to the results of specific research studies.

By asking each author to analyze a common set of scenarios from his or her specific area of expertness, we hope to enable you to see more clearly how the same educational situation can be viewed from many different perspectives. We believe that this approach can increase your understanding of, and hopefully your ability to deal effectively with, classroom events.

Finally, the writers of each essay have provided some guidelines to help you learn and apply the content of each chapter. At the beginning of each chapter, the writers have listed the concepts that they consider the most important ones for you to concentrate on while reading and studying their chapter. These are the major content areas you should remember and apply when you engage in the act of teaching. After each chapter the writers have suggested some activities for you to perform that involve the principles and concepts presented in the chapter. These activities should increase your understanding of the teaching–learning process and help you to analyze this process from a number of different frames of reference. These analytic skills should, in turn, increase your effectiveness as a teacher.

At this time we would like to introduce you to the three scenarios and the case studies of selected students that will be used throughout the book. Before you proceed to the essays, you should become thoroughly familiar with these scenarios and case studies. Even after you have become thoroughly familiar with them, you will probably find it necessary to refer to them for certain details during the course of reading the different essays.

The scenarios are designed to capture the essence of three representative types of schools and communities in America today. Although fictitious, the three illustrative scenarios represent very real schools. Probably, you went to a school very much like one of them.

From each of the three schools, two students, also fictitious but real, are focused on for closer study. The case studies of these six students contain information similar to what you might find in the pupils' cumulative records or to what you might learn from conversations with teachers in the schools. Hopefully, as you read and reread these scenarios and the personal profiles that accompany them, the schools, the teachers, and the students will become very real to you. It is most probable that you will teach, or have already taught, students who are like those described in these case studies and attend schools like those described in these scenarios. Also, it is very likely that you will have, or already have had, colleagues like the teachers described in the scenarios.

The first scenario, Knightcrest Middle School, describes an innovative, comprehensive school in a suburb near a large metropolitan area. The second scenario, Bridges Elementary School, describes an inner-city school in a large industrial city. The third scenario, Midview Elementary School, describes a small-town school in a quasi-rural setting.

KNIGHTCREST MIDDLE SCHOOL

Knightcrest Middle School is an innovative, comprehensive school located in Pine Valley, an affluent bedroom community near a Far West metropolitan area. Students who would ordinarily be in grades six, seven, and eight attend Knightcrest. At Knightcrest, however, there are no sixth, seventh, and eighth grade labels, because this school is based on a continuous progress system for each student. Rather, there are only the general labels of Pluto, Saturn, and Mars, which indicate a flexible home base for particular pupils. A large proportion of each student's day is spent in independent study or "contract" work, with the pupil taking a major responsibility for selecting the subject matter he pursues and the method he uses to pursue it.

The building that houses Knightcrest reflects the philosophy of the school. It is designed with large open spaces that allow the pupils to move easily from one area of the school to another. The media and resource center is the hub of the learning areas. It is designed for the self-directed, flexible, continuous progress educational program that the majority of the faculty, administration, and parents in Pine Valley want.

The community of Pine Valley has long been known throughout the West as a town of great community pride, especially for a commuter's suburb, and as a town with many outstanding examples of modern architecture, both in public buildings and in privately owned homes. The median income in Pine Valley is in the upper 10 percent nationally, and the residents are primarily white Protestants with a sprinkling of Jews plus two Mexican-American families. The median number of years of education completed by family heads in the suburb is 15.5 years. Most of the men in Pine Valley work in the nearby metropolitan area and have executive level positions. A number of physicians and lawyers who live in Pine Valley maintain an office both in the city and in Pine Valley. The parents have high achievement expectations for their children, and one sixth grader (oops, Saturn inhabitant) at Knightcrest was overheard describing Pine Valley as the perfect environment for *The Graduate's* Mrs. Robinson.

Nancy Carter teaches mathematics–science to the Pluto-level students at Knightcrest. To be more precise, Miss Carter is part of the Pluto-level mathematics–science teaching team. Since she just graduated from Redwood State University (formerly Redwood State Teachers College) and has had no previous teaching experience, Nancy's primary duties are aiding the master teacher, Mrs. Holmes, in preparing material for her large-group presentations and in working with small groups of students to clarify any misconceptions that might have arisen during Mrs. Holmes' presentations. Nancy hopes someday to have the theatrical-like skills Mrs. Holmes uses in her large-group presentations but is content for now to work with the small groups and help prepare the learning materials. In fact, Nancy is very happy to have a job in a progressive school like Knightcrest in an affluent suburb such as Pine Valley. Her own educational experiences were much more traditional, and the most affluent people in her small hometown could not afford the life-style of Pine Valley's most modest-living persons. Nancy frequently returns to her hometown to shop for clothes, because she cannot afford the prices at the Pine Valley shops. Although she has taught at Knightcrest for 7 months, Nancy is still very uneasy when she finds herself in a situation that requires her speaking with the parents of her students. She is very much aware of the class distinction between the wealthy parents and the teachers. She not only feels that the parents look down on her, but frequently has the suspicion that many of the students are making derogatory remarks behind her back about her clothes, manner of speech, and lack of culture and sophistication. In a number of instances Nancy has had to restrain herself from trying to get back at these "snobby little rich kids." Nancy has often commented to the other teachers that these students don't know how lucky they are to have the advantages that their wealthy parents have given them. Nancy's statement invariably causes the other teachers to reminisce about how hard they had to work in order to get an education and to talk about how kids get everything on a silver platter.

Although the majority of the students at Knightcrest would be classified as academically talented pupils (verbal IQ range is from 121 to 148), there are certain achievement levels within this relatively homogeneous group. For example, the Pluto group is about one grade level behind the Saturn group in reading skills, and the Saturn-level students are roughly one grade level behind the Mars group in reading skills. The Pluto group is still working on advanced arithmetic; whereas the Saturn-level students are beginning to solve some algebraic equations, and the Mars pupils are working on problems involving plane geometry. Although the Pluto-level students are about 11 years old, the Saturn-level students 12 years, and the Mars students 13 years, there are four 11-year-olds in the Saturn group and three in the Mars group. Also, there are three 13-year-olds in the Pluto group and six in the Saturn group. Much the same pattern is found in the English and social studies groupings as well as in the mathematics–science sections. Two Knightcrest students, Marvin Blake and Linda Grey, are described in more detail in the following case histories.

MARVIN BLAKE

Marvin Blake is an 11-year-old Pluto-level student who has very poor eyesight. He is rather small for his age and is very reluctant to take part in any physical activities at school. He is sometimes teased by the other boys because of his frail physique and the owl-like appearance created by his thick glasses. Marvin's father is a field representative for a large advertising firm, and was graduated from a small, highly selective liberal arts college, which he hopes Marvin will attend. Mr. Blake receives an excellent salary plus commissions, and he is determined that Marvin and his 8-year-old sister, Jane, will have the best opportunities he can afford. Marvin has mentioned to some of the teachers at Knightcrest that his father was very opposed to the family of Mexican-Americans who moved into the house two blocks down the street from the Blake house. Although Mr. Blake perceives himself to be a very liberal person, he is quite concerned that the property value of his home will drop drastically if the neighborhood gets overrun with "wet backs."

Marvin's favorite hobbies are reading and playing the trumpet. He hopes that he will be good enough to play in the marching band when he gets to high school, because the band gets to take long trips and once even got to march in the Tournament of Roses Parade. He would like to join the Forensic Society but is too shy to talk in front of people. Marvin has had some difficulty getting along with his sister, because he feels that his parents give her too much attention and that they frequently ignore him.

Marvin's language IQ is reported to be 128, and his nonlanguage IQ is 122. He ranked at the 74th percentile in Reading Achievement and at the 62nd percentile in Math Achievement. His favorite subjects are English and social studies.

The following comments were taken from Marvin's cumulative record:

Grade	Teacher	Comments
1	Fieldberg	Marvin is a very inquisitive student. He has shown much initiative in class. He does well in most subject areas.
2	Maxwell	Marvin is alert and tries very hard. He sometimes seems overly dependent on the teacher to tell him what to do. He has shown amazing growth in vocabulary this year.
3	Rosewell	Marvin is very impulsive and seems to lack self-restraint. He has good ability, especially in problem-solving areas, but he needs close supervision in completing his work.
4	Cove	Marvin is a very lazy student. He requires constant prodding to get good work out of him. He should be working at a higher level. He seems very restless.
5	Roberts	Mrs. Cove's remarks still remain true of Marvin. He is an extremely likable person with a good disposition and a helpful nature. However, he doesn't always seem to use his abilities.

Note that before Marvin went to Knightcrest, his first 5 school years were spent in a traditional elementary school, which was organized on the traditional grade level plan.

LINDA GREY

Linda Grey is a classmate of Marvin Blake's at the Knightcrest Middle School. She is the youngest daughter of Mr. and Mrs. Dean Grey, who have three daughters and no sons. Mr. Grey is a certified public accountant, who has worked his way up to a very responsible and financially rewarding position with a large firm located in a metropolitan area about 35 minutes from Pine Valley. The Greys have traveled throughout the United States and most of Europe during their vacations. They have made a special point of taking Linda and her two older sisters with them and have always gone out of their way to see historical and educational points of interest.

Linda is a very talented student academically. Her *California Test of Mental Maturity* nonlanguage score is 135, and her language score is 147. She was given the *Stanford-Binet (Form L-M)* in the fourth grade and scored 143. She ranks at the 92nd percentile in Math Achievement and at the 96th percentile in Reading Achievement.

Linda is very interested in politics and hopes someday to become the first woman representative from her district. Many of her teachers find this desire hard to believe, because Linda is so quiet and shy in class. She rarely responds unless called upon but always knows the correct answer. She also tends to deliberate a long time before answering any questions that could have equally correct answers. Rarely is she wrong on these questions, however.

Linda reports that social studies and biology are her favorite subjects in school. She has indicated that if she does not become a politician she might like to go into oceanography.

Linda is a very attractive girl with dark hair and brown eyes. She is more mature in terms of physical development than most of the other girls, who envy her nicely developed figure. She has begun to spend considerable time thinking about boys and discussing them with some of her classmates. She is particularly attracted to two of the ninth grade students, who are classmates of her older sister, and feels that they are much more mature than the silly boys in her age group.

The following comments were taken from Linda Grey's cumulative record:

Grade	Teacher	Comments
1	Green	She is a very attentive student, although she seems very slow and plodding in her work. She rarely talks unless called on.
2	Owens	Linda is a very good student. Extremely quiet but makes outstanding contributions in class when called on. She is a very cooperative student and seems most enthusiastic about learning. Has a wonderful attitude toward school.
3	Parker	An excellent student in all areas. A joy to teach. She does seem somewhat anxious on occasion.
4	Barber	A number one citizen in every way. A good student. Very quiet but makes an outstanding contribution to class. Seems to have a number of friends, despite a somewhat shy personality.
5	Adams	Linda continues to be very quiet. Her overall work is superior. I have noticed that recently she tends to "have the giggles" especially when she is around boys. A few special interest subjects have sparked Linda in class discussion, when generally she is more passive than active (vocally). Her mother says she is opposite at home. I feel that the more encouragement she can get to be more outspoken in class as a normal fifth grader—the better. She will say what she thinks on sticky issues and feels that students have too much homework.

BRIDGES ELEMENTARY SCHOOL

Bridges Elementary School is an inner-city school in a large Eastern seaboard city. The city is a major industrial center that has attracted many blacks and some poor whites from the rural regions of the South who are in search of a better life. Like most urban areas, this city has developed with unskilled migrants moving into the center of the city and the economically more prosperous moving farther and farther from the center of the city. Consequently, people with similar incomes tend to be clustered together with the lowest income groups in the central part of the city. The type of industry located in the city and the lack of skill and experience of those who live in the central area have resulted in chronic unemployment. Operation of assembly line equipment in factories and service work are the most common occupations. Even during times of near full employment, the median family income for residents of the area served by Bridges Elementary School is in the lowest 10 percent nationally. The median number of years of education completed by family heads is 7.2 years.

John Bellamy teaches the sixth grade at Bridges Elementary School. Mr. Bellamy was graduated last spring from the teachers college located in the city, and this is his first year of teaching. He is black, grew up in the same downtown area, and attended public schools similar to Bridges Elementary School during his elementary school years.

Bridges Elementary School is organized so that Mr. Bellamy's sixth grade class receives all of its instruction from him except for art, music, and physical education. He has thirty-one students in his class. Twenty-six are black, three are Puerto Ricans, and two are whites who just last year moved to the city from the southern Appalachians. Mr. Bellamy is the first male teacher the children in this sixth grade have ever had.

Since this is Mr. Bellamy's first year teaching at Bridges Elementary School, he has been quite eager to get to know the children in his class as well as he possibly can. As soon as he was assigned to Bridges School, he began to ask teachers who had taught at this school for some time about their views of the current students at Bridges.

The teachers with whom he talked painted a rather gloomy picture. They described the typical student as inattentive, not interested in learning, and irresponsible. The teachers reported that students rarely had pencils, notebooks, or books ready when needed. Furthermore, the teachers indicated that most of the students would do little schoolwork unless threatened by the teachers. Students were reported to be frequently tardy and hypochondriacal before tests. The teachers also indicated that many students believed they were unjustly picked on by teachers and other school administrators.

During a break at the fall teachers' workshop, held before school began, Mr. Bellamy stated that he found the picture of students at Bridges painted by several teachers hard to believe. Mrs. Cravens, who has taught fifth grade at Bridges for four years, assured Mr. Bellamy that the picture was accurate and pointed to Rick Washington, one of Mr. Bellamy's students, as a typical student. Mr. Bellamy checked out Rick's cumulative folder along with that of another student in his class, Julia Clark. The following case histories describe these two students.

RICK WASHINGTON

Rick Washington is the oldest of five children. There is no father in his home. His mother depends primarily on money from Aid to Dependent Children for support. Over his school years a rather large discrepancy between his ability scores and his achievement in school has developed. On the *Primary Mental Abilities Test* given at the end of the fifth grade, he scored at the 50th percentile in Verbal Meaning, 35th percentile on Spatial Relations, 55th percentile on Number Facility, 40th percentile on Perceptual Speed, and 45th percentile on the total test. On the *Metropolitan Achievement Test* given at the end of the fifth grade, he was at the 5th percentile in Word Knowledge, 3rd percentile in Word Discrimination, 20th in Spelling, and 5th percentile in Reading. His Arithmetic Computation was at the 40th percentile. Rick has never failed a grade, because the school system has a policy of automatic promotion; however, his grades have been the lowest possible.

The following comments were taken directly from Rick Washington's cumulative record:

Grade	Teacher	Comments
1	Strum	Rick is not ready for the first grade. Although he is a physically mature boy, he needs considerably more work on the skills prerequisite to reading.
2	Ballentyne	Rick has little interest in schoolwork. He has poor motivation.
3	Star	Rick is a master of shifting blame for his failures to someone else. He is impulsive and gives snap answers that even he knows are wrong after he has given them.
4	Brown	I believe that Rick is capable of doing schoolwork if he wanted to. He is just not interested in what this school has to offer. I cannot capture or hold his attention.
5	Eddy	Rick has a poor self concept in school but sees himself as king of the hill when he is in the streets. Indeed, he is the most popular boy in the class, which is unfortunate for the teacher, because he is a born troublemaker.

JULIA CLARK

Julia has four brothers, all older than she, and two sisters, both younger than she. Her father drives a delivery truck for a local merchant's delivery firm. He has worked on this job for the past four years. Before that the family lived in the rural South, where her father had worked as a sharecropper. Julia, a black student, attended an all-black first grade in the rural South.

At the end of the fifth grade, Julia obtained the following percentile scores on the *Primary Mental Abilities Test:* Verbal Meaning 40th percentile, Spatial Relations 10th percentile, Number Facility 47th percentile, Perceptual Speed 5th percentile, and total 20th percentile. Her scores on the *Metropolitan Achievement Test* given at the same time were also low. She obtained percentile rank scores of 30th percentile in Word Knowledge, 35th percentile in Word Discrimination, 28th percentile in Spelling, and 18th percentile in Reading. Her Arithmetic Computation grade equivalent score was 20th percentile.

The following comments were taken from Julia Clark's cumulative record:

Grade	Teacher	Comments
1		None available.
2	Harris	Julia seems eager to put it all together. However, she still feels uneasy about living in the big city.
3	Zrinski	Julia is too shy. I don't think we can expect too much from her in schoolwork. Early deprivation on the farm has caused irreparable damage.
4	Drake	Julia does beautiful artwork. I believe she could make a contribution in this area if she but had some training. I recommend that special provision be made for her to pursue a special curriculum in art.
5	Weiss	Julia is highly motivated to do art but nothing else. She is shy and consequently does not cause trouble. Still she is wasting time at school. Her mind is elsewhere. Although she responds when asked a question, she gives the first answer that comes into her head.

MIDVIEW ELEMENTARY SCHOOL

Katherine Fowler is reminiscing with Dorothy Cummings in the teacher's lounge of Midview Elementary School about her 17-year teaching career. Mrs. Fowler, a heavy-set lady in her early forties, has been employed in the Midview system for fifteen of those seventeen years. She mentions to Dorothy that she is starting to feel her years creeping up on her. She tells Dorothy "I am just beginning to get students who are the children of people I taught when I first started teaching." The fact that she has a 16-year-old son and a 13-year-old daughter may also be adding to Katherine's increasing awareness of her age. As the Fowlers look ahead to the years when both of their children will be in college at the same time, it seems even more imperative that Katherine retain her teaching position in order to supplement the income that her husband, Bob, receives from operating the pharmacy he inherited from his father.

As Katherine and Dorothy continue their conversation in the lounge, they begin to discuss their current classroom problems and particular students who are of concern to them. Dorothy mentions that this year's group of sixth graders is reputed to be the brightest group in Midview in recent years, but she is just not able to get them interested in anything. Katherine sympathizes with Dorothy and says, "I know just what you mean. I am having the same difficulty with Mary Cairns. She just won't do anything that I ask her."

Dorothy nods her head and replies, "Well, I guess we are just lucky she is able to get herself dressed and get to school on time as frequently as she does considering her homelife. I've taught two of her brothers and one of her sisters, and they have been pretty much all the same."

Katherine says, "I guess Mary is doing just about what we would expect from a person in her position. I was just looking at her cumulative record yesterday. She has a low IQ. We can't expect too much from her."

The Fowlers feel very comfortable living in Midview, a town of 8,000 located in a Mid-Western Border State. Three large manufacturing firms employ the majority of the labor force of Midview, and the economy is rather stable, because these firms produce materials that are basic to the present technological society. The local churches and the schools are the center of much of Midview's social activity. Although the Fowlers do not travel in the social circle of the executives and board of directors of the three major manufacturing firms, they do rank quite high in the Old Guard society by virtue of the position of Mr. Fowler's father as one of the town's earliest merchants.

Midview has recently begun to feel some tension between the lifelong residents, who compose the majority of the merchants of the town; and the newly arrived industrial executives and workers. This friction has surfaced in a number of Lions Club and Civitan Club meetings as well as at meetings of the Chamber of Commerce. Nowhere, however, is it felt more strongly than in the school system. The industrial faction is putting pressure on the local school administration to provide special classes and enriched curricula for their sons and daughters so that they will be better prepared for the College Boards Examination and thus more likely to be accepted at a preferred college or university.

Midview is also the home of a small, church-supported, 4-year college. Although this college has had, and is having, financial problems, many students from Midview who lacked the funds to go to another school have had an opportunity to obtain a college degree. The faculty of this college is small in number and does not exert a great amount of influence in Midview society except in a few church-related areas and on some educational issues.

Most of the people who live in the country around Midview are farmers, although an increasing number of these people are taking jobs as unskilled or semiskilled laborers on the assembly line at one of the three manufacturing firms.

The students in Mrs. Fowler's class come from very diversified home environments. Stanley Robinson, for example, is the son of the executive vice-president of Holden Technological Enterprises, Midview's largest manufacturing firm. It is estimated by the "people who know" that Mr. Robinson's income is in the $40,000–$60,000 bracket. The Robinsons live in a large colonial home and also maintain a cottage on a nearby lake. They have taken two European trips since Stanley was old enough to accompany them, and he often mentions the things he has seen in Europe when the class discussion moves anywhere near this topic. The Robinsons debated for some time about sending Stanley to a private school but finally decided that the advantages of doing this were outweighed by the disadvantage of having him leave home at such an early age. They have decided that if the public school system of Midview does not improve by the time Stanley reaches high school, they will definitely send him to Cutter Military Academy.

Mary Cairns is a classmate of Stanley Robinson's. Mary's father works for Stanley's father as a custodian at Holden Technological Enterprises. The Cairns live in a government-subsidized housing project, which was built at least ten years ago and has deteriorated steadily since. Most of the people who live in this development, like the Cairns, are minimum-income families. Mary has never been outside of the state, although she says she once did get near the state line, when her family went to visit her uncle, who lives in a small town two counties removed from Midview.

The Cairns have four boys and three girls in addition to Mary. Mrs. Cairns works as a domestic for two different families in Midview in order to supplement the meager income Mr. Cairns receives from his job as custodian. Mr. Cairns is frequently "between jobs," because he is often fired for failing to report to work after a weekend of heavy drinking, and Mrs. Cairns' job has been especially important to the family on these occasions. Mary has told her only close friend that her family is very worried about whether or not her father will keep his present job, because of his drinking. She said that her father becomes very hard to live with when he isn't working, because he feels that it is the man's job to support the family, and it hurts him to see his wife work to support the family.

Stanley Robinson and Mary Cairns represent two extremes, but they are indicative of the range of backgrounds, interests, and abilities of the students in Mrs. Fowler's class.

The range in IQ from the lowest student in the class (Martha Lamb) to the highest students (Evelyn Martin and Stanley Robinson) is 59 points. The students range from the 7th percentile to the 96th percentile in Math Achievement and from the 1st percentile to the 99th percentile in Reading. A number of the students, such as Robert Green and John Beckham, have won statewide recognition at science fairs, but some of the students, Elaine Knight and Albert Kersey in particular, rarely attempt to do any of the schoolwork assigned them.

Two students, Sheila Smith and William Baker, are described in greater detail in the following case histories.

SHEILA SMITH

Sheila Smith is an 11-year-old black girl in Mrs. Fowler's class. Her father is a salesman for a paper products company, and her mother is a housewife, who spends a large portion of her time taking care of Sheila's 3-year-old sister, Libby. Sheila has an older brother, Steve, in the eighth grade, who is very close to Sheila and serves as her protector.

Sheila is somewhat of a tomboy and is very interested in finding out how things work. Her nonlanguage IQ on the *California Test of Mental Maturity* was 126 (86th percentile), and her language IQ was 120 (73rd percentile). She is at the 90th percentile in Math Achievement and at the 55th percentile in Reading.

Sheila loves to work around animals and says that she hopes to be a veterinarian when she grows up. She is very popular with her classmates, and has twice been elected vice-president of her 4-H club. Her parents have occasionally expressed some concern about her tomboy tendencies but feel that she is just going through a stage that she will soon outgrow.

These comments appeared in Sheila's cumulative folder:

Grade	Teacher	Comments
1	Copely	Sheila entered school at age five and does not apply herself with diligence, because she is still immature. She needs to spend more time on her schoolwork and pay more attention in class.
2	Barker	Does not work up to her potential. Spends too much time fooling around with the things on her desk. Doesn't appear very interested in the material assigned to her.
3	Reed	She is an intelligent, eager student, but she would have better results if she worked slower and more carefully. She is a real talker. Seems to have made a number of friends throughout the year.
4	Turner	She is quite good at arithmetic but has very little interest in reading. She frequently fails to ask for help with her work when she needs it and consequently has to redo it. Her handwriting could stand improvement. She is a vivacious and creative person.
5	Black	Sheila is a talkative, friendly girl. She enjoys doing schoolwork that interests her but has to be prodded to do work she doesn't enjoy. I feel she has great potential to be a good student if she is given individual attention.

WILLIAM BAKER, JR.

William Baker, Jr., is a small, rather handsome, 13-year-old, the middle child in a family of three children. His father, William, Sr., is a long-distance truck driver, employed by a local trucking company. His mother, Sarah, is currently unemployed, although she was a part-time clerk in a local supermarket as recently as 6 months ago. His sister, Ruth, is in the eighth grade. James, his younger brother, is in the first grade. The Bakers live in an attractive five-room home, about 2 miles from Midview Elementary School. We might consider the Bakers to be in the lower middle-class socioeconomic status classification.

During his 6 years of formal schooling, Bill has had his ups and downs. His cumulative record indicates that he completed the first grade twice, and even then was promoted to the second grade over his teacher's "better judgment"; she believed he was "still not doing first grade work." Bill is generally described as slightly below average in mathematics and has exhibited persistent reading problems. Even he is painfully aware of his reading problems. Although he was enrolled in a remedial reading class for several months in the third grade, his performance apparently did not improve much. A year later his fourth grade teacher summed up the situation: "William has not acquired basic reading skills —he has difficulty reading even the simplest passages and cannot follow the class in reading assignments." This same teacher also felt that William would be "better off" in a special education class.

Behaviorally, Bill appears moderately attentive and interested in class assignments; he politely and adequately answers the teacher's questions, although his manner of responding is rather slow—"naturally deliberate in nature," as one teacher has observed. Although at times he displays disruptive behavior, he would not be considered a discipline problem. When working with small groups of classmates, he appears alert, good-humored, and interested. In a small group he talks freely and seems to be at ease; his behavior toward group members, as well as their behavior toward him, is generally that of respect.

Bill is judged by both his teachers and his peers to be above average in sports. Although short in stature he is well coordinated and rather muscular for his age. These psychomotor traits, coupled with his easygoing and at times enthusiastic manner, result in his being ranked near the top of his peers in physical activities. In short, although he is not a leader, he is a very good participant on the playground and athletic field.

On the most recently administered individual intelligence test, the *Stanford-Binet (Form L-M)* (given by a school psychologist at the request of his third grade teacher), Bill scored in the low average range with an IQ of 91. The psychologist reported that he was "especially successful with items of similarities and differences and with items involving manual dexterity. He had problems with vocabulary items and found it very difficult to read sentences." This behavior, as well as the overall IQ level, is consistent with his performance on a Binet test given a year earlier.

On the *California Mental Maturity Test,* a group test administered during the fourth grade, Bill had a total IQ score of 87, with a language score of 79 and a nonlanguage score of 89. The *Sequential Test of Educational Progress,* administered during the last quarter of fifth grade, gave Bill a mathematics score at the 9th percentile and a reading score at the 1st percentile. His overall grade level placement, as indicated by the *Stanford Achievement Test* (administered during the last month of the fifth grade), was 4.3.

Of further interest are the comments made by Bill's teachers as they evaluated his total performance at the end of each academic year. These comments appeared in his cumulative folder:

Grade	Teacher	Comments
1	Jones	William has shown very little interest in learning this year. He is very active and playful. He doesn't work up to his ability—needs stronger motivation.
1	Smith	William has made very slow progress this year. He is very shy and withdrawn around adults. At the end of school he was still not doing first grade work.
2	Hogan	Cooperative, quiet student. Well liked by classmates. Shows some interest in learning, but makes little progress.
3	Taylor	Well-liked and cooperative. Shows sporadic interest in learning. Showed willingness to be part of low reading group toward end of year and enjoyed participation. Has shown considerable progress since beginning of year; yet he is still very much below grade level in reading. Retaining the child, however, will certainly create "problems." He needs to be told what he is responsible for doing at all times—he is not able to sit in his seat without a task for any length of time.
4	Horton	Bill has limited abilities because of a reading handicap. He needs special work assignments because his ability is below grade level. He is very good in sports and is well liked by the students.
5	Brooks	The above comments still hold true. The work at this grade is entirely too difficult for him. He enjoys participation in physical education, and he is helpful in taking care of the room.

In concluding this chapter, we will use one of the scenarios, Knight-crest Middle School, and a sample from one of the case studies to illustrate how these materials are used in this book, how the different writers examine the same situation from different perspectives and arrive at the implications that psychological concepts hold for the classroom.

In his chapter, "Power and Influence Variables in the Classroom," Professor Schlechty looks at Nancy Carter, a teacher at Knightcrest Middle School, in the following manner:

> Nancy Carter seems to perceive the role of the teacher, at least in part, as that of a moral leader. She apparently believes that teacher expectations should be important to the students. Nancy is aware that this set of beliefs is creating a problem because most of her students do not share her view of what the teacher's role ought to be. Her students' view of her role is doubtlessly conditioned by their social position. The social position of the students' families makes it likely that few, if any, of Nancy's students will ever be teachers, and of those few most will be girls. For Nancy's students, becoming a teacher would be to lower themselves in terms of prestige, status, income, and power. Thus to accept Nancy or any other teacher as an important social referent, students would have to reject many of the values and beliefs that have come to them through the socialization process to which they have been exposed. It is very unlikely that many students at Knightcrest will be willing to make such a dramatic break from the values and beliefs they have come to accept. For example, Brookover's research indicates that in spite of the impact of peer groups and teachers, parents are for most students the primary source of direction, particularly in matters of personal value, career plans, and future orientation.

Professors Good and Brophy, in their chapter, "The Influence of Teacher's Attitudes and Expectations on Classroom Behavior," see Nancy from a different viewpoint:

> Although the preceding model describes how teachers may react differentially to individual students as a result of their performance expectations, the same process sometimes operates for a whole class or a whole school. For example, Miss Carter apparently feels that her students are "pampered" at home, and she may feel that she must "make it hard" on them so that they will become mature, responsible adults (like her, presumably). Also, her expectation that the parents and students will reject her may lead her to behave in ways that will cause this expectation to be fulfilled. (For example, she may apologize for her clothes, apologize or try to fake interest and knowledgeability when cultural topics are discussed, or give long sermons on "how you kids don't appreciate what a dollar's worth because you've never had to work for one.")

Similarly, the various authors look at the students in the different case studies from their own particular frames of reference. Consider one of Miss Carter's potential students, Marvin Blake.

In her chapter on behavioral analysis, Professor Wasik has the following to say about Marvin:

> One of the students, Marvin Blake, has been described as one who "should be working at a higher level," "is a very lazy student," and "doesn't always seem to use his abilities." Let us accept the teacher's description that Marvin is not performing at an acceptable level. Also notice that

Marvin has several favorite hobbies; among them are reading and playing the trumpet. A relationship between certain activities Marvin does not do well or does not attempt to do and those he does enjoy can be arranged and made a part of the contract. The teacher and Marvin can agree on a set amount of work to be completed, with a free-choice time to follow the work. If, during the work period, Marvin completes an arithmetic assignment with over 90 percent accuracy, then, he can be rewarded with 20 minutes of free time to read from a book of his choice. His parents could become part of the contract arrangement and take Marvin to see a marching band or give him trumpet lessons based on the completion of a certain number of assignments on his contract.

Drs. Solomon and Oberlander analyze Marvin from the viewpoint of how he considers his efforts to be related to his successes and failures.

Marvin Blake is presented as an individual who uses realistic differential perception in gearing his behavior toward situations where he can maximize his success. He apparently does have an internal control orientation; that is, he considers success and failure as depending on his own efforts. He shows an interest in musical matters and develops his musical talents (where he believes he can be successful), while shying away from athletic activities (where he expects failure). It appears that Marvin is realistic in his assessment of what his efforts in different areas are likely to produce, and he is fortunate to find himself in a school setting where such differential choices are possible.

These examples of how the different principles and concepts described in this book can be used to increase your understanding of the classroom and the work of the teacher are, of course, taken out of context. Consequently, considerable clarity and comprehensiveness have been lost. However, we hope they have helped you to see the intended goal of this book—the demonstration of the practical utility of principles and concepts for increasing your competence as a teacher. As you read the essays in this book, we hope you will expand the application of these principles and concepts beyond the scenarios and case studies to your own educational career, both as a student and as a teacher. Furthermore, as you read each essay, we hope you will become increasingly aware of the complexity of the classroom. Finally, you should become increasingly aware of how principles and concepts are related to each other and how, when they are considered together, a wider, more meaningful view of the classroom emerges.

REFERENCE

Bruner, Jerome S. *On Knowing: Essays for the Left Hand.* New York: Atheneum, 1966.

2 · Power and influence variables in the classroom

PHILLIP SCHLECHTY
University of North Carolina at Chapel Hill

PHILLIP SCHLECHTY
University of North Carolina at Chapel Hill

<u>KEY CONCEPTS</u>

significant and important others
leadership
social position of teachers
power
compliance

Theories of teaching have their basis in learning theories and philosophies of education. The practice of teaching has its basis in the *social* and *psychological* realities of the classroom and the school.

Educators are generally aware that social and psychological factors have important implications for teaching. The typical teacher education program requires that the student preparing to be a teacher take a course in the social foundations of school and society and a course in psychological foundations in which these social and psychological factors are treated. Such courses usually deal with social and psychological differences at a very general level, and the beginning teacher often has difficulty in seeing how these general social and psychological differences relate directly to classroom practice.

The structure of the scenarios presented in this book, for example, implies that where the school is located makes a difference in the schooling process. Midview is a small, rural, village school; Bridges is an inner-city school; and Knightcrest Middle School is located in an upper middle-class suburb.

It is true that children from some types of communities do seem to differ in important ways from children from other types of communities. It is the assumption that differences in school communities create differences in schoolchildren that has led to some of the categories of students that are found in social foundations' textbooks. For example, in writing of the children of the slum, small town, suburb, and peasant village, Brembeck (1971) observes that children from these environments experience quite different sets of human interactions. The schools they attend reflect quite different cultural styles, and the students view the school from different perspectives.

Accepting, for the moment, that the life that the child experiences in an inner city is different from the life the child experiences in a small town or a suburban community, we must still ask the question: What difference do these differences make? For example, outside of the fact that Stanley Robinson happens to reside in Midview rather than Pine Valley and thus attends a small-town school, what real difference is there between Stanley Robinson and the bulk of the students who attend Knightcrest Middle School? Stanley's father's income places him in a socioeconomic position equivalent to the residents of Pine Valley. What Stanley's family expects of the school does not differ markedly from what the parents of the students at Knightcrest expect. The difference, therefore, is not solely Stanley or his family, for in Knightcrest Stanley would be a typical student. Stanley stands out only because *in Midview* he is atypical. The culture of the school defines Stanley as different; the difference is not inherent in Stanley.

Katherine Fowler, the teacher in Midview, and Nancy Carter, the teacher at Knightcrest, are also very similar. They are different in age and experience, but these differences are probably trivial in terms of impact on the women's attitudes toward what students should be expected and required to do in class. The big difference is that Katherine Fowler teaches in a school system that tends to support her style of life, manner of thinking, and value system. Nancy Carter, however, is teaching in a situation that constitutes a threat to her life-style and her system of values. Not only do the students seem to her to be unappreciative of their good life, but Nancy cannot afford to live in the community or participate in community life.

Educational theory encourages the teacher to concentrate on the differences among students. Yet the realities of the classroom and the practicalities of school life force attention on similarities. Ability grouping, for example, is usually defended as a means of taking into account the differences that exist among students. Another way of looking at ability grouping is to view it as a mechanism whereby convenient similarities are created. Students are put together *because they are assumed to be alike somehow.* Thus ability grouping works against the confusion and messiness that differences create for teachers.

Any effort to place a large number of individuals into a single category forces one to emphasize similarities and overlook or deny differences. Yet without categories that extract similarities we would have no way to think about differences. A most appropriate use of social categories is as a backdrop against which the nature and meaning of difference can be articulated. For example, Stanley Robinson is indeed different from most of the students in Midview Elementary School, or as the editors put it, Stanley Robinson represents an extreme. But as suggested earlier, Stanley Robinson is only different when viewed in terms of the social context of Midview, that is, the similarities among other students at Midview.

To speak of a small-town school without clearly delineating the kinds of individuals who comprise the populace of that small town tells one very little about the quality of the education or of the schools. A small public school system in a university community would probably be qualitatively different from a public school system in a mining town of equal size. To make qualitative distinctions between schools, one needs to know much more than whether the school is a small-town school, inner-city school, or a suburban school. Among the things one needs to know is the relative mix of the attitudes, values, beliefs, aspirations, economic potentials, and limitations of the populace that the school serves. The differences between small-town, inner-city, and suburban schools have much more to do with the tendencies of the particular types of people living in these areas than they do with any other factor.

One of the most significant differences between Midview and Knightcrest is that Knightcrest has *many* families like the Robinsons, whereas Midview has very few. That quantitative difference explains a great deal about any real or perceived qualitative differences between the two schools. You should not conclude, however, that we are arguing that the only way to improve the quality of the schools is to "get a better grade of student." Indeed, there is little that can be said for certain about a better "grade" of student. But students do differ, and within a given school these differences do make a difference. Stanley Robinson, for example, is different from the type of student that the Midview school is designed to teach or accommodate. So, it can be added, is Mary Cairns. In Midview both Mary and Stanley exhibit differences that are significant, and the school apparently does not accommodate these differences, for neither of them seems to be in a position to get what he or she wants, needs, thinks he wants, or thinks he needs. Nor do they receive what the teachers and the school think students should want or need.

EXPECTATIONS: GREAT AND OTHERWISE

The impact of expectations on behavior has long been of interest to social psychologists. In recent years educators, particularly educational researchers, have given attention to the subject. For example, the now famous Rosenthal and Jacobsen studies (1968) were efforts to show how a teacher's expectations affect student performance. Wilbur Brookover's research on academic ability and self concept deals with the effect of the student's expectations about himself on his educational success. There is also a growing body of literature relating parental expectations and aspirations to student performance in the classroom (Brookover et al., 1962). Although there is a great deal of controversy concerning the precise nature of the impact of expectations on classroom performance, two things seem to be beyond controversy: (1) Expectations have a definite impact on behavior, and (2) if one perceives a person as important (to oneself), the expectations of that person will have a greater impact than the expectations of individuals who one does not perceive as significant and important people. Most teachers assume that students do or should view the teacher's expectations as important.

Theories of schooling are generally based on the assumption that teachers are significant to students. It seems reasonable to infer, therefore, that when students share the belief that the teacher *is* a significant and important person, the teacher will have considerably more impact on the students than he or she will have if the students do not share the belief that the teacher is a significant and important person.

Consider the case of Nancy Carter and Knightcrest School. Nancy Carter seems to perceive the role of the teacher, at least in part, as that of a moral leader. She apparently believes that teacher expectations should be important to the students. Nancy is aware that this set of beliefs is creating a problem because most of her students do not share her view of what the teacher's role ought to be. Her students' view of her role is doubtlessly conditioned by their social position. The social position of the students' families makes it likely that few, if any, of Nancy's students will ever be teachers, and of those few most will be girls. For Nancy's students, becoming a teacher would be to lower themselves in terms of prestige, status, income, and power. Thus to accept Nancy or any other teacher as an important social referent, students would have to reject many of the values and beliefs that have come to them through the socialization process to which they have been exposed. It is very unlikely that many students at Knightcrest will be willing to make such a dramatic break from the values and beliefs they have come to accept. For example, Brookover's research (1962) indicates that in spite of the impact of peer groups and teachers, parents are for most students the primary source of direction particularly in matters of personal value, career plans, and future orientation.

For various reasons—for example, wealth, parents' educational level, and parental aspirations for children—schools in communities like Pine Valley are in a better position than other schools to employ teachers with high academic and professional qualifications, purchase the most recent educational materials and equipment, and provide up-to-date physical facilities. It is also probable that such schools will be more innovative than schools in large cities or rural areas. But the observer is confronted with a chicken-and-egg question. If one accepts most conventional measures of academic quality as having some validity, it seems fair to argue that the quality of education in upper middle-class suburbs is generally superior to the quality of education in most other schools. Given the fact that schools in upper middle-class suburbs can generally acquire better qualified teachers and facilities, it is tempting to argue that the better quality of schools, teachers, and programs accounts for or causes the high quality of educational output. It is not that simple. If one controls for the sociocultural composition of the student population (for example, deals only with upper middle-class schools), the nature of the programs and facilities seems to make little difference, and teacher behavior seems to be only slightly important, if it is important at all (Jencks, 1972).

Put simply, who the teacher is and what the teacher does is less important in schools like Knightcrest than it might be in other school settings. The cultural advantages enjoyed by students at Knightcrest largely account for any real or imagined academic superiority. For most of the students in Knightcrest, the teacher is a functionary to be used—not a model to be emulated. Yet most of what the teacher does, including variations of what could be done—for example, the use of different methods or teaching styles—is based on the assumption that the teacher is a significant other. In schools like Knightcrest—and even more so in high schools in communities like Pine Valley—most present pedagogy is indeed based on questionable assumptions.

Over the past several years the author has had the opportunity to travel to a wide variety of public schools in the United States and engage in extensive and intensive observations. These observations indicate that there may be some exceptions to the argument just presented. Generally, it does appear that in upper middle-class schools, who the teacher is and what the teacher does make little difference in what the students learn. But some few teachers do seem to make a great deal of difference to some students in these schools. Most of the teachers who make a difference, however, are nonacademics, such as coaches, special education teachers, remedial reading teachers, art teachers, and drama teachers. Furthermore, the students to whom these teachers make a difference appear to be atypical compared to the bulk of the student population; for example, these atypical students include the turned-on artist, the self-styled hippie, and the nonintellectual mechanic.

School communities like those represented by Bridges Elementary School present a marked contrast to Knightcrest. In Knightcrest the teacher's expectations are probably less important than educational theory would indicate the case should be. (For the most part the students do share the school's expectations regarding the schooling process itself.) If nothing else, most students and parents of students in schools like Knightcrest expect the school to prepare the young for college. It is probable that in Bridges few students share the values of either the teachers or the school. Furthermore, given the ways schools are organized and the values implicit in these organizations, without some planned intervention these students probably never will come to identify with the schooling process itself. Whether the students will come to view the teacher as a human being worthy of personal attachments and thus respond to her expectations is another matter.

For the students, and probably most parents, in schools like Bridges the school system and the teachers, principals, and guidance counselors represent one more of the many capricious, arbitrary agencies that must be contended with in order to survive. Parents tend to stay away from the school. There are probably many reasons for this, such as the demands of day labor and a lack of interest, but fear and anxiety must be among them. For many, if not most, of the parents of children in Bridges, school was a failure experience. The median grade level that parents of Bridges students attained was 7.2. Certainly, economic factors, along with other sociocultural variables, account for the relatively low level of educational attainment, but one would be naïve to think that the parent of a typical student at Bridges expects the school to be a warm and happy place where success is met at every turn. Also, it is clear from the reports that Mr. Bellamy received from the other teachers that the school is living up to the parents' expectations. There is little indication in the scenarios that most of the teachers perceive anything wrong with the school's expectations regarding students. The difficulty rests in the students' inability and unwillingness to meet these expectations.

Wehling and Charters (1969) report a study of teachers' beliefs indicating that teachers hold very similar views concerning the aims and methods of classroom instruction. In looking at the three scenarios, one cannot help but be struck by the similarity in the expectations of most of the teachers, regardless of the schools in which they teach, particularly the similarities among the expectations of Nancy Carter (Knightcrest), Katherine Fowler (Midview), and Mr. Bellamy's anonymous colleagues (Bridges). Yet one cannot help but feel that the nature of the teacher's expectations, if they are to be realized, must be shaped and molded by the sociocultural context of the situation in which the expected behavior is to be shown. It seems doubtful, for example, that the teacher's expectation that students should be successful in academic matters would have the same meaning or consequences for a child in Knightcrest and for a child in Bridges. Martin Deutsch (1964) puts it this way:

For the lower-class child there is not the same contiguity or continuity, and he does not have the same coping mechanisms for internalizing success or psychologically surviving failure in the formal learning setting. If the lower-class child starts to fail, he does not have the same kinds of operationally significant and functionally relevant support from his family or community—or from the school—that his counterpart has.

To expect a child in Knightcrest to succeed academically is to reinforce the expectations of most parents and a significant proportion of the student subculture. The teacher's expectation that a student should succeed academically in Bridges *may* run directly counter to the expectations of the student subculture, forcing the student to make a choice between his peer group and the school or even between his parents and the school. Regarding the student's rejection of peer group expectations, Mr. Bellamy's personal biography might well provide an interesting case study. The case study would be even more interesting if one could contrast Mr. Bellamy's biography with Miss Carter's and Mrs. Fowler's.

If one looks at the data concerning the social origins of elementary school teachers, it is clear that individuals with social backgrounds similar to those of Mrs. Fowler and Miss Carter constitute a significant proportion of the total teacher population. Although the statistics vary from study to study, it seems reasonable to say that between 45 and 60 percent of all elementary school teachers are females from middle-class small-town families. In contrast to this figure the number of black, male elementary school teachers is small indeed. For teachers like Mrs. Fowler and Miss Carter teaching represents little or no change in social status. It is possible that for Mr. Bellamy entry into the teaching profession was an upwardly mobile social move. Of course, there is no sure way of knowing about this matter. It may very well be that Mr. Bellamy's father was also a teacher.

What is being suggested is that for Katherine Fowler and Nancy Carter entry into the teaching profession did not represent a break with their prior social experience. Teaching represents one of the expected and respected alternatives for young girls from backgrounds similar to theirs. For Mr. Bellamy, however, success in school may well have precipitated a serious disruption in his social experience. His peers, upon noticing his success in school, may well have called him such endearing names as "brown nose," "candy ass," and "pansy." If you doubt that this is possible, imagine for a moment the potential social consequences for Rick Washington should Mr. Bellamy find some means of turning Rick's considerable talents to the attainment of academic success. Yet if Mr. Bellamy or one of his counterparts fails to establish a significant relationship with Rick, the odds are that Rick will suffer other negative social consequences, which in the long run could be more harmful than peer rejection. As Bill Cosby puts it: "In my neighborhood kids were going to grow up to be killers or priests." The dichotomy between killers and priests is certainly an oversimplification, but the implication and meaning are clear.

Another point that is often overlooked when dealing with schools like Bridges and students like Rick is that many of the values implicit in academic success and the schooling process are direct assaults on family loyalties and other primary social relationships. Mr. Bellamy may well become personally important in Rick's life. In many ways this outcome would probably be desirable. But one should not forget that even this development would be a serious criticism of the nature of the family life to which Rick is accustomed. Furthermore, when a student like Rick does attain academic success, he rejects other family values. Some even go so far as to suggest that one of the reasons some students opt to fail in school is to avoid such consequences (Bettelheim, 1961).

What teachers expect of students, what parents expect of their children, and what students expect of each other all go into the makeup of classroom behavior and affect the nature and consequences of schooling. The social context of the school shapes and forms the meaning and significance of these consequences. Whether the teacher's expectations regarding himself or his students are great or not so great, it cannot be denied that expectations are differences that make a difference.

PERCEPTIONS—THE EYE OF THE BEHOLDER

The author is not a perceptual psychologist, nor does he aspire to be an expert in the area. In the previous section the word *perception* was used quite loosely, and in this section there will be no greater restriction. *Perception* is used to mean the images that people hold of things, nothing more.

What the teacher is perceived to be and what the teacher perceives himself or herself to be have been the subject of considerable discussion among educators. One can scarcely find a book on teaching that does not discuss at some point stereotypes of the teacher (Waller, 1967).

The intent in this section is to discuss:

1. The image of the teacher from the point of view of teachers, students, and parents.
2. The image of the student from the point of view of students and teachers.
3. The image of the school community from the point of view of teachers, students, and parents.

In a following section the consequences of these images on classroom behavior will be discussed.

The image of the teacher certainly has much to do with the personal characteristics of individuals who are teachers. But equally important is the social structure of the community and the school in which the teacher teaches. It is probable that in the Bridges community the image of the teacher is that of a representative of an impersonal and threatening authority system. In Knightcrest the prevailing community image of the teacher is probably that of a well-qualified civil servant. In both the Bridges community and the Knightcrest community, teachers are "sociological strangers." In both communities the teacher is important, but the importance is not a personal importance. It is probable that in the Bridges community most parents and students cannot think of the teacher as a person—the teacher is an authority position. The position of teacher is important, but the person of the teacher is not known, or is seldom known.

In Knightcrest the image may be somewhat different. Most of the parents undoubtedly aspire for their children to be "something better" than a teacher. Teachers and schools may be necessary for the attainment of that "something," and thus the teacher is important. But for the most part teaching is a failure belt, "the refuge of unsalable men and unmarriageable women" (Waller, 1967).

Those who teach in schools like Knightcrest and Bridges tend to live outside of the community—in Knightcrest, because costs are too great; in Bridges, because the teacher's life-style is at odds with the conditions in the neighborhood. In any case, the position of the teachers in both Knightcrest and Bridges and the image that that position creates are largely impersonal.

The image of the teacher in Midview is probably different. Undoubtedly, many of the teachers in Midview are, like their counterparts in Knightcrest and Bridges, sociological strangers. But Katherine Fowler probably has no counterpart in Bridges, and the odds are she has no counterpart in Knightcrest (unless it would be the wife of one of the residents of the community, who "came back to teaching after she raised her family"). Katherine Fowler is a teacher in the school, but her image has more to do with the fact that she is the pharmacist's wife than with the fact that she happens to teach. In the community she is Mrs. Fowler, who teaches, not the teacher, who is Mrs. Fowler.

Some years ago the author undertook a research project in a small town much like Midview. One of the purposes of the research was to determine what images community leaders held of teachers in the local school. The data proved to be most perplexing. The only way one could organize the data into a sensible pattern was to divide the teachers into two broad categories—one group that the respondents referred to impersonally as teachers and one group that the respondents referred to with more personal symbols, such as Old Red or Joe's wife.

Once the teachers were placed in one of these two broad categories
—that is, those referred to personally and sympathetically and those
referred to impersonally (strangers)—some interesting relations were
discovered. It became clear that those teachers that the community
leaders perceived as "strangers" were also more apt to be discussed in
stereotypic terms. The other group of teachers were not viewed consistently, but they did have one characteristic in common: They all had
some significant role in the community that was independent of their
position as teacher, for example, the wife of a minister, a farm owner
and operator, or shoe salesman. The fact that a teacher from outside the
community participated in community affairs—for example, joined the
Lions Club or taught Sunday school—did not seem to affect his being
placed in the stranger category (Schlechty, 1960).

In addition to the community image of the teacher, teachers themselves are a source of teacher images. And as studies like those reported
by Wehling and Charters (1969) seem to indicate, the images teachers
hold of themselves seem to vary remarkably little from school to school,
community to community. If it is true that teachers teaching in different
schools hold common images of the role and function of teachers, it is
little wonder that some teachers have difficulties in school and in the
community.

Perhaps one of the most important images of the teacher is the view
that the teacher is a moral leader. Teachers generally seem to favor this
image. The study by Wehling and Charters (1969) indicates that many
teachers believe they should behave in ways that provide sound moral
leadership. Many sociologists and educational philosophers have taken
cognizance of the moral qualities of the teacher's leadership role
(Waller, 1967).

In a community like Midview the image of the teacher as a moral
leader is relatively consistent with the prevailing community perceptions. In fact, the origins (in America) of the professional educator's
image of himself (in the experience of rural and small-town education)
gave rise to the image of the teacher as a moral leader in the first place.
One of the assumptions (in this case *assumption* is a kind word for
mythology) of small-town life is the idea of a shared core of values.
This assumption is characterized by such statements as, "We're all
equal here." A corollary dimension of the mythology of small-town life
is the belief that "our town is different from all other towns, and these
differences make our town qualitatively better than other towns"
(Vidich and Bensman, 1958).

The image of the teacher as a moral leader carries with it the expectation that the teacher will enhance and reinforce the town's unique
values, for it is the teacher's task to prepare the young to become
effective and active citizens in the life of the community. It seems clear

that in Midview Katherine Fowler sees herself as participating in the dominant mode of life typical of the community. What she believes about the school and what she believes about the community are synonymous. Just as Katherine Fowler sees herself as a part of the life of the community, she sees the school as a reflection of that same life.

Both Mary Cairns and Stanley Robinson come from families that are on the fringes of community life. Mrs. Fowler's tendency to interpret any problems these students might have with schooling in terms of their families' position in the community is indeed great.

Undoubtedly, much of what Mrs. Fowler does in the classroom is shaped by her views of what a "good citizen" of Midview should want and need. So long as the students and parents share her values, problems of motivation are minimal. Students who are committed to the same moral symbols that she is will respond to her as a moral leader. Her approval is encouragement. Indeed, even her unstated desires will serve as sources of direction, control, and inducement for these students. But with students like Mary Cairns, who has no way of identifying with the central values of the community, it is no wonder that Mrs. Fowler must complain, "She won't do anything I ask her."

Attempting to motivate Stanley Robinson by appealing to his sense of school pride or community spirit is useless. Moral symbols will become even less compelling to Stanley as he comes to expect and demand that the school prepare him for college and for life in the world beyond Midview. The position of Stanley Robinson's and Mary Cairns' families makes it difficult, if not impossible, for Mary and Stanley to feel a sense of moral identity with the social milieu of the school in Midview. Yet without some degree of moral commitment on the part of students in her class, Katherine Fowler, at least as she seems to view her role, is relatively helpless in motivating students. The question is: Is the problem created by these circumstances the problem of Stanley Robinson, Mary Cairns, Katherine Fowler, Midview School, or the community itself? This question will be taken up in the following section.

Another set of images that is important to the life of the school includes the images that teachers and students hold of the students' position. Here we are not concerned with the image particular teachers have of particular students. Rather, we are concerned with the generalized image teachers and students hold regarding what is expected of the students and their obligations.

In a previous section attention was given to the effect of expectations on behavior. Many factors shape the expectations that teachers have of students and that students have of themselves. But chief among these factors must surely be the images teachers and students "carry around" concerning the position of the student in the school organization.

For the most part the ideology of teaching supports the notion that a student ought to be a member of the school organization or a citizen of the school community. Such a view of the student is quite compatible with the image of the teacher as a moral leader. It seems logical, though data are lacking, that teachers who view themselves as moral leaders are also apt to give considerable attention to the membership image of the student. For example, one would expect that in Midview School teachers like Katherine Fowler would be apt to weigh the nebulous qualities of citizenship, responsibility, cooperativeness, and so on in their evaluations of student performance in the classroom. Many of the teachers in Bridges Elementary School would employ similar criteria. Indeed, one is tempted to suggest that it is probable that a primary cause of academic failure in many inner-city schools is the inability of students to live up to the teachers' image of a responsible member of the school community.

The situation in Knightcrest may be very different from Bridges or Midview. Although it is probable that teachers like Nancy Carter believe a student *ought* to be evaluated in terms of membership criteria, the hazy quality of these criteria makes them difficult to defend to parents. It is one thing to tell a socially powerless parent that the reason his child's grades are lower for this 6-week period is because he was uncooperative and belligerent. It is another thing to tell the same thing to the local pediatrician's wife, who also has her degree in education. Put bluntly, the teacher in Knightcrest may be forced to be specific in defending himself against the criticisms of irate parents. The parents' apathy and fear of authority may protect the teachers in Bridges from ever being confronted with this awesome task.

Perhaps a more typical view of students in schools like Knightcrest would be the view of the student (or the student's parents) as client. This is suggested for two general reasons. First, schools like Knightcrest tend to be academically oriented, and it is probable that teachers who are attracted and recruited to such schools would have a strong inclination to emphasize their role as professional teachers. At the high school level in particular there is a tendency for teachers in the academic areas to see their roles as something approaching a "lower level" college professor. The author's experience with high school teachers in communities like Pine Valley leads to the belief that most junior high school and high school teachers in academically oriented settings are upset by the notion that they should be anything other than semiprofessional biologists, historians, or chemists. The view of the student as client is relatively compatible with the idea of professionalism in teaching, at least some narrowly defined ideas of professionalism.

Second, as a new teacher like Nancy Carter finds efforts to exercise moral leadership constantly thwarted by the social structure of the school and the community, some other meaningful definitions must be substituted if notions of personal worth are to be maintained. The teacher who views the student as client is probably less apt than her colleagues to be concerned with motivation. Motivation is assumed to exist a priori. Lack of motivation, although a problem, is something of concern to other specialists in the system, such as guidance counselors, school psychologists, and the assistant principal.

In schools like Knightcrest students, particularly successful students, have a tendency to impose the client image on the teacher. Over the past 5 years the author has been engaged in a series of undertakings designed to introduce inquiry-oriented curriculum materials into the secondary school classroom. One of the greatest sources of resistance to the introduction of these materials is the "A" and "B" student in upper middle-class schools. As teachers report the story, the "clincher" question can be summarized as follows: "This inquiry stuff is all right, but how's it going to help me pass the college boards?" In other words, the teacher as a professional is seen as failing to provide the service the student *as client* expects her to provide.

Another image that teachers may hold of the student is that of the student as product. The student is seen as raw material to be worked on, molded, and shaped. In the product orientation considerable emphasis is given to quality control. Couched in the terms suggested here, few teachers would admit that their view of the student is that of a student as product. Yet appropriately cast in the garb of science and the idiom of recognizing individual differences, many teachers embrace the notion of the student as product.

It is not clear whether or not Knightcrest evidences a product orientation toward the student. It is clear, however, that in schools like Bridges there is a crude and heavy-handed kind of product orientation. Specifically, schools like Bridges often serve chiefly as quality control agencies. They do very little to change the student, but they do serve as a selecting and sorting agency that gives an official stamp of approval to the decisions society and its agencies have already made (Goslin, 1965).

The students may have some very different images of the position of the student. Students can, and probably do, see themselves as members, clients, and products of the school, although it is doubtful that students would voluntarily use these labels. When one considers the students' image of the position of students in the school, the personalistic, affective connotations of the term *involvement* seem to provide a better set, than do the terms *client, member,* and *product.*

Etzioni (1961) suggests that involvement can be usefully viewed in terms of three types. His typology and a description of each type are as follows:

Alienative Involvement—Alienative involvement designates an intense negative orientation; it is predominant in relations among hostile foreigners.

Similar orientations exist among merchants in "adventure" capitalism, where trade is built on isolated acts of exchange, each side trying to maximize immediate profit. . . . Such an orientation seems to dominate the approach of prostitutes to transient clients. . . . Some slaves seem to have held similar attitudes to their masters and to their work. Inmates in prisons, prisoners of war, people in concentration camps, enlisted men in basic training, all tend to be alienated from their respective organizations.

Calculative Involvement—Calculative involvement designates either a negative or a positive orientation of low intensity. Calculative orientations are predominant in relationships of merchants who have continuous business contacts. Attitudes of (and toward) permanent customers are often predominantly calculative, as are relationships among entrepreneurs in modern (rational) capitalism. Inmates in prisons who have established contact with prison authorities, such as "rats" and "peddlers," often have predominantly calculative attitudes toward those in power. . . .

Moral Involvement—Moral involvement designates a positive orientation of high intensity. The involvement of the parishioner in his church, the devoted member in his party, and the loyal follower in his leader are all "moral" [p. 10].

Alienative involvement is in fact noninvolvement. The participation of the individual in the behaviors required of him rests entirely on the constraints of the organization, not on some positive attraction the organization holds for the alienated individual. In a situation where lower level participants, such as recruits in the army or inmates in prison, are totally alienated, force is the only means whereby required behaviors can be induced. This is the case precisely because alienative involvement is a condition in which the organization has *no* positive attraction.

Rick Washington at Bridges provides a good example. Whether Rick indeed perceives the position of the student at Bridges as an alienative position is a matter of conjecture. From what one can glean from the scenario, however, such an inference does have some basis. Two of the teachers' comments about Rick stand out: "Rick has a poor self concept in school but sees himself as king of the hill when he is in the streets." "Rick is capable of doing schoolwork if he wanted to. He just is not interested in what this school has to offer."

Students may also see the position of the student as a calculative position. A student with such an image is willing to do what the school requires of him because by so doing he can get something he feels he needs. For example, Stanley Robinson will probably come to view himself in a calculative position vis-à-vis Midview School. His parents apparently already hold such a view. If the school cannot provide the desired services as Stanley progresses in school, his parents seem to be entirely willing to remove him from the school setting. There are undoubtedly many students in Knightcrest who will come to view themselves in calculative positions.

A final image students may hold of the position of student is that of moral involvement. Moral involvement includes the notion of the student position as an "insider" position. To some extent the student who sees himself in a morally involved position sees the school as an extension of himself and significant others, such as his family and friends. Symbolic notions like school pride, school spirit, and a generalized perception of community go along with the image of the student position in the school as a moral position. The school is socially as well as legally in loco parentis. Many students in Midview are apt to see their position in school as a moral position. Nancy Carter probably finds some source of remorse in the fact that so few students at Knightcrest have such an image of the students' position. It is clear that Nancy Carter and many of her colleagues at Knightcrest would consider it a significant "spiritual" uplift if the calculative "snobs" at Knightcrest had one-half the moral commitment to schooling that students had in the good old days (4 or 5 years ago).

A final set of images that should be discussed includes the images that teachers, students, and community members hold of the community itself. In the small town like Midview teachers probably become quite aware of the community power structure. Some of the young teachers, particularly the more cosmopolitan young teachers, may deprecate the provincial attitudes of local leaders, but they will know who the local leaders are and recognize their importance. In suburban schools like Knightcrest the community structure may not be so clear to those who occupy teaching positions. And the community structure that surrounds Bridges Elementary School will be largely unrecognized by any but the most socially sophisticated teachers in the Bridges School. Put more bluntly, when teachers make decisions concerning children in Midview, it is highly probable that the teacher's perception of the community power structure will intervene. It is also probable that teachers share a common perception of this power structure, and thus the effect of the power structure on the teachers' decision making may be very systematic.

The structure of the community surrounding Knightcrest makes the effects of the teachers' view of the power structure somewhat different. Suburban communities often *appear* to have less coherent or more diffuse community power structures. Appearance is often not reality, however, and it is this knowledge that may affect the teacher. Indeed, teachers will probably be quite anxious about the structure and make many decisions that are safe and "won't upset anyone," precisely because there are few indicators about who it is that should not be upset. In Bridges, however, teachers generally will be unaware that there is indeed a community "out there." To the extent that they are aware of the community structure, it will be viewed largely as a problem to be dealt with, a handicap to overcome, a condition to be conquered. The street life of the students will be viewed not as a resource but as a threat. For example, one teacher considers it unfortunate that Rick Washington is a leader.

It is difficult to be precise about the images that students hold of their community. Thus far in social research the imagery of the young, outside of works like *Elmtown's Youth* (Hollingshead, 1945) and *The Adolescent Society* (Coleman, 1949), has not received the attention the subject deserves. But some reasonable speculations are possible. First, it is probable that children and young adults in places like Midview largely share their parents' perceptions of their town: "just plain folks," "there is not a place I'd rather live," "the best little town in the United States." In the language of the young, these adult perceptions may be translated into "the best school," "the finest football team," "the best band," or "the best vocational agriculture program." But here one is presented with an interesting puzzle. The data suggest that most of those who succeed in the small-town high school betray their loyalties and leave the community to return only on short visits to see the folks. (Unless, of course, one's father happens to be the local pharmacist, and one can return to Fowler's drugstore after spending some time at the state university.) Even more perplexing is the fact that those who "stay behind" tend to be precisely those that the school has labeled failures.

The notion of loyalties to a suburban community and the image students hold of such communities are more difficult to pinpoint. Suburban families tend to be more mobile than do rural families, although rural to urban migration is a significant pattern. But the mobility tends to be from the suburb of one city to a similar suburb of another city. Thus one is led to suspect that loyalty to a suburban community and perceptions related to that loyalty have more to do with abstract symbols than with the experience of the student body. The fact is that in many suburban communities there is a significant number of new arrivals both geographically and socially, for example, the nouveau riche. Most of the community images these persons hold must come from symbolic and reputational data rather than from concrete experience. The notion that Knightcrest Middle School is a progressive and innovative school will be perpetuated, in coffee klatches for new arrivals, by ambitious real estate salesmen and the public information office of the local school system. In these situations it is difficult to distinguish myth from reality, and in spite of the recent tendency to worship the wisdom of the young, it is doubtful that the children of the nouveau riche are any more sure what the realities are than their parents are.

In the high school it is probable that many of the brighter, more aggressive students will attempt to convince the teachers that they view

Pine Valley as a striving, grasping, status-conscious environment, which they reject. But the teacher who accepts these confessions of guilt as accurate portrayals of the students' image of a suburban community may well be in for some surprises.

In an attempt to describe the image a student might hold of the inner-city community, it might be well to quote at some length the words of an informed observer of the scene. Jean Dresden Grambs (1965) writes:

> The city neighborhood was not and is not the same as the idealized village or suburban neighborhood. The neighborhood for a dweller in a high density area might be his apartment house. Some high-rise apartments may have as many residents as a small town. With high population density has come high transiency. Urban renewal often has removed local landmarks which once helped to establish the feel of a neighborhood. But increasingly, greater concentrations of people have resulted in greater movement of people. The transiency itself may be due to a feeling of rootlessness, or the rootlessness may produce the transiency, but observers have noted that city families move often. They do not move far away, maybe only a few blocks, but they move. In one study, for instance, it was found that sixth grade children in the center of the city had moved 1.58 times in five years and attended 2.3 schools; those in suburban areas had moved .89 times and attended 1.8 schools. Most of the mobility was confined to one third of the sixth grade population, and of this mobile one-third, three-fourths lived in the central city area. Five percent of these students had attended from five to nine schools.
>
> Administrators of public education in big cities typically insist that a child relocate in a new school if he moves into a new district; and in a big city this may mean that a move of only four blocks is into a new school district. Yet, the same administrators complain about the problem of transiency because it interferes with the educational progress of a child [p. 264].

Whatever images students hold of the inner-city school, the images probably come from direct and immediate experience with the local environment. The community includes the people with whom the student associates, and the structures and relationships that define that community are those structures and relationships that directly impinge on him. Thus the reported importance of Rick Washington's street life should not be surprising, for Rick's street life probably constitutes much of his community. As books like The Vice Lords (Keiser, 1969) make so eminently clear, the street life of the child in the inner city has many of the salient characteristics we normally attribute to the notion of community, such as shared symbols, rituals, and values.

THE CLASSROOM—WHERE IT'S AT

All the forces and factors that have been discussed in the previous sections come to bear on the classroom, along with many other psychological and social factors that have not been touched on. It is in this web of relationships and emotions, perceptions and expectations that teachers must teach and students are supposed to learn. The strategies that teachers develop to induce students to behave in ways that are assumed to lead to learning and the responses students make to these strategies are shaped and formed by all of these factors. This shaping and forming occurs whether the teacher is aware of it or not. The purpose of this section is to present some of the strategies teachers develop and some of the responses students make to these strategies. Particular attention will be given to the impact the social context of the school has on the strategies that teachers develop and the responses that students are apt to give.

The teacher who holds the view that the dominant role of the teacher is that of moral leader and that the proper position of the student is that of moral involvement is apt to employ teaching strategies that fall under the broad category of *normative inducements*. Normative inducements are efforts to direct, control, or motivate student behavior through the use of morally compelling symbols of approval. For example, when a teacher suggests to a student that he is a good student or a bad student, the teacher is employing a normative strategy. When the teacher rewards a student with prestige, status, or privilege *or* takes these away, the teacher is employing normative strategies.

The perplexing aspect of the employment of normative strategies is that the effectiveness of these strategies is dependent on the teacher's and the student's shared meanings and estimations of worth and value. If meanings are not shared or if estimations of worth and value are highly divergent, what the teacher sees as a symbolic reward may well be seen by the student as a punishment. The author recalls observing one situation where a student very much like Rick Washington wrote a bit of poetry and quietly submitted it to the teacher. Since the teacher was committed to teaching poetry, she decided that this student's behavior should somehow be rewarded. The teacher's total lack of awareness of the context of the school and her overestimation of her power as moral leader turned what might have been a beautiful introduction to the romance of poetry into a traumatic finish to a budding interest in "poms." The teacher read the poem out loud in class and proudly announced her elation with the student's fine work. Immediately after class some of the student's peers snickered at him and called him names. Perhaps this student was able to weather the psychosocial storm the teacher's approval generated, but the odds are he never was so "dumb" as to write poetry again.

A second kind of inducement strategy teachers may resort to is coercion. *Coercive strategies* include those activities that involve the infliction of pain, the limitation of mobility, or the denial of access to physical and social activities. The public ideology of schoolteachers, research evidence, and common decency all indicate that coercive strategies should seldom if ever be employed by a professional educator. Yet the continued use of detention, the denial of access to extracurricular activities unless the student is academically successful, and the continued significance of the paddle in the hand of the teacher or the assistant principal in charge of discipline (sometimes endearingly called the chief head knocker), all indicate that coercive strategies continue to be used in the public school. As late as 1956, 77 percent of schoolteachers were in favor of elementary teachers having the authority to use corporal punishment; 84 percent were in favor of principals having such authority in elementary school; 37 percent were in favor of high school teachers having such authority; and 55 percent were in favor of high school principals having such authority (Nash, 1963).

In spite of preachments against coercive strategies and in spite of research that indicates the harm coercion does to positive learning, coercive strategies continue to be employed. Why? The easy answer is that teachers tend to manifest personality characteristics that result in sadistic authoritarian behavior. One could undoubtedly muster some evidence for such a view. It is possible, however, that coercive strategies continue to be employed precisely because they are so convenient, so utterly simple, and do not depend for their effectiveness on the cooperation of the student or the social context of the application, although in some schools it may be a mark of manhood and status to be paddled. If one views the difficulty the alienated student creates for the teacher whose image of his role is that of a moral leader, the tendency to rely on coercion is more understandable. Students like Rick Washington drive the moral leader teacher nearly to apoplexy. Every normative inducement tried will probably fail. Since Rick is apparently bright and certainly has leadership ability, he will probably be referred to at first as an "underachiever." But as he continues to fail to respond to normative strategies, teachers will more systematically make moral judgments concerning Rick's personal character and his destiny. "He'll come to a no good end" may never show up in his permanent record, but it will be heard in the teachers' lounge. Some of the moral leader types may even justify their use of coercion by pointing out that the minor pain or limitations in mobility that they and the school are causing Rick are nothing compared to the systematic coercion of the penal institution that will be his destiny if he fails to respond. Indeed, the moral leader teacher may even argue that coercion is used "for the student's own good." Probably Rick, or some student like Rick, would respond to the teacher as a moral leader if the teacher understood the social context in which he was working. *To Sir with Love* (Braithwaite, 1960) is a romantic and simplistic presentation of a teacher–moral leader who was able to use his position to direct student behavior with only minimal coercion. But he was able to do so only when he adjusted his leadership strategies to square with the symbolic meanings held by the students.

A third type of strategy that classroom teachers may employ can be labeled *remunerative strategies*. Remunerative strategies involve giving and taking away material rewards. Most teachers probably use few remunerative strategies, because few material rewards are available to the school system. In the days of the little red schoolhouse the practice of giving pencils and candy to the winners of the spelling bee or ciphering match was a remunerative strategy. Recently, some attention has been given to the systematic employment of remunerative strategies by educators interested in behavior modification. (See Chapter 4 by Wasik.) Remunerative strategies might be quite effective with children who for cultural or psychosocial reasons have difficulty in deferring gratification and even more difficulty in making connections between symbolic rewards and behavior. One might object to the use of remunerative strategies on philosophical grounds, but it is doubtful if one could argue that the use of remunerative strategies is as questionable as coercion.

A fourth and final set of strategies to be discussed includes *psychological-affective strategies*. Psychological-affective strategies involve presumed personal relationships between the teacher and the student. Calling on words like *rapport* and *meaningful relationships*, we get a feel of what is implied by psychological-affective strategies. The teacher presumes she is a significant and important person to the child and acts on that assumption to induce, direct, or motivate behavior. In actual practice it is often quite difficult to separate normative strategies from psychological-affective strategies. Perhaps the most crucial distinction is that morally involved students will respond to normative strategies even if they dislike the teacher or do not hold the teacher to be a significant other. On the other hand, it would be difficult to imagine the alienated student responding to normative strategies. But the alienated student may respond to psychological-affective strategies if indeed the teacher is able to establish a significant personal relationship with the student.

It is important to keep in mind that students, like teachers, are engaged in inducing behavior on the part of others—that is, teachers and peers—and in this activity they develop strategies quite similar to those employed by the teacher. In responding to the teacher's inducement strategies, students probably behave in a variety of ways. (Merton, 1968, suggests the ideas of conformity, retreatism, rebellion, innovation, and ritualism. The author's use of these ideas may represent something of a distortion of Merton's initial intent.)

Most typically, students respond by conforming, that is, by doing what the teacher indicates should be done. Another response is to retreat. *Retreat* as the term is used here involves withdrawal from the interaction situation. For example, it is likely that Mary Cairns would engage in considerable retreatist behavior in Mrs. Fowler's class. Mary does not seem to be the type of student who would openly challenge the teacher's authority or direction; yet Mrs. Fowler reports that "she won't do anything I ask her."

Another type of response students could make is rebellion. As the term *rebellion* is used here, it means something similar to the more general notion of nonconformity. Like the retreatist, the rebel refuses to comply with the directives of the teacher, but unlike the retreatist, his refusal is overt. Furthermore, the rebel is likely to offer alternative behaviors. Sometimes these behaviors may be a simple challenge to the teacher to "make him do it." At other times the rebel may say, "Oh, I don't want to—why don't we . . .?" Probably, Stanley Robinson would be apt to engage in such behaviors in a class in Midview.

Students may also make an innovative response. *Innovation* includes the acceptance of the teacher's general direction, but it also includes a modification or expansion of that direction. The student does what the teacher indicates but in his own way.

Ritualism, another type of response, is difficult to distinguish from conformity. Ritualism involves doing what is required but not for the reasons officially indicated. Teachers are sensitive to the presence of ritualism in their classrooms. Such statements as "You should study in order to understand, not just for grades" and "Now I don't want you to cram for this exam" carry the teacher's warnings against ritualism. The moral leader teacher probably has more difficulty with ritual behavior than he might otherwise, for he tends to concentrate on looking for "outward signs of internal grace." Katherine Fowler, dear lady that she might be, would probably be much more pleased with Mary Cairns if Mary just turned in her homework assignment. At least then the teacher would know she was "trying." There is considerable research evidence suggesting that teachers tend to reward conformity and ritualistic behavior much more freely than they do creative and innovative behavior.

These categories include most of the classroom behaviors that are interesting and often misunderstood by the classroom teacher. It is worth our time to examine more closely at least one of these patterns—the pattern of *strategic deviancy.*

Given the superordinate-subordinate nature of most classroom relationships, the teacher is expected and comes to expect himself to establish and enforce the rules of appropriate classroom behavior. Such a view may lead the teacher to believe that any time he or she perceives a violation of a rule, the student who is violating the rule is engaging in some active rebellion or open challenge to authority. So long as the student does not have support from his peers, the teacher's evaluation is probably valid. There are other times, however, when particular students are expected to be innovative. When the student rebels or innovates because rebellion or innovation is expected by his peers, such behavior indicates what is here called strategic deviancy. For example, in the junior high setting some students gain status with their peers by disrupting the normal flow of classroom activity, for example, by dropping a book, flipping a paper wad, or shuffling their feet. As student alienation from the ongoing classroom activities increases, the incidents of such deviancy will increase, and the status and prestige that such acts bring students will increase also. It is highly likely, for example, that Rick Washington will become increasingly effective at engaging in such acts of strategic deviancy.

A more conventional and often accepted act of strategic deviancy is "getting the teacher off the subject." Students who engage in this type of action may be relatively bright and accepted by the teacher as being a leader. There is no way of knowing for sure, but we would not be too far wrong if we suspected that Stanley Robinson might engage in this type of strategic deviancy rather systematically and quite effectively in Mrs. Fowler's class. In schools similar to Midview the author has observed students like Stanley directing classroom activities like a master of orchestration. At the same time the teacher continues with the pleasant myth that she is really in charge.

WE HAVE MET THE ENEMY AND IT IS US

Recently teachers and schools have come under a great deal of attack. Teachers have been called callous, insensitive, stupid, and bores. Undoubtedly, there are teachers who deserve such labels. These people should be isolated and removed from the teaching profession. Unfortunately, there are many teachers who are basically intelligent, sensitive, and utterly decent but who behave very much like their more callous and insensitive colleagues. They behave this way because they are ignorant of the social context of the school and have few conceptual tools with which to overcome this ignorance. This discussion should provide the teacher with some crude framework that will serve as a starting point for understanding what might be going on between teachers, students, and schools.

It is not enough, however, to know what the facts are and to understand the conditions of the teacher's work. One must act on that knowledge, even when the knowledge is incomplete, speculative, and imprecise. For too long teachers have hidden behind the convenient shelter that "it's fine in theory, but it won't work in practice." Some things that will work in practice should not be practiced, and some practices that will work are employed too infrequently. It is the task of the professional teacher to develop a theory of instruction that establishes practices that are sensitive to the social context of the school but do not violate what we know about conditions conducive to learning.

SOME SUGGESTED ACTIVITIES

1. Visit three or four different schools that seem to you to serve clienteles that come from communities that differ in important ways. For example, you might visit an inner-city school, a rural school, and a suburban school. During your visits attempt to determine the ways in which the communities are different, and make a list of these differences. You might also want to make a list of the ways in which the communities are similar. Using this list, develop a series of speculative statements concerning how these differences might be reflected in the classroom behavior of teachers and students. Finally, revisit the schools and observe classrooms to see if you can find any evidence to support your speculations.

2. Observe a first grade class, a sixth grade class, and a senior high class, and see if the strategies the teacher employs are different at different grade levels. For example, do elementary teachers rely as much on statements of right and wrong, good and bad, as do high school teachers? Or do high school teachers frequently use words like *right* and *wrong*, and elementary teachers more frequently use words like *good* and *bad*?

3. Develop an interview schedule in which you attempt to assess the images teachers have of themselves, particularly in regard to the impact they think they have on the lives of students. Develop a similar interview schedule in which you attempt to assess the images students hold of teachers, particularly in terms of the impact students believe teachers have on their lives. Using the two interview schedules you have developed, interview some teachers and students from the same schools and compare your findings.

REFERENCES

Bettelheim, Bruno. "The Decision to Fail." *The School Review* 69 (Winter 1961): 377–412.

Braithwaite, E. R. *To Sir with Love.* Englewood Cliffs, N. J.: Prentice-Hall, 1960.

Brembeck, Cole S. *Social Foundations of Education: Environmental Influences in Teaching and Learning,* 2d ed. New York: Wiley, 1971.

Brookover, W. B. et al. "The Relationship of Self-Image to Achievement in Junior High School Subjects." Final Report of Cooperative Research Project No. 845, Michigan State University Office of Education, U.S. Department of Health, Education, and Welfare, 1962.

Coleman, James S. The Adolescent Society. New York: Crowell Collier and Macmillan, 1949.

Deutsch, Martin. "Early Social Environment: Its Influence on School Adaption." The School Drop Out. Washington, D.C.: National Education Association, 1964, pp. 90–91.

Etzioni, Amitai. A Comparative Analysis of Complex Organizations. New York: Free Press, 1961.

Goslin, David A. The School in Contemporary Society. Glenview, Ill.: Scott Foresman, 1965.

Grambs, Jean Dresden. "The Neighborhood School Revisited: A Sociological Journey." In Society and Education, edited by James R. Raths and Jean Dresden Grambs, pp. 260–269. Englewood Cliffs, N. J.: Prentice-Hall, 1965.

Hollingshead, August B. Elmtown's Youth. New York: Wiley, 1945.

Jencks, Christopher; Smith, Marshall; Ackland, Henry; Bane, Mary Jo; Cohen, David; Gintis, Herbert; Heyns, Barbara; and Michelson, Stephen. Inequality: A Reassessment of the Effect of Family and Schooling in America. New York: Basic Books, 1972.

Keiser, R. Lincoln. The Vice Lords. New York: Holt, Rinehart, and Winston, 1969.

Merton, Robert K. Social Theory and Social Structure, 1968 enlarged ed. New York: Free Press, 1968.

Nash, Paul. "Corporal Punishment in an Age of Violence." Educational Theory 13, 1963: 295–308.

Rosenthal, R., and Jacobsen, L. Pygmalion in the Classroom. New York: Holt, Rinehart, and Winston, 1968.

Schlechty, Phillip C. "The School and the Community Power Structure." Unpublished research report, Ohio State University, 1960.

Vidich, Arthur J., and Bensman, Joseph. Small Town in Mass Society. Princeton, N. J.: Princeton University Press, 1958.

Waller, Willard. The Sociology of Teaching. New York: Wiley, Sons, 1967.

Wehling, Leslie J., and Charters, W. W. Jr. "Dimensions of Teacher Beliefs About the Teaching Process." American Education Research Journal 6 (January 1969): 7–30.

3 · The influence of teachers' attitudes and expectations on classroom behavior

THOMAS L. GOOD
University of Missouri at Columbia

JERE E. BROPHY
University of Texas at Austin

KEY CONCEPTS

Teachers' expectation
Teachers' attitude
Differential teacher behavior
Self-fulfilling prophecy

Teachers develop attitudes toward their students and hold expectations about student performance. In our three scenarios these expectations are negative and rigid. At Midview School we witness a conversation between Mrs. Fowler and Mrs. Cummings in which they compared students with their older brothers and sisters, and we hear teachers freely state that students with low IQs cannot be expected to perform in the classroom. At Bridges Elementary School we listen as Mr. Bellamy is told that students are inattentive, not interested in learning, irresponsible, and unwilling to work unless threatened. At Knightcrest Middle School we see that Miss Carter resents her students' superior social status and openly expresses hostility about parents who provide "too much" for their children.

Negative, rigid expectations and invidious comparisons of students with older siblings often lead teachers to treat students in ways that guarantee poor performance. Of course, there is no direct data in these case studies to show that the teachers did this, and it is possible for teachers to hold low expectations for students and yet treat them fairly and effectively. However, it is the rare teacher who behaves this way. Teachers who expect students to do poorly typically behave in ways that minimize learning opportunities for these students.

The following pages present data showing that the teacher's behavior is sometimes influenced by the expectations and attitudes he holds about students. After discussing these data, we shall present a model to illustrate how the teacher's expectations may act as self-ful-

Then we shall return to the protocols to discuss how ⌐tations, biases, and attitudes represented there are

MENT
TEACHER BEHAVIOR

ations influence the students' behavior, motivation, it should be possible to show how teachers treat students y as a result of their expectations. The studies reviewed in the next few pages have attempted to determine if teachers treat students that they like or hold high expectations for differently than they treat students about whom they feel indifferently or for whom they hold low expectations.

A student's achievement level figures heavily in whether or not he responds frequently. Good (1970) and Kranz, Weber, and Fishell (1970) found that high-achieving elementary school students were asked more questions and received more praise from the teacher than low-achieving students. Similarly, Mendoza, Good, and Brophy (1971) and Horn (1914) reported that high-achieving students in secondary schools received more opportunities to respond than low-achieving students. Jones (1971), studying student teachers in secondary schools, also reported that high achievers were asked more questions than low achievers. Good, Sikes, and Brophy (1972) reported that in comparison to other students, low-achieving males in junior high received inferior treatment, and high-achieving males received more frequent and more favorable contacts with the teachers.

Several studies suggest that in addition to these differences in the frequency of the teachers' contacts with students, the quality of teacher–child interaction varies with the students' achievement level. Rowe (1969) found that teachers waited significantly longer for more capable students than for less apt students before giving the answer or calling on another student. Thus slower students had to respond more quickly to avoid losing their turn. These results surprised the teachers, who were not aware that they were behaving in this fashion. One teacher said, "I guess we just don't expect an answer, so we move on to someone else."

Brophy and Good (1970) studied the behavior of four first grade teachers with high- and low-achieving students. They reported only minor differences in the *frequency* of the teachers' contacts with students of differing achievement levels, but found important variations in the quality of these contacts. For example, Brophy and Good found that teachers were much more likely to praise high-achieving students than low-achieving students, even when differences in success and failure were taken into account.

When high-achieving students gave a right answer, they were praised 12 percent of the time. Low-achieving students were praised only 6 percent of the time following a right answer. Even though they gave fewer right answers, low-achieving students were less likely to be praised when they did so. Similarly, low-achieving students were more likely to receive criticism from the teacher for a wrong answer. Following an incorrect response low-achieving students were criticized 18 percent of the time, and high achievers were criticized 6 percent of the time.

An additional finding of interest was that when high-achieving students made no response, said they didn't know, or answered incorrectly, teachers were more likely to stay with the students (that is, repeat the question, provide a clue, or ask a new question). In contrast, teachers were more likely to "give up" (that is, give the answer or call on another student) under similar circumstances with low-achieving students. The teachers were twice as likely to stay with high achievers as they were to stay with low achievers. These results, in combination with Rowe's data, suggest that some teachers expect and demand performance from high-achieving students, but give up on low-achieving students and accept only minimal performance.

This is not to suggest that all teachers categorically favor their high-achieving students. Brophy and Good (1973), in another study of first grade classrooms, showed that some teachers are quite responsive to low achievers and actively provide them with frequent and helpful contacts. Also, teachers who favor high achievers and low achievers do not necessarily express their preferences in similar ways. Kranz et al. (1970) showed that sometimes teachers interacted much more frequently with high achievers than with medium- or low-achieving students, but that in other classes teachers had similar contact patterns with high- and medium-achieving students but noticeably fewer contacts with low-achieving students. In general, low achievers have fewer chances to respond than other students.

Rist (1970) presented an interesting, but distressing, longitudinal case study of a group of children progressing from kindergarten through second grade. He explained how teachers created a caste system within this group of students: High-status children learned and communicated disrespect for low-status children. Interestingly, students who needed the most help from the teacher, the ones who were shy and not very verbal, were seated in the rear of the room when they began kindergarten. The teacher was not aware that this would reduce their contacts with her and slow their classroom progress. Yet these unfortunate circumstances did result from the teacher's decision to separate and "exile" children that were perceived to have little learning potential. Such rigid grouping patterns also prevent low-achieving students from learning from their classmates.

These studies suggest that teachers should improve their contact patterns with low achievers. If the low achiever is relatively ignored and given second-class status, he will continue to fall progressively further and further behind his peers as long as he stays in school. Physically separating such students into rigid groups increases the probability that the teacher will treat them differently and inappropriately. Much of this is done unwittingly by teachers, but it is done nevertheless.

TEACHERS' ATTITUDES
AND DIFFERENTIAL TEACHER BEHAVIOR

There is some evidence to suggest that differential teacher attitudes are also associated with differential teacher behavior. Silberman (1969) asked a sample of ten female, third grade teachers, who had taught in upper middle-class suburban school systems for at least 3 years, to respond to the following interview items:

1. *Attachment.* If you could keep one student another year for the sheer joy of it, whom would you pick?
2. *Concern.* If you could devote all your attention to a child who concerns you a great deal, whom would you pick?
3. *Indifference.* If a parent were to drop in unannounced for a conference, whose child would you be least prepared to talk about?
4. *Rejection.* If your class were to be reduced by one child, whom would you be relieved to have removed?

Following these interviews, 20 hours of observational data were collected in each class to see how teachers treated the students they nominated and to see what the students were like. Profiles of the characteristics of the four types of students and of the teachers' behavior toward them are presented in the following paragraphs.

ATTACHMENT. Children in this group conformed, fulfilled the personal needs of the teachers (volunteered, answered questions correctly), and made few demands on the teachers' energies. Even though the teachers preferred these students, they did not interact with them or call on them more frequently than the others. However, the teachers did praise these students more and held them up as models to their classmates.

CONCERN. Children in this group made extensive but appropriate demands on the teacher's time. Of the groups studied these children received the most attention from the teacher. Teachers initiated frequent contacts and placed few restrictions on these children, who were allowed to approach them freely in most circumstances. Teachers praised their work frequently and were careful to reward effort. However, at times the teachers did express their concern directly and openly; "I don't know what to do with you next."

INDIFFERENCE. These children were seldom noticed by the teachers, who had much less contact with them than with other children. Other than infrequency and brevity of contacts, no differences in the teachers' behavior toward these children were observed.

REJECTION. The teachers viewed these children as making illegitimate or overwhelming demands on them. In contrast to the students the teachers were concerned about, these children often received criticism when they approached the teacher. Whereas students in the concern group could do no wrong, students in the rejection group could no nothing right. These children were under continual surveillance, and much of the teacher's behavior directed at them involved attempts to control their behavior. However, the teachers had frequent contact with these children and frequently praised and criticized their behavior in public. Interestingly, eight of the ten students in this group were asked to leave the room at least once when an observer was present.

Attitudes toward individual students significantly affected the teachers' behavior, although there were differences in the behaviors of teachers holding the same attitudes toward students. The teacher's concern and indifference were more readily expressed than rejection and attachment. Silberman suggests that the teacher role may interact with the teacher's preferences to prevent the expression of rejection and attachment. Feelings of indifference and concern present less of a role conflict, and therefore it is easier for the teacher to express these in the classroom.

Good and Brophy (1972b) replicated Silberman's study in nine first grade classrooms. Three classes were studied in each of three types of schools: upper middle-class white, lower-class white, and lower-class black. In Silberman's study knowledge of the relevant variables might have led teachers to distort their behavior during observation periods. (For example, they may have masked favoritism toward preferred children or demonstrated concern for children described as objects of special concern.) In the replication study Good and Brophy collected attitude information from the teachers *after* each class had been observed for sixteen 2 ½-hour periods.

Teachers were told that the investigators were interested in observing differences in the classroom behavior of children who varied in achievement. In late September each teacher supplied a list, ranking her children in order according to the level of achievement she expected from them. Other than this achievement rank and a seating chart, no information was requested from the teachers until all behavioral observational data were collected. This eliminated the possibility that the teachers' knowledge of the relevant attitude variables could influence the behavioral data.

Data on the sex and achievement status of the children in the four attitude groups show some distinct patterns. Roughly, equal numbers of boys and girls were in the attachment, indifference, and concern groups, but the teachers nominated twice as many boys as girls for the rejection group. Achievement status was related to all four attitudes. The attachment group was composed mostly of high achievers, and the other three groups included mostly low and average achievers. Thus teachers get to know and like high achievers. Children in the middle range of achievement appear to be less salient to the teachers; they were mentioned frequently only on the indifference item. Low achievers were mentioned most often as objects of teacher concern (especially if they were girls) or rejection (especially if they were boys).

Although the data in this study were drawn from first grade classrooms and from schools representing three distinct socioeconomic levels, they confirm and extend Silberman's findings.

Teachers in this study did interact in distinct ways with the students they were attached to. Although there was no gross favoritism, the teachers provided these students with additional support in subtle ways. Teachers may also reward such students in ways that were not examined in this study. For example, Hadley (1954) has shown that teachers grade the students they like the most higher and the students they like the least lower than they deserve on the basis of standardized achievement test scores.

The findings for the students in the concern group parallel Silberman's, and the data for students in the indifference group confirm, but extend somewhat, his conclusions. Specifically, both studies showed that students in the indifference group do not approach the teacher, nor does the teacher approach them. However, Good and Brophy also noted that these children were seldom praised or criticized in academic work situations, even though their performance was similar to other students. Thus these children have little contact with the teacher, and when they do have contact, it seldom results in strong evaluative comment.

The findings for the rejected students differ somewhat from the data reported by Silberman. He reported that the frequency of the teachers' contact with rejected students was similar to the frequency of contact with other students, but that the teachers both praised and criticized the rejected students more frequently. However, in this study the teachers avoided initiating contacts with rejected students. Also, they often failed to provide these students with feedback about their work, and when they did provide feedback, it was much more likely to involve criticism than the feedback given to other children.

These studies show that the attitudes teachers hold toward students do influence the ways in which they interact with those students. As Jackson and Lahaderne (1967) have reported, classroom life is an uneven affair, with some students having much more contact with the teacher than others. Teachers' attitudes toward students affect the quality and quantity of contacts they have with students.

More studies are needed, particularly at the secondary level, to achieve a clearer understanding of how teachers' attitudes structure teacher–child interaction. Available data suggest that teachers prefer bright but docile students and are indifferent toward passive students of average achievement. Interestingly, except for sex, the characteristics of the students in the concern and rejection groups appear to be similar; yet certain unknown differences cause teachers to become concerned about and work harder with the first group and to reject and avoid the second group.

We have reviewed several studies showing that some teachers provide high achievers with interaction that is quantitatively and qualitatively superior to their interaction with low achievers, and that differential teacher attitudes toward students often result in differential teacher behavior. We now present studies to show that in some situations differential teacher behavior affects student behavior and/or achievement.

IMPACT OF THE TEACHERS' EXPECTATIONS ON THE STUDENTS' BEHAVIOR

Palardy (1969) studied the reading achievement of the students in the classes of two groups of first grade teachers. Using a questionnaire, Palardy identified ten teachers who thought that boys could learn to read just as successfully as girls in the first grade and fourteen who thought that boys could not learn to read as successfully as girls. This information was gathered from a single item on an extensive questionnaire, so that the teachers were not aware of the nature of the study.

Five teachers from each group were selected for further study, because they were closely matched on several important variables. These teachers were all white females with bachelor's degrees and at least three years of teaching experience in the first grade. All taught in middle-class schools and used the same basic reading series, working with three reading groups in heterogeneously grouped, self-contained classrooms. Reading readiness and reading achievement scores were obtained from the ten classrooms involved, and the two groups were compared.

The students were exactly comparable on the reading readiness scores taken in September, so that there was no initial group difference. However, differences were apparent among the boys in reading achievement scores obtained in March. Boys in classes in which the teacher believed they could achieve as well as girls averaged 96.5 on these reading achievement tests, whereas those in classes with teachers who did not believe they could do as well as girls averaged only 89.2. The girls in these classes averaged 96.2 and 96.7 respectively. Thus in the classes where teachers did not think boys could achieve as well as girls, the boys did, indeed, achieve at a lower level.

Another study of this type was conducted by Doyle, Hancock, and Kifer (1971). These investigators asked first grade teachers to estimate the IQs of their students, shortly before an IQ test was given. The teachers' IQ estimates were then compared to the IQs obtained from the tests. The comparisons showed that the teachers tended to overestimate the IQs of girls and to underestimate the IQs of boys. Also, these estimates were related to the children's reading achievement. Even though there was no difference between the boys' IQs and the girls' IQs, the girls showed higher reading achievement. Furthermore, within the two sexes the children whose IQs had been overestimated by the teachers had higher reading achievement scores than those whom the teachers had underestimated. All of this might simply mean that the teachers were heavily influenced by the children's reading abilities in making judgments about their general intelligence. However, it is likely that the teachers' expectations affected their teaching of reading. In addition to the previous findings, it was discovered that the classes of teachers who generally overestimated the children's IQs achieved more than the classes of teachers who generally underestimated, regardless of sex.

These studies show that school achievement is not simply a matter of the child's native ability; the teachers' expectations are also involved. Several other studies have shown the same result with different types of students in different settings. Douglas (1964), in a massive study of the tracking system used in the British schools, found that children who were clean and well-clothed, and who came from better kept homes, tended to be placed in higher tracks than their measured ability would predict. Once they were in these tracks, they tended to stay there and to perform acceptably. Mackler (1969), studying a school in Harlem, also found that children tended to stay in the tracks in which they were placed, even though initial placement was affected by many factors other than measured ability. Douglas' and Mackler's findings show that: (1) teachers' expectations about a child's achievement can be affected by factors having little or nothing to do with his ability; and (2) these expectations can determine the child's level of achievement by confining his learning opportunities to those available in his track. A student who is stuck needlessly in a low track is unlikely to reach his potential, because his teachers do not expect much from him and his self-concept and achievement motivation are likely to deteriorate over time.

Studies in three very different settings showed that the students' learning was affected by the expectations induced in their instructors. Beez (1968), working with adult tutors who were teaching Head Start children, Burnham (1968), working with swimming instructors teaching pre-adolescents how to swim, and Schrank (1968), working with Air Force mathematics instructors teaching airmen mathematics, all found the same results. In each study the experimenter manipulated the teachers' expectations. Sometimes the teachers were led to believe that the children or classes they would work with had high learning potentials; sometimes they were led to believe the students had low learning potentials. There was no factual basis for these expectations, because the groups had been matched or randomly selected. Nevertheless, in each case students of instructors who had been led to have high expectations learned more than the students of instructors who had been led to expect little. In his study Beez (1968) monitored the teaching behavior and found that the achievement differences were a direct result of differences in the teaching to which the children were exposed. Tutors who had high expectations attempted to teach more than those with low expectations and succeeded in doing so.

TEACHERS' EXPECTATIONS
AS SELF-FULFILLING PROPHECIES

The studies presented in the preceding section each illustrated how teachers' expectations can function as self-fulfilling prophecies. That is, teachers' expectations affect the ways they treat their students, and over time the ways they treat the students affect the amount that the students learn. In this sense, then, expectations are self-fulfilling: Teachers with high expectations attempt to teach more, and teachers with low expectations tend to teach less. As a result, both groups of teachers tend to end up with what they expected, although not with what they might have achieved if they had had different expectations in the first place.

Robert Rosenthal and Lenore Jacobson's *Pygmalion in the Classroom* (1968) created wide interest in and controversy about this topic. Their book describes research in which they deliberately tried to manipulate teachers' expectations about their students' achievement to see if these expectations would be fulfilled. The study involved several classes in each of the first six grades of school. The teachers' expectations were created by claiming that a test (actually a general achievement test) had been developed to identify late intellectual bloomers. The teachers were told that this test would select children who were about to bloom intellectually and, therefore, could be expected to show unusually large achievement gains during the coming school year. A few children in each classroom were identified as late bloomers. They had actually been selected randomly, not on the basis of any test. Thus there was no real reason to expect unusual gains from them. No factual basis existed for the expectations induced in the teachers.

However, achievement test data from the end of the school year offered some evidence that these children did show better performance (although the effects were confined mostly to the first two grades). Rosenthal and Jacobson explained their results in terms of the self-fulfilling prophecy effects of the teachers' expectations. They reasoned that the expectations they had created about these special children somehow caused the teachers to treat them differently, so that they really did do better by the end of the year.

Controversy has raged over this topic ever since. The findings of *Pygmalion in the Classroom* were widely publicized and discussed, and for a time they were accepted enthusiastically. Later, however, after critics (Snow, 1969; Taylor, 1970) had attacked the study and a replication (Claiborn, 1969) failed to produce the same results, the idea that teachers' expectations could function as self-fulfilling prophecies began to be rejected.

We think the evidence now available supports the idea that teachers' expectations are sometimes self-fulfilling. However, this statement requires some explanation, both about the research available and about the way the process is defined and described.

Regarding research, one must make a distinction between two types of studies in this area. The first type, which includes Rosenthal and Jacobson's work as well as that of others who have tried to replicate their study, involves attempts to manipulate or induce teachers' expectations. That is, the investigators try to create expectations by identifying "late bloomers," using phony IQ scores, or providing some other fictitious information about students' ability. The second type of study uses the teachers' own expectations as they exist naturally. No attempt is made to induce expectations. Instead, the teacher is simply asked to make predictions or to rank, or group, students according to achievement or ability.

Studies involving induced expectations have produced mixed, mostly negative results. Two recent studies suggest that the failures in some studies involving induced expectancies occurred because the teachers did not acquire the expectancy that the experimenter wanted them to have. The most obvious case is where teachers know that the basis for the expectancy is not true. This was shown by Schrank (1970) in an adaptation of his earlier study of Air Force mathematics courses. For this second study Schrank merely simulated the manipulation of teachers' expectations; the teachers knew that the students had been grouped randomly rather than by ability levels. Under these conditions, even when the teachers were given instructions to teach the groups as if they had been tracked by ability level, no expectation effects were observed. Similar results were found by Fleming and Anttonen (1971), who tried to falsify IQ information about some children by adding sixteen points to the actual scores. They found that the teachers did not accept the phony IQs as real, and, therefore, did not allow the IQs to affect their treatment of the students. When the teachers were faced with too great a discrepancy between what they saw in their everyday contacts with their students and what a test purported to reveal about them, the teachers rejected the test data.

These results suggest that attempts to induce expectations in teachers will fail if the expectations are too obviously and sharply discrepant from the students' observable characteristics. The credibility of the source is probably another important factor. Teachers are much more likely to accept the opinions of the principal or of the teacher who worked with the students the previous year than the opinions of a researcher who comes in, administers a test, and leaves without acquiring any more personal knowledge of the students.

Thus the negative results in studies using induced teachers' expectations should not necessarily be taken as disproof of the self-fulfilling prophecy idea. The negative results are more likely due to failure to induce the desired expectations in the teachers than to failure of the teachers' expectations to affect the teachers' behavior. Naturalistic studies using teachers' real expectations about their students have usually yielded positive findings. These studies show that teachers' expectations do tend to have self-fulfilling prophecy effects, causing the teachers to behave in ways that tend to make their expectations come true. It is likely that many students in most classrooms are not reaching their potential, because their teachers don't expect much from them and are satisfied with poor or mediocre performance, when they could obtain something better.

Overenthusiastic popular accounts of *Pygmalion in the Classroom* have sometimes misled people about the self-fulfilling prophecy idea. Sometimes these accounts imply that the mere existence of an expectation will automatically guarantee its fulfillment or that a magic and mysterious process is involved (just make a prediction and it will come true). Most teachers rightfully reject this idea as utter nonsense. However, this is not what we mean when we say that teachers' expectations can act as self-fulfilling prophecies. We refer here to something resulting naturally from a chain of observable causes, not to something akin to magic or ESP.

HOW THE PROCESS WORKS

The fact that teachers' expectations can be self-fulfilling is simply a special case of the principle that any expectations can be self-fulfilling. The process is not confined to classrooms. Although it is not true that "wishing can make it so," *our expectations do affect the way we behave in situations, and the way we behave affects how other people respond.* In some instances our expectations about people cause us to treat them in a way that makes them respond just as we expected they would. (See Chapter 7 by Coopersmith and Feldman for examples of how this process works in the area of self concept.)

For example, look ahead to the time when you accept your first teaching job and receive notice about which school you are being assigned to (or look back on this experience if you have gone through it already). Unless you already have information, you will probably want to find out as much as possible about the school and the principal you will be working with. Often, information can be gathered from a friend already teaching at the school. Suppose the friend says: "Mr. Jackson is a wonderful man. You'll love working for him. He's very warm and pleasant, and he really takes an interest in you. Feel free to go to him with your problems; he's always glad to help."

If you heard this about Mr. Jackson, how do you think you would respond to him when you met him? Think about this situation for a few moments. Now let's think about another situation. Suppose your friend said: "Mr. Jackson? Well, uh, he's sort of hard to describe. I guess he's all right, but I don't feel comfortable around him; he makes me nervous. I don't know what it is exactly; it's just that I get the feeling that he doesn't want to talk to me, that I'm wasting his time or irritating him." How do you think you would act when meeting Mr. Jackson after you had heard this?

If you are like most people, your behavior would be quite different in these two contrasting situations. Given the first information about Mr. Jackson, you would probably look forward to meeting him and would approach him with confidence and a friendly smile. Among other things, you would probably tell him that you have heard good things about him and that you are happy to be working with him and are looking forward to getting started. Given the second set of expectations, however, you would probably behave quite differently. You would be unlikely to look forward to the meeting in a positive sense, and you might well become nervous, inhibited, or overly concerned about making a good impression. You would probably approach with hesitation, wearing a serious expression or a forced smile, and speak to him in rather reserved, formal tones. Even if you said the same words to him, the chances are that they would sound more like a prepared speech than a genuine personal reaction.

Now, put yourself in Mr. Jackson's place. Assume he knows nothing about you as a person. Take a few moments to think about how he might respond to these two, very different approaches.

Chances are that Mr. Jackson would respond quite differently. In the first instance, faced with warmth, friendliness, and genuine-sounding compliments, he is likely to respond in kind. Your behavior would put him at ease and cause him to see you as a likable, attractive person. When he smiles and says he looks forward to working with you too, he will really mean it.

But what if Mr. Jackson is faced with a new teacher who approaches him somewhat nervously and formally? Again, he is likely to respond in kind. Such behavior is likely to make him nervous and formal, if he isn't already. He is likely to respond in an equally bland and formal manner. This response is likely to be followed by an awkward silence that makes both you and Mr. Jackson increasingly nervous. As the authority figure and "host," Mr. Jackson will probably feel compelled to make the next move. In view of your behavior, attempts at small talk would appear to be risky, so he probably will "get down to business" and begin to speak in his capacity as principal, talking to you in your capacity as one of his teachers.

These examples show how expectations can influence behavior and how the behavior can, in turn, help produce the originally expected results. Teachers who expect Mr. Jackson to be friendly and who approach him in a warm manner make it easier for him to feel at ease and to be friendly. On the other hand, teachers who expect him to be cold and who approach him formally tend to make him nervous, so that he responds in a way that does appear cold.

We can see parallel examples in the scenarios that you have read previously. Before meeting his students at Bridges Elementary School, Mr. Bellamy obtained information about them: Teachers consistently informed him that his students would be disinterested in school and irresponsible. Given this expectation, Mr. Bellamy may approach his students in a distant, formal way, and initially he may emphasize the need for students to understand the rules of *his* classroom. By consistently conveying his mistrust and feelings that students need to be controlled, Mr. Bellamy may undermine his chance for establishing rapport with his students and for developing a classroom where students assume responsibility for establishing classroom rules and where students can study materials that are relevant and useful for them. (That is, if he never expresses his desire to create a classroom that is responsive to their needs, students are unlikely to express their needs to him.) Given the picture that the other teachers paint, Mr. Bellamy could be influenced so that he will bring about the forecasted undesirable student behavior by communicating low expectations (threatening punishment for inattention, reminding the students unnecessarily and excessively that they must not mutilate textbooks or other school property, suggesting that anybody absent on test day better have a good written excuse, and so on).

Similarly, it is easy to see that when Miss Carter talks with parents at Knightcrest School, her perception of herself (as someone who doesn't belong in the community) and the children's parents (people who suspect that she's incompetent) may lead her to behave awkwardly, incoherently, and submissively. The parent may well treat her as an incompetent inferior, not because she is a teacher, but because she behaves as an incompetent inferior.

The examples show that it is not just the existence of an expectation that causes self-fulfillment; it is the behavior that this expectation produces. This behavior then affects the other person, making him more likely to act in the expected ways. In the classroom the process works like this:

1. The teacher expects specific behavior and achievements from particular students.
2. Because of his different expectations, the teacher behaves differently toward the different students.
3. The teacher's treatment tells each student what behavior and achievements the teacher expects from him and affects his self concept, achievement motivation, and level of aspiration.
4. If the teacher's treatment is consistent over time, and if the student does not actively resist or change it in some way, it will tend to shape his achievement and behavior. High-expectation students will be led to achieve at high levels, and the achievement of low-expectation students will decline.
5. With time the student's achievements and behavior will conform more and more closely to what was originally expected of him.

This model clearly shows that the teacher's expectations are not automatically self-fulfilling. To become so, they must be translated into behavior that will communicate the expectations to the student and shape his behavior in the direction of the expected patterns. This does not always happen. The teacher may not have clear-cut expectations about a particular student, or his expectations may continually change.

Even when he has consistent expectations, he may not necessarily communicate them to the student through consistent behavior. In this case, the expectation would not be self-fulfilling, even if it turned out to be correct. Finally, the student himself might prevent expectations from becoming self-fulfilling by overcoming them or by resisting them in a way that makes the teacher change his expectations. Although most classroom research has focused on the impact of teachers on students, there are arguments and data to suggest that the students' behavior does influence teachers' behavior (Emmer, Good, and Oakland, 1971; Martin, 1972; Oppenlander, 1969; Jenkins and Deno, 1969; Klein, 1971; Jones, 1971). Thus more than the mere existence of a teacher's expectation is required in order for that expectation to become self-fulfilling. It must lead to behavior that will communicate the expectation to the student, and this behavior must be effective in moving the student in the expected direction.

Similarly, teachers' attitudes may influence their teaching behavior and ultimately the progress of their students. For example, we have seen that teachers behave more desirably toward students they like than toward students they reject. Rejection of students can be seen in the three scenarios. Note especially at Bridges School how Rick Washington's previous teachers have described him. Each teacher's statement communicates a rejection of him as a person and complete abandonment of any attempt to teach him. The low achiever whom the teacher is concerned about may escape this fate, if the teacher's concern leads him to diagnose and remedy the student's learning difficulties. For the most part, however, students who benefit from a teacher's attitude of attachment or concern are those who are already well adjusted to the classroom (Silberman, 1969; Good and Brophy, 1972a; Feshback, 1969; Good and Grouws, 1972).

Although the preceding model describes how teachers may react differentially to individual students as a result of their performance expectations, the same process sometimes operates for a whole class or a whole school. For example, Miss Carter apparently feels that her students are "pampered" at home, and she may feel that she must "make it hard" on them so that they will become mature, responsible adults (like her, presumably). Also, her expectation that the parents and students will reject her may lead her to behave in ways that will cause this expectation to be fulfilled. (For example, she may apologize for her clothes, apologize or try to fake interest and knowledgeability when cultural topics are discussed, or give long sermons on "how you kids don't appreciate what a dollar's worth because you've never had to work for one.")

There is also evidence in the scenarios that the following attitude is implicitly accepted: "Students from low-income families won't learn." Note that Mr. Bellamy, a beginning teacher in a low-income school, has full instructional responsibility and that Miss Carter, also a beginning teacher but in a high-income neighborhood, has no responsibility for planning the instructional program of her students. In a high-income school young teachers are often "tutored" by experienced team leaders, so that they will teach more effectively. But in low-income schools the beginning teacher is often left to his own devices and told: "Don't worry. It's an impossible job. No one will blame you when you fail." Furthermore, it is well known that disproportionate numbers of beginning teachers begin their teaching careers in low-income areas and then move from these areas as soon as they have enough tenure to do so. Thus low-income schools have fewer veteran, effective teachers and lack the community–school stability and credibility that good teachers and good administrators build up. School systems implicitly support the view that low-income students are "poor investments" by sanctioning practices that allow (and at times encourage) experienced teachers who "show promise" to switch to "better" schools.

It is also interesting to contrast the heavy emphasis at Knightcrest on independent study and the belief that students should take a major responsibility for determining the subject matter they study with the emphasis at Bridges on student irresponsibility and the need for external threats and rewards. Obviously, the low expectations and lack of trust for students at Bridges will make it difficult for any teacher to experiment with student-centered methods.

Such school-wide norms, expectations, and teaching practices make it likely that teachers' behavior will be systematically influenced by the school they teach in. Failure expectations can be a problem in any school, however, even a generally good one. A teacher at Knightcrest might feel that six of his students can't make it, whereas a teacher at Bridges might feel that fifteen of his students can't make it. In either case, if the teacher categorically accepts his expectations, he will find ways to communicate them to his students.

Teachers' attitudes are expressed in similar ways in different school environments (Good and Brophy, 1972a). Teachers were found to treat students in the concern, indifference, attachment, and rejection groups in similar ways in three distinct school settings (lower-class black, lower-class Anglo, and upper-middle Anglo).

In summary, if teachers hold *strong* expectations or attitudes toward students, they communicate these attitudes in similar ways. However, not all teachers allow their low expectations for students to affect their classroom behavior. The authors have observed teachers who treat low achievers in fair and helpful ways (Brophy and Good, 1973). However, many teachers do hold low expectations for student performance (Good and Dembo, 1972), especially teachers in low-income schools (Becker, 1952; Fuchs, 1968; Davis and Dollard, 1940), and some do allow their low expectations to become self-fulfilling prophecies.

PRACTICE EXAMPLES

We have provided some practice examples you can use to sharpen your understanding of the self-fulfilling prophecy concept. Read each example and see if you think a self-fulfilling prophecy was involved. If so, you should be able to identify: (a) the original expectation, (b) behaviors that consistently communicated this expectation in ways that made it more likely to be fulfilled, and (c) evidence that the original expectation was confirmed. If the example does not contain all three elements, it does not illustrate a self-fulfilling prophecy.

1. Judy, a junior education major, tells her roommate, "I'll bet Ralph brings me flowers for our pinning anniversary." On their Monday night date Judy remarks, "Ralph, the funniest thing happened. Ann knitted a sweater for her boyfriend for their pinning anniversary, and it practically reached his knees." During another conversation the same evening, she says, "Yes, the initiation went perfectly. It was lovely, absolutely lovely. I love the sorority house at initiation time. The flowers are so nice, especially the roses. They are so special. They make me feel warm and happy." When Ralph arrives Saturday night for their anniversary date, he presents Judy with a lovely bouquet of roses.

2. Mrs. Explicit is giving directions to John Greene, a second grader who is frequently in trouble. Mrs. Explicit has no confidence in John's responsibility, so she gives him detailed instructions: "John, take this note to Mrs. Turner, whose room is at the end of the hall, across from the room where our fire drill exit is. This is a big responsibility, and I want you to remember . . . you will not make noise in the hall . . . don't stop to look in any other classrooms . . . and above all, don't go outside." With an obviously pained look, John responds, "Mrs. Explicit, don't you trust me?"

3. Dean Helpful counsels a few students in addition to his other, administrative duties. He does so because he is very interested in current student problems, and he enjoys the opportunity to stay in tune with student life. In September the dean begins to counsel Tom Bloom. The dean knows that Tom will probably flunk out of school at the end of the semester. His entrance scores are very low, and his writing skills are particularly poor. He is also socially withdrawn and shy, making it unlikely that he will get to know his instructors very well or receive much special help from them. The dean tells Tom that he may encounter academic difficulty, and urges him to enroll in the reading

clinic and to devote extra time on Saturdays to his studies. In addition, he has Tom report to his office once a week. Tom realizes that the dean expects him to have trouble unless he works hard. He begins to work as hard as he can and keeps it up for the whole semester. When the grade slips are mailed in January, Tom finds he has made a B average.

4. Mrs. Graney knows that Bill Burton will be a problem. She had his older brother the year before, and he was uncontrollable. Trying to keep Bill out of trouble, Mrs. Graney seats him at a table far away from the other third graders in the room. Before long, though, Bill begins to throw things at the other children to attract their attention.

5. Mal Chauvin is a young physics professor teaching undergraduates for the first time. He is especially concerned about reaching the girls in his class, because he expects them to have a difficult time. He thinks that most of the girls at the college are there just to get a husband, and he doesn't think they have much interest in or aptitude for physics. To avoid embarrassing them, he never calls on them to answer a mathematical question or to explain difficult concepts. He also shows his concern by looking at one of the girls after he introduces a new point and asking, "Do you understand?" However, the girls usually find this more embarrassing than helpful, and in general they don't do very well in his course.

6. Miss Ball is concerned about Dick Stewart's adjustment to his peer group. Dick is one of the boys in her second grade class, and although he participated all year long in the races and group games conducted during recess, he began to withdraw from the group in the spring, when she started the boys playing baseball. Although Dick was coordinated well enough, he hadn't played much baseball and had difficulty in both hitting and catching the ball. As a result, he was usually one of the last boys to be chosen when teams were selected. After this happened a few times, Dick began to withdraw, claiming that he didn't want to play because he had a headache, a stomachache, or a sore foot. This didn't fool Miss Ball, who recognized that Dick's embarrassment was the real reason.

To help Dick compensate for his deficiencies and to see that he didn't lose status with his peers, Miss Ball began allowing him to serve as umpire for ball games. This way he had an important and active role. She reinforced this by praising him and calling the other children's attention to his umpire work. In private contacts she reassured Dick that he shouldn't feel bad because he was not playing, and that there can't be a ball game without an umpire.

In the last few days of school Miss Ball decided to let Dick play again, now that his confidence was built up. She was gratified to see that he was chosen earlier than usual by the team captain. However, his batting and catching were just as bad as they had been before. The next day he was the last one chosen, and he begged off, complaining of a headache.

ANSWERS

Let's see if you were able to identify the self-fulfilling prophecies. If we have been successful in describing the process, you should have correctly identified each example.

Case 1 is an example of a self-fulfilling prophecy. Judy expected to receive flowers and consciously or unconsciously communicated this expectation to Ralph. Ralph took the hint and fulfilled her original expectation.

In Case 2, Mrs. Explicit's original expectancy is "If I don't give Johnny explicit instructions, he will take advantage of the situation and misbehave." She unconsciously communicates this expectation in her behavior toward Johnny. However, even though Johnny gets her "real message," his behavior does not change in the direction of her expectation. Thus this is not an example of a self-fulfilling prophecy. However, if Mrs. Explicit were to continue to treat Johnny this way, he might begin to behave as she expects. At this point, her expectations would become self-fulfilling.

Mary Cairns at Midview School may be a similar case. The teacher says that Mary "won't do anything I ask." Feeling this way, the teacher may communicate that she expects Mary to disobey. ("Mary, don't forget to sign your name." "Turn in the paper on time." "Be neat.")

Case 3 is an especially interesting and instructive example. The dean fears that Tom will flunk out, and he communicates this expectation to Tom. Tom gets the message, but reacts by working as hard as he can to prove himself. He ends up doing very well, despite the dean's original expectation. Similar examples occur every day in doctor's offices. A doctor who fears that his patient is about to have a heart attack will quickly place him on a strict diet and exercise program. He also schedules the patient for regular appointments so he can check the patient's progress. In this way a heart attack is avoided and the person's general health improves. Both the doctor and the dean communicate serious concern, but they follow this up with attempts to deal with the problem. If, instead, they communicated hopelessness and did nothing to change the situation, their expectations would probably be fulfilled.

Case 4 is a classic illustration of a self-fulfilling prophecy. Mrs. Graney expects the boy to be a problem and therefore begins to treat him like one. Her treatment involves separating him from his peers and forcing him to misbehave to get peer attention, so that her expectations become fulfilled. Case 4 is similar to the problem that we witnessed in the teachers' lounge at Midview School, where one student was being compared with an older sibling. These comparisons are typically incorrect, because there are many differences in the interests and learning styles of any sibling pair. The teacher who "pegs" students on the basis of his interactions with older siblings often forces students into inappropriate molds.

Case 5 is another example of a teacher's expectations becoming self-fulfilling prophecies. Despite his good intentions, the teacher's treatment of the girls in his class tends to erode their confidence and reduce their opportunities to learn through participation in class discussions. The result is low motivation and low performance, just as the teacher expected.

Case 6 also illustrates how a teacher's expectation can be self-fulfilling, even though the expectation itself might be unformulated and unrecognized by the teacher. Miss Ball's conscious intention is to build Dick's confidence so that he will participate in ball games. However, her approach takes into account only his attitude and not his need for practice in hitting and catching the ball. Although she may never have thought about it this way, her approach follows from the basic expectation that Dick can't hit or catch, and therefore needs some alternative role. This is very different from the idea that Dick can't hit or catch and therefore needs to be taught to do so. Miss Ball's attempt to solve the problem involves many good things for Dick, but not the thing he needs most—practice at hitting and catching the ball. As a result, by the end of the year he is even further behind his classmates in these skills than he was earlier.

This last example is one of many that could have been given showing how teachers adopt inappropriate strategies because they define a problem improperly. This is often done by teachers who are concerned about their students' self concepts. These teachers sometimes confuse the relationship between self concept and abilities, thinking that they have to improve the student's self concept before his abilities will improve. Usually, the opposite is true. A low self concept results from low abilities, and improvement in abilities will produce improvement in self concept. When students show handicaps, inhibitions, or lack of skill, the appropriate teacher strategy is to provide remedial instruction and extra practice or opportunities to learn. Although well-meant, attempts to provide the student with compensations in other areas without changing his problem are not what he needs.

Marvin Blake at Knightcrest School is a similar example of this problem. Marvin is a shy student who secretly has an interest in the Forensic Society but lacks the self-confidence to join activity groups and to speak in front of people. Look closely at the teachers' notes to see how Marvin's confidence has progressively deteriorated. His band interest (hiding in the crowd) won't solve his problem. It is useful and fulfilling in its own right, but it won't improve his speaking skills. The problem will remain until it is attacked directly by a teacher who helps him to develop the skills that he wants and needs.

APPROPRIATE TEACHER EXPECTATIONS

How can the classroom teacher apply his knowledge of the self-fulfilling prophecy effects of teachers' expectations? Several suggestions are presented in later sections of this chapter. Before getting to them, however, we wish to discuss two frequently made suggestions that we do *not* think are appropriate. Either suggestion would effectively eliminate undesirable self-fulfilling prophecies if teachers could follow it. However, we do not believe teachers can follow either suggestion. The first is that teachers should have only positive expectations; the second is that they should have no expectations at all.

The suggestion that teachers should have only positive expectations is appealing on the surface. Confidence and determination are important qualities for a teacher, and a "can do" attitude helps cut large problems down to workable size. However, this must not be carried to the point of distorting reality. Students show large individual differences in learning abilities and interests, and these cannot be eliminated through wishful thinking. Some are capable of more than others, and a teacher will only frustrate both himself and his students if he sets unrealistically high standards that some or all cannot reach.

Expectations should be appropriate rather than high, and they must be followed up with appropriate behavior. This means that the teacher should provide planned learning experiences that take the student at the level he is now and move him along at a pace he can handle. The pace that will allow continued success and improvement is the correct pace, and this will vary with different students. The teacher should not feel guilty or feel that he is stigmatizing a student by moving him along at a slower pace because he is a slower learner. As long as the student is working up to his potential and progressing at a steady rate, the teacher has reason to be satisfied. There will be cause for criticism only if the slow student is moved along at a slower pace than he can handle because the teacher's expectations for him are too low and are not changed because they are never tested out or reevaluated.

Some authors have suggested that teachers try to avoid self-fulfilling prophecy effects by avoiding forming expectations altogether. This means refusing to discuss students with their previous teachers and avoiding or ignoring cumulative records or test information. This is not a good suggestion, however, for two reasons. First, expectations cannot be suppressed or avoided. Experiences tend to stay with us and make an impression on us. When events occur repeatedly, they gradually come to be expected and are seen as normal, and expectations are reinforced every time repetition occurs. Thus teachers build up expectations about their students simply from interacting with the students, even if they try to avoid other sources of information. Second, the question of whether other sources of information are solicited is not as important as the question of how information is used. Information about students will create expectations about them, but such information is also useful in the planning of individualized instruction to meet the students' specific needs. The teacher should try to get information and use it in this way, rather than to avoid it. Suggestions about how teachers can profitably use the information in school records and test data are presented by Brubaker (1968).

As a case in point, consider Mr. Bellamy, who knows that the other teachers feel the students don't learn and can't be trusted. This is not bad ipso facto. Conceivably, he could take this to mean that the students aren't learning because of the way they are being taught, and he might be motivated to try new approaches. Thus the key is not whether teachers have information, but how they use it. Cumulative file data and teachers' remarks are potentially useful for the forming of *initial* hypotheses about what students need.

Mr. Bellamy apparently has not completely accepted the views of the other teachers. He notices that some students perform better than others, so that he cannot accept a single general stereotype. However, based on the reports from other teachers, he may be persuaded to develop different expectations for the two sexes, so that he may begin to see boys and girls as being more different than they actually are. If he accepts as fact the idea that boys won't learn, this could lead to undesirable expectancy effects. His expectations could be helpful, though, if they lead him to ask, "What can I do to make the classroom more relevant to the learning needs of the boys?".

Expectations built up through repetition can be very compelling. If John has turned in completed homework every day this year, he probably will do so again tomorrow. If Susan has been among the bottom five in the class on every math test this year, she probably will be on the next one too, unless her teacher provides extra math instruction and practice and gives shorter but more frequent tests to Susan and other students like her.

Regular repetition of student behavior will build up strong expectations in all teachers, including (and perhaps especially) teachers who try to deny or suppress them. Inevitably, some of these expectations will be pessimistic. However, teachers can avoid undesirable self-fulfilling prophecy effects, if they remain alert to their own expectations as these expectations form and change, and if they monitor their own behavior to see that negative expectations are not communicated. To the extent that such expectations are communicated, the communication should be of the "Dean Helpful" variety, combining expressions of concern with behavior geared to remedy the difficulty. Saying that a student needs help is bad only if the teacher does not provide that help in a positive, supportive way.

FORMING AND CHANGING EXPECTATIONS

Teachers form some expectations about their students before they even see the students. The individual cumulative record files provide IQ data, achievement scores, grades, and teachers comments that create expectations about achievement and conduct. Other expectations are picked up in chats with colleagues who taught the students in earlier grades. The family's reputation or the teacher's prior experience with an older brother or sister may also condition what he expects from a particular student. Some teachers deliberately try to avoid being influenced by the past. They do not look at records or seek information about their students until they have had a chance to see them and form their own impressions. This is not necessarily an improvement, however, since a lack of information from the files does not prevent most teachers from forming strong and general impressions very quickly.

In one study, for example, first grade teachers were able to rank their children in order of expected achievement after the very first day of school. Furthermore, these rankings, which were made without benefit of any test data, were highly correlated with achievement scores from tests given at the end of the year (Klinger and Dollar, 1972). Thus first impressions lead to specific and largely accurate expectations about students, even in teachers who are aware of the phenomenon. Rather than trying to eliminate expectations, teachers must remain aware of them and see that they do not lead to inappropriate treatment of certain students.

If low expectations lead to inappropriate teacher behavior, they may well become self-fulfilling. For example, a first grade teacher who expects a particular child to have great trouble in learning to read may begin to treat the child differently from the way he treats other children. To avoid pressuring or embarrassing the child, he may call on him infrequently and only to read easy passages, and whenever the child has trouble reading, the teacher may give him the word and quickly move on to another student. Over the year this will mean that the child will receive fewer opportunities to practice. So long as this keeps up, the child will gradually fall further and further behind his class-mates in reading ability.

This will happen even if the teacher attempts to compensate by allowing the child to be the first in the lunch line, to sit near him, or to take notes to the office frequently. Like the efforts of Miss Ball in our earlier example, these are misdirected and inappropriate intervention strategies for the low-achieving reader. The child may enjoy these activi-ties and may become more receptive to the teacher and the teacher's instruction efforts, but he will not improve in reading unless he gets the instruction and practice he needs.

A teacher who behaves this way is reacting to a label (low achiever, low potential, slow learner) instead of to the student as he is. A subtle shift has taken place in which the teacher has lost his focus on instruct-ing the student, on taking him from where he is to some higher level of progress, and has become fixated on the status quo. This fixation some-how makes the lack of progress acceptable and at the same time rein-forces the teacher's low expectations.

To avoid falling into this rut, teachers need to keep their expecta-tions open and to bear in mind their role as instructor. If expectations are allowed to become too strong or too settled, they can begin to distort perception and behavior. The teacher may begin to notice only those things that fit his expectations and may start deviating from good teach-ing practice.

Once formed, expectations tend to be self-perpetuating, because expectations guide both perceptions and behavior. When we expect to find something, we are much more likely to see it than when we are not looking for it. This is part of the reason why teachers often fail to notice good behavior in students who are frequent discipline problems in the classroom. The teachers are used to misbehavior from these stu-dents and are on the lookout for it, so they tend to notice most of the misbehavior that occurs. With a set toward misbehavior, however, the teachers miss a lot of the good behavior that someone else might have noticed and reinforced. Think about Mr. Bellamy and his expectation that the students are irresponsible. Given that he is looking for signs of irresponsibility, he may crack down too harshly when students care-lessly omit homework problems and at the same time fail to reinforce good responses on the completed questions. Mistaken beliefs and atti-tudes about other people are self-perpetuating and difficult to correct, because of their tendency to influence how we interpret what we see. If we are convinced that a person has particular qualities, we often "see" these qualities in him when we observe him.

Consider the teacher who asks a complex, difficult question and then gives his students some time to think about the answer. After a while he calls on Johnny Bright, whom he sees as an intelligent and well-motivated student. Johnny remains silent, pursing his lips, knitting his brow, and scratching his head. The teacher knows that he is working out the problem, so he patiently gives Johnny more time. The teacher has an attentive and eager expression as Johnny begins to speak. Johnny responds with a question: "Would you repeat that last part again?" The teacher is happy to do so, because this indicates that Johnny has partially solved the problem and may be able to do it by himself with a little more time. He asks Johnny what part he wants repeated and then obliges. He then waits eagerly, but patiently, for Johnny to respond again. If someone interrupted the teacher at this point to ask him what he was doing, he might say that he was "challenging the class to use creativity and logical thinking to solve problems."

Suppose, however, that the teacher had called on Mary Cairns (Midview School) instead of Johnny Bright. The teacher knows that Mary is a low achiever, and he doesn't think she is very well motivated, either. When called on, Mary remains silent, although the teacher notes her pursed lips, her furrowed brow, and the fact that she is scratching her head. This probably means that Mary is hopelessly lost, although it may mean that she is merely acting, trying to give the impression that she is thinking about the problem. After a few seconds the teacher says, "Well, Mary?" Now Mary responds, but with a question instead of an answer: "Would you repeat that last part again?" This confirms the teacher's suspicions, making it clear that any more time spent with Mary on this question would be wasted. After admonishing Mary about not listening more carefully, he calls on someone else. If interrupted at this point and asked what he was doing, the teacher might say that he was "making it clear that the members of the class are expected to pay close attention to the discussion, so that they can respond intelligently when questioned."

In this example the teacher's expectations regarding these two students caused him to "see" much more than was objectively observable to a more neutral observer. The observable behavior of the two students was the same, and they made the same response to the initial question. Yet the teacher interpreted the behavior quite differently by reading additional meaning into it. His interpretations may be correct, but we (and he) can't tell for sure, because he didn't check them out. Instead, he acted on them as if they were observable facts, so that his treatment of Mary was grossly inappropriate.

The fact that a student couldn't do something yesterday doesn't mean that he can't do it today, and the teacher won't find out whether or not the student can do it today unless he gives the student a chance. Expectations stress the stable or unchanging aspects of the world. The teacher, however, is a change agent who is trying to make his students into something different from what they are today. Therefore, he must keep his expectations in perspective. To the extent that they are negative, expectations represent problems to be solved, not definitions of reality to which he must adapt. Unfortunately, the teachers in the three case studies do not think this way.

Consider the teachers' statements about Mary Cairns at Midview Elementary School. They use her family background and low aptitude as the *explanation* for her difficulties, rather than as descriptions of influences and problems that are potentially modifiable. Similarly, we see in the teachers' notes throughout the case studies that teachers speak in final, categorical terms rather than in tentative, problem-solving terms. For example, why does the teacher at Midview feel that William would be better off in a special education class? Is there some definable problem that she can't solve, or is it because she doesn't want to deal with him and sees the special education class as a convenient way out?

BASIC TEACHER EXPECTATIONS

The following sections present certain basic attitudes and expectations teachers must have to do their jobs successfully. Descriptions and examples of how these expectations are communicated to students through observable behavior are also provided.

The teacher should enjoy teaching

Teaching brings many rewards and satisfactions, but it is demanding, exhausting, and sometimes frustrating. It is hard to do well unless you enjoy doing it. Teachers who enjoy their work will show this in their classroom behavior. They will come to class prepared and will present lessons in a way that suggests interest in and excitement about their teaching. They will appear eager for contact with students, will keep track of the students' individual needs and progress, and will take pride and satisfaction in helping the students' overcome learning difficulties. The students' difficulties and confusion will be perceived as challenges to be met with professional skills, not as irritations. When the student does achieve success, the teacher will share in his joy. In general, the teacher who enjoys his work sees himself as a benevolent resource person for his students, not as a warden or authority figure.

Teachers who don't enjoy teaching also show it in their classroom behavior. They appear apathetic or negativistic and act as if they are "putting in their time" on the job. They seem eager to escape the students or the classroom when opportunities arise and may frequently assign busywork or needless recitations, because they are unprepared or unwilling to teach. They seem to be unconcerned about students who are not learning the material, being content to rationalize rather than accept the challenge of finding another way to teach them. They may seem mildly pleased when a student achieves success after struggling with a concept, but they don't light up with joy or excitement. It is evident that Dorothy Cummings at Midview School no longer enjoys teaching and continues in the classroom only because it is financially necessary to do so. Although the scenario does not include information about her classroom behavior, it is likely that her apathy and disinterest will be communicated to students.

What about yourself? If you are student teaching, how do you feel in the classroom? Do you feel at home and enjoy yourself there, or would you really rather be someplace else? If you are a student observer, how do you feel about the work of a teacher? Is this work that you would enjoy as a career?

If your personal response to these questions has been negative, or reflects doubt, some careful thought and reassessment are in order. If you think you cannot and will not really enjoy teaching, you should avoid going into it, or should get out of it if you can. If you don't enjoy it but are open to change, don't give up. You may have been operating with inappropriate attitudes and expectations about teaching, which may have prevented you from enjoying the satisfactions that the job offers. Practice systematic observation of your own and other teachers' classroom behavior. You may become aware of facts about yourself that you never realized before. Once awareness exists, change is possible. Miss Carter, at Knightcrest School, is a teacher whose inappropriate attitudes interfere with her progress in the classroom. It is not difficult to see that her feelings about "pampered and snotty" students make her tense and perhaps ineffective in her classroom interactions. She should attempt to view these students in terms of the complex demands that their environment places on them and try to be more sympathetic toward their needs. If she cannot overcome her resentment toward these students and her feelings of inadequacy, she should think about moving to a different school where the students come from lower middle-class homes.

The teacher's main responsibility is to teach

The teacher's job involves many roles besides that of instructing students. At times the teacher will serve as a parent surrogate, an entertainer, an authority figure, a psychotherapist, and a record keeper, among other things. All of these are necessary aspects of the teacher's role. However, they are subordinate to and in support of the major role of teaching. Important as they are, they must not be allowed to over-shadow the teacher's basic instructional role.

It sometimes happens that teachers working with young children will become more concerned with mothering or entertaining the children than with teaching them. In classes with such teachers much of the day is spent in reading stories, playing games, working on arts and crafts projects, singing and listening to records, show and tell, and "enrich-ment" activities. Often the teachers basically do not like to spend time teaching the curriculum and feel that they must apologize to or bribe the children when lessons are conducted. This type of teacher is meeting his own needs, not those of the children. By the end of the year they will have acquired negative attitudes toward the curriculum and will have failed to achieve near their potential.

Research by Thomas (1970) suggests that this tendency to apologize for the curriculum is peculiar to adults. Thomas studied the tutoring behavior of college tutors and fifth and sixth grade tutors working with second grade students in reading. Even though the college students were senior education majors enrolled in a reading methods course, the fifth and sixth grade tutors were just as effective in producing reading gains. The college students spent much time trying to coax the children into liking them, into enjoying the reading materials, and into practicing the reading skills. In contrast, the fifth and sixth graders were more direct and businesslike. Children tend to see teaching and learning as normal, expected activities that do not require explanation or apology.

Teachers must have empathy and respect for their students. How-ever, they must also expect students to learn and treat them so that they realize their potential for succeeding in school-related tasks. Kleinfield (1972) found that some teachers were ineffective because their sym-pathy for certain students led them to treat these students in ways that defeated their purpose. For example, when these students failed to respond to public questions, teachers quickly called on someone else (presumably to save them from public embarrassment). In contrast, more effective teachers would smile confidently at the unresponsive student, wait for him to respond or rephrase the question for him, and stay with him until he gave a correct response.

At the higher grades teachers sometimes fail to teach because they have low expectations about their own ability to manage the class or about the learning abilities of a particular class. When homogeneous grouping is practiced in a junior high or high school, for example, teachers assigned to a period with a low-achieving class may sometimes abandon serious attempts to teach their subject. They may, perhaps, attempt to entertain the class or merely act as a sort of proctor, who is interested only in seeing that the noise doesn't get out of hand. Such behavior indicates that the teacher has a serious lack of confidence, either in his own ability to motivate and control the class or in the students' ability to learn or become interested in the subject matter. The behavior represents a total surrender to expectations of failure; in this surrender emphasis has been switched from reaching the class to merely keeping the class happy. Mr. Bellamy may fall into this trap at Bridges School. His expectations that students are irresponsible and that they won't learn may eventually lead him to define his teaching role as simply that of a proctor.

Teachers must understand the crucial aspects of teaching

Failure to be clear about the crucial aspects of teaching (task presentation, diagnosis, remediation, and enrichment) characterizes teachers who favor high achievers over low achievers or who pay more attention to answers than to the thinking processes that a student goes through in reaching an answer. Such a teacher sometimes acts as if the students were expected to learn on their own with no help from him. If a student doesn't catch on immediately after one demonstration or does not do his work correctly after hearing the instructions one time, the teacher reacts with impatience and frustration.

Such behavior represents a fundamental misunderstanding of the teacher's basic role. The teacher is in the classroom to instruct. This involves more than just giving demonstrations or presenting learning experiences. Instruction also means giving additional help to those who are having difficulty, diagnosing the source of their problem, and providing remedial assistance to correct it. It means evaluating the students with an eye toward identifying and correcting difficulties, not merely as a prelude to passing out praise or criticism. It means keeping track of each student's individual progress, so he can be dealt with in terms of where he was yesterday and where he should be tomorrow. It means finding satisfaction in the progress of the slower students as well as the brighter ones.

There are many aspects of the teacher's behavior that help to indicate whether or not he clearly understands what he is supposed to be doing with his students. The handling of seatwork and homework assignments is one good indicator. The purpose of such assignments is to provide students with practice in the skills they are learning and to provide the teacher with information about the students' progress. Teachers should monitor the students' performance on seatwork and homework, noting the particular error patterns that occur. These patterns will suggest the nature of the individual student's learning problems and the nature of the remedial actions the teacher should take. However, some teachers fail to use seatwork and homework in this way.

They simply pass out the work and then collect and score it, without following the scoring with remedial teaching. Students who succeed are praised, and those who need help receive only criticism or low marks. Seatwork thus does not lead to diagnosis and remediation.

Teachers can create negative attitudes toward seatwork assignments by giving assignments that are inappropriate or that are not adjusted to individual differences within the class. Seatwork assignments should be made with specific instructional objectives in mind. This may mean separate assignments for different groups of students in a class. Assignments that are too difficult or too easy for a given student will not fulfill the teacher's instructional purpose. In particular, students will rightly regard overly simple and repetitious seatwork as annoying busywork. Teachers sometimes create this attitude in otherwise well-motivated and bright students who tend to do the seatwork quickly and correctly. If the teacher's method of handling students who finish quickly is to assign more of the same kind of exercises, the students will learn to slow down their pace or hide the fact that they have finished. Teachers would do much better to allow the students to choose alternative activities or to move on to more challenging problems of a similar type.

Another important indicator is the way the teacher responds to right and wrong answers. When the teacher has the appropriate attitude, he accepts either type of response for the information it gives about the student. He neither becomes overly elated about correct answers nor becomes overly depressed about incorrect answers. He uses questions to stimulate thinking and to acquire information about the students' progress. Questions should come in sequences designed to see that both the students who answer them and the others in the class, who are listening, develop a deeper understanding of the concepts being discussed. They should not be a series of disjointed "tests" or spot checks on the students' memories.

Inappropriate expectations can even be communicated through praise. Although praise and encouragement are important, they should not interfere with basic teaching goals. If the teacher responds with overly dramatic praise every time a student answers a simple question, the class will likely be distracted from the content of the lesson. A contest in which the more confident and outgoing students compete for the teacher's recognition and approval will probably result. A better strategy is simply to acknowledge that an answer is correct. The teacher should then advance the discussion by asking another question or adding information to expand on the previous question. Praise can be saved for times when it can be given more effectively and meaningfully, especially during contacts with individual students. Criticism, of course, should be omitted entirely. In general, the teacher's behavior during question and answer sessions should say, "We're going to discuss and deepen our understanding of the material," and not, "We're going to find out who knows the material and who doesn't."

When praise is given to students, it should be specific praise that reinforces their feelings of progress in obtaining new knowledge and learning new skills. Empty phrases like "how nice" or "that's good" should be avoided in favor of more specific statements. Praise should stress appreciation of the student's efforts and the progress he is making, and usually should be focused on his more general progress rather than on single isolated successes. All of this helps to reinforce the teacher's role as a resource person who facilitates learning, as opposed to a judge who decides who has learned and who hasn't.

Teachers should expect all students
to meet at least the minimum specified objectives

Although all students cannot reasonably be expected to do equally well, reasonable minimal objectives can be established for each teacher's class or for each individual student. Naturally, most students will be capable of going considerably beyond minimal objectives, and the teacher should try to stimulate this development as far as their interests and abilities allow. However, in doing so, teachers must not lose sight of basic priorities. Remedial work with students who have not yet met minimal objectives should not be delayed in favor of enrichment activities with those who have. Ways in which teachers can use grouping, peer tutoring, and other techniques to make time for such remediation are discussed elsewhere. (See Good and Brophy, 1972.)

Teachers with appropriate attitudes will spend extra time working with the students who are having difficulty. Their behavior when interacting with these students will be supportive, patient, and confident. In contrast, teachers with inappropriate attitudes will often spend less time with the students who most need extra help. When they do work with these students, these teachers will tend to do so in a half-hearted way that communicates disappointment and frustration. Such teachers are often overly dependent on achieving easy success and eliciting many right answers. They need to change this attitude if they are to acquire the patience and confidence needed to do effective remedial teaching with slower learners. Teachers who teach in schools where there is a wide range in student ability within one classroom (for example, at Midview where the range in IQ is 59 points) will have to continuously plan and revise remediation and enrichment strategies, if they are to be effective with students who have diverse achievement levels and aptitudes.

Teachers should expect students
to enjoy learning

Teachers can and should expect students to enjoy learning activities, including practice exercises, and should back these expectations with appropriate behavior. This is one of the most common areas where teachers' expectations become self-fulfilling. When teachers have the appropriate attitude toward schoolwork, they present it in ways that make their students see it as enjoyable and interesting. Tasks and assignments are presented without apology as activities that are valuable in their own right. There is no attempt to build up artificial enthusiasm or interest; the interest is assumed to be there already. Comments about upcoming assignments stress the specific ways in which they extend or build on present knowledge and skills. Comments about present work reinforce the students' sense of progress and mastery. The teacher doesn't try to give learning a "hard sell" or to picture it as fun. He doesn't expect the students to enjoy it in the same way they enjoy a trip to the circus or a ride on a roller coaster. Instead, he expects the quieter but consistent satisfactions and feelings of mastery that come with the accumulation of knowledge and skills.

The teacher with a negative attitude toward school learning behaves very differently. He sees learning activities as unpleasant but necessary drudgery. If he believes in a positive approach toward motivation, he will be apologetic and defensive about assignments and will frequently resort to bribery, attempting to generate enthusiasm artificially through overemphasis on contests, rewards, and other external incentives. If he is more authoritarian and punitive, he will present assignments as bitter pills that the student must swallow or else. In either case, the students will quickly acquire a distaste for school activities, thus providing reinforcement for the teacher's expectations.

Other evidence of a teacher's having inappropriate attitudes toward school activities include a heavy stress on the separation between work and play with work pictured as an unpleasant activity one does in order to get to play; a tendency to introduce assignments as something the class has to do rather than merely as something they are going to do; the use of extra assignments as punishments; and practices such as checking to make sure that everyone has signed out one or more books from the library. Teachers with negative attitudes also have a tendency to discuss academic subjects in a way that presents them as dull and devoid of content. For example, they tend to say, "We're going to have history," instead of "We're going to discuss the voyage of Columbus," or "Read pages seventeen to twenty-two," instead of "Read the author's critique of Twain's novel." All these behaviors tell the student that the teacher doesn't see school activities as very interesting or pleasant. At

Bridges School one of the elementary teachers wrote the following in Rick Washington's folder: "Rick is capable of doing schoolwork if he wanted to. He just is not interested in what this school has to offer." This comment again shows a teacher's willingness to blame the students for their failures, and it shows little sensitivity to the fact that the school should at times be interested in providing Rick with materials that turn him on. Similarly, at Midview School the first grade teacher's comment that William "needs stronger motivation" implicitly suggests that any change will have to come from inside William instead of from outside influence.

The teacher should expect to deal with individuals, not groups or stereotypes

As a rule, teachers should think, talk, and act in terms of individual students. This does not mean that they should not practice grouping or that terms such as *low achievers* should not be used. It does mean that teachers must keep a proper perspective about priorities. Grouping must be practiced as a means of meeting the individual student's needs. Similarly, labels and stereotypes are often helpful in thinking about ways to teach individuals better. Ultimately, however, the teacher is teaching John Smith and Mary Jones, not group A or low achievers. The way teachers talk about the students in their classes is an indication of how they think about them. If the teacher continually mentions groups to the exclusion of individuals, he may well have begun to lose sight of individual differences within groups and to overemphasize the differences between groups. If this has happened, observers will note that the teacher asks for too many choral responses and not enough individual responses in group situations, that he has not changed the membership in the group for a long time, that group members are seated together and spend most of the day together, or that the teacher spends more time with the high-achieving group than with the low-achieving group.

Similarly, observers should be alert to the teacher's use of oversimplified, stereotyped labels in describing certain students (immature, discipline problem, slow learner, and so on). The teacher may be reacting more to the stereotypes than to the students' individual qualities, and he may fail to notice behavior that doesn't fit the stereotype. If the teacher is reacting this way, it will show up in behavior such as labeling or criticizing the student directly, describing problems without trying to do anything about them, or treating the student on the basis of untested assumptions rather than observed behavior. These behaviors suggest that the stereotyped label has begun to structure the teacher's perception of the student.

Occasionally, common beliefs (classrooms should be quiet; girls don't like math, and so forth) or mythical norms (all students should participate regularly in classroom discussion) lead teachers to treat students inappropriately. Some teachers, for example, place undue emphasis on frequent participation in classroom discussions, and they view suspiciously students who don't participate regularly. Linda Grey at Knightcrest School provides a good example of the potential dangers in pressing a student to talk more.

Linda is apparently a well-balanced, capable student, who is doing well in school. She has unique career interests, which she expresses freely, and is able to express herself (by complaining about homework, for instance) when she wants to do so. If someone took the fifth grade teacher's suggestion seriously and attempted to get Linda to participate more frequently, Linda might react to the increased pressure (to speak when she is not ready to speak) by not doing as well on her work assignments, because she *might* see more frequent participation as a threat to her social position.

One may wonder where common shibboleths, such as "Students should talk," develop. Much of this particular belief stems from the fact that it is basically (but not completely) true. Most students should be encouraged to participate (especially students who want to participate but are afraid to do so and whose silence is a means of coping with anxiety), because participation allows students to become actively involved in the discussion, gives them a chance to compare their opinions with other students, and gives them a chance to develop skills for presenting their ideas.

However, if a student has developed a mature way of expressing his opinions and sees increased participation as a threat to his social position (and it may well be!), efforts to obtain higher frequencies of participation may do more harm than good. The point here is that when teachers attempt to categorically apply normative statements (even basically good ones like "Students should frequently participate in discussions") to *all* students without recognizing the unique needs of individual students, they are likely to act inappropriately.

The teacher should assume good intentions and a positive self concept

Teachers must communicate to all of their students the expectation that the students want to be, and are trying to be, fair, cooperative, reasonable, and responsible. This includes even those students who consistently present behavior problems. The rationale here is that the teacher's basic faith in the student's ability to change is a necessary (although often not sufficient by itself) condition for such change. If the student sees that the teacher does not have this faith in him, he will probably lose whatever motivation he has to keep trying. Thus teachers should be very careful to avoid suggesting that students deliberately hurt others or enjoy doing so, that they cannot and probably will not ever be able to control their own behavior, or that they simply don't care and are making no effort to do so. Even in cases where this might actually be true, there is nothing to be gained and much to be lost by saying so to the student. Such statements will only establish or help reinforce a negative self concept and will lead to even more destructive behavior. ("If they think I'm bad now, wait until they get a load of this.")

If the teacher realizes he has failed in this area, he may be able to salvage the situation somewhat by convincing the student that he spoke in anger and really didn't mean what he said. However, if the student is convinced that the teacher did mean what he said, the teacher's chances of establishing a productive relationship with the student are seriously and perhaps permanently damaged.

The teacher should expect some difficulties and take responsibility for them

Despite what has been said in this chapter about confidence and positive expectations, difficulties are inevitable, and teachers must expect them and be prepared to deal with them. This statement may, at first, appear to contradict what has been said previously, but a careful analysis will show that it does not. Granted, positive expectations will go a long way toward solving and preventing problems, but they will not prevent or solve all problems. Expectations are not automatically self-fulfilling. For example, Cohen and Roper (1971) have suggested that in addition to the teacher's expectations regarding student behavior it is necessary to consider and perhaps modify the student's expectations regarding his own behavior and the peer group's expectations regarding a given student's behavior. In trying to change the status, assertiveness, and influence power of black students who were working with white students on experimental problem-solving tasks, Cohen and Roper found that the behavior of black students was not enhanced if the blacks were merely provided with high expectations for their own performance and then put in contact with white students. Only when blacks were taught the skills necessary for the task and both their expectations and the expectations of whites regarding them were manipulated were the blacks able to assume positions of cooperative leadership while working with white students on experimental tasks. Similarly, teachers can expect to change students' expectations and the expectations of other students regarding them only when students are helped to learn usable skills.

However, positive expectations are necessary and important. Without them the situation would be considerably changed. To the extent that positive expectations initiate behavior that does lead to self-fulfilling prophecy effects, they help prevent and solve problems that would otherwise appear. The benefits of self-fulfilling prophecy effects result-ing from positive expectations simply would not be gained if such expectations were not there in the first place.

In addition, the self-fulfilling prophecy effects of negative expecta-tions must be considered. When no negative expectations exist, un-desirable self-fulfilling prophecy effects cannot occur. When negative expectations do exist, however, some of these expectations are likely to result in behavior that will produce self-fulfilling prophecy effects, thus adding to the teacher's burden. Besides the problems that would have been there anyway, additional problems are caused by the teacher's own negative expectations.

An additional benefit of consistent positive expectations is that they cause the teacher to examine his own behavior and to ask what he could be doing differently to help the situation. This is an important function, because teachers, like everyone else, are strongly tempted to take credit for success and to blame failure on things other than them-selves. This was shown, for example, in a study by Good, Schmidt, Peck, and Williams (1969). They asked fourteen fifth grade teachers and fourteen eighth grade teachers to describe the students in their classrooms who presented the biggest problems and to explain why the students presented problems. In responding to these questions, teachers mentioned themselves as part of the problem in only four of seventy-four cases. The other seventy problems were seen as resulting from limited student ability, poor student attitude, or a home life that did not support the school. Most of these cases were described as if the situation were permanent and unchangeable.

Similar results were found in a study by Quirk (1967). Quirk manipulated the teachers who were the subjects in his experiment, so that some thought they had succeeded (their students learned) and others thought they had failed (their students didn't learn). He then asked the teachers to assess their performance. He found a strong tendency for teachers who had experienced success to take credit for it by attributing it to their own presentation. In contrast, teachers who had been led to experience failure usually blamed it on the students or on factors other than their own teaching presentation.

The teachers in all the schools in the scenarios show that they are willing to blame the students and the students' environment for the students' failure or lack of interest. The teachers show little inclination to study their own behavior as a factor contributing to the problem. For example, Mrs. Fowler complains that although her students are reputed to be brighter than in the past, they are not interested in any-thing. However, rather than engaging in a problem-oriented discussion in which they attempt to find ways to interest students, the teachers begin discussing a particular student's inability to cope with school demands. Such scapegoating discussions are common in teachers' lounges. Rare are discussions about the teachers' inability to cope with school problems and purposeful searches for ways to cope with these problems. At Bridges School we see that the teachers consistently tell a young teacher not to expect much from his students, and at Knight-crest School we see that teachers join the bandwagon when Miss Carter suggests indirectly that parents give their children too much. Such attitudes make it easy for teachers to blame parents rather than themselves when they have problems communicating with the students.

Such rationalizing is not particularly malicious, and it is not confined to teachers. We all want to see ourselves as likeable, competent, and successful, and we all tend to repress or explain away the things that don't fit this self-image. Such defensiveness is not necessary in teachers who adopt positive, but appropriate, expectations for their students. Because his expectations are appropriate, the teacher does not need to feel guilty or dissatisfied if slow students do not do as well as better students. Success is defined as progress in terms of the students' capabilities. Since the expectations are also positive, they remind the teacher continually to think in terms of progress forward and, when progress is not evident, to analyze the problem and to question his teaching approach. This helps him to stay on top of the situation and to adapt quickly to changes as they appear. The teacher will recognize and exploit breakthroughs as they occur, and he will respond to failure with a search for another way to do the job rather than for an excuse or "explanation."

In summary, even though appropriately positive attitudes and expectations are not automatically or totally effective by themselves, they are necessary and important teacher qualities. Teachers won't always succeed with them, but they won't get very far without them. Attitudes and expectations cannot be observed directly, of course, but a teacher's behavior can be observed and measured. Observation instruments used for recording teacher behavior related to basic teaching attitudes and expectations are discussed elsewhere (Good and Brophy, 1972a). By observing inappropriate behavior in other teachers and by becoming conscious of it in your own teaching, you can learn to detect and eliminate the undesirable self-fulfilling prophecy effects that result when inappropriate attitudes and expectations are present.

SUMMARY

In this chapter we have shown how teachers' attitudes and expectations about different students can lead teachers to treat students differently, so that teachers' attitudes and expectations sometimes become self-fulfilling. A particular danger is that low expectations combined with an attitude of futility will be communicated to certain students, leading to an erosion of their confidence and motivation for learning. This will confirm or deepen their sense of hopelessness and cause them to fail, when they could have succeeded under different circumstances.

Expectations tend to be self-sustaining. They affect both perception, by causing the teacher to be alert for what he expects and less likely to notice what he doesn't expect, and interpretation, by causing the teacher to interpret (and perhaps distort) what he sees, so that it is consistent with his expectations. In this way, some expectations can persist even though they don't fit the facts (as seen by a more neutral observer).

Sometimes low expectations or defeatist attitudes exist because the teacher has given up on certain students, accepting their failure rather than trying to do anything about it. In these instances, inappropriate attitudes and expectations help the teacher to take his mind off the problem or to explain the problem away. The attitude or expectation ("Johnny's limited intelligence, poor attitude, and cumulative failure in school have left him unable to handle eighth grade work; he belongs in a special education class") "explains" and, therefore seems to justify, the teacher's failure with this student, and it psychologically frees him from continuing to worry about the student's progress and from seeking new and more successful ways to teach him.

Once a teacher and student become locked in such a circle of futility, they tend to stay there. The teacher's behavior causes the student to fall even more behind than he might have otherwise, and this failure in turn deepens and reinforces the teacher's already low expectations.

Teachers can avoid such problems by adopting appropriate general expectations about teaching and by learning to recognize their attitudes and expectations about individual students and to monitor their treatment of individual students. In particular, it is essential that teachers remember that their primary responsibility is to teach, to help each student reach his potential as a learner. It is natural for teachers to form differential attitudes and expectations about different students, because each student is an individual. To the extent that these attitudes are accurate and appropriate, they are helpful for planning ways to meet each student's needs. However, they must constantly be monitored and evaluated, to ensure that they change appropriately in response to changes in the student. When teachers fail to monitor and evaluate their attitudes, expectations, and behavior toward students, they can easily get caught in a vicious circle of failure and futility.

Remember, attitudes and expectancies can be your allies and tools if properly maintained and used. However, if unquestioningly accepted and allowed to solidify, they can become defense mechanisms that lead you to ignore or explain away problems rather than solve them. Therefore, learn to control your attitudes and expectations—don't let them control you!

SUGGESTED ACTIVITIES

1. List the students (or teachers at your school) in your preservice teacher education course who are the brightest. What behavioral evidence and information have you used to form your attitude? How accurate do you think your estimates are?

2. In your opinion, when teachers form their expectations about how students will perform in their classes, do they tend to underestimate or overestimate the following types of students: loud, aggressive males; quiet, passive males; loud, aggressive females; quiet, passive females; students who are neat and follow directions carefully; students with speech impediments; and students who complain that schoolwork is dull and uninteresting? Why do you feel that teachers would tend to over- or underestimate the ability of these student "types"? Check your predictions by interviewing teachers about their expectations for these types of students whom you have observed in their classrooms.

3. Write an original example of a self-fulfilling prophecy. Give an example of a self-fulfilling prophecy that happened to you, a relative, or a classmate. Be sure that you include each of the following: an original expectation, behaviors that consistently communicate this expectation, and evidence that the original expectation has been confirmed.

4. Identify the ten student characteristics or behaviors that will delight you most when you are a teacher. What does this list tell you about your personal likes and your teaching personality? Closely *observe* children that you like and dislike and try to discover the child behaviors that affect your attitudes toward children.

5. List the ten student characteristics or behaviors that are most likely to irritate you or make you anxious. Why do these behaviors bother you? How can you deal fairly with students who exhibit behaviors that are bothersome to you?

6. Observe teachers interacting with high- and low-achieving students. Do teachers interact with these students differentially? If so, how? Observe teachers' interaction patterns with male and female students. See if the teacher holds or communicates different expectations for boys and girls.

REFERENCES

Becker, H. "Social Class Variations in the Teacher–Pupil Relationship." *Journal of Educational Sociology* 25 (1952): 451–465.

Beez, W. V. "Influence of Biased Psychological Reports on Teacher Behavior and Pupil Performance." *Proceedings of the 76th Annual Convention of the American Psychological Association,* 1968, 605–606.

Brophy, J., and Good, T. "Brophy–Good System (Teacher–Child Dyadic Interaction)." In *Mirrors for Behavior: An Anthology of Observation Instruments Continued, 1970 Supplement.* vol. A, edited by A. Simon and E. Boyer. Philadelphia: Research for Better Schools, 1970a.

Brophy, J., and Good, T. "Teacher's Communications of Differential Expectations for Children's Classroom Performance: Some Behavioral Data." *Journal of Educational Psychology* 61 (1970b): 365–374.

Brophy, J., and Good, T. *Classroom Interaction: The Influence of Teacher Perception.* New York: Holt, Rinehart, and Winston, 1973 (in press).

Brubaker, H. "Are You Making the Best Use of Cumulative Records?" *Grade Teacher* 86 (1968): 96–97, 222.

Burnham, J. "Effects of Experimenter's Expectancies on Children's Ability to Learn to Swim." Unpublished master's thesis, Purdue University, 1968.

Claiborn, W. "Expectancy Effects in the Classroom: a Failure to Replicate." *Journal of Educational Psychology* 60 (1969): 377–383.

Cohen, E., and Roper, S. "Expectation Training II: Modification of Interracial Interaction Disability." Technical Report No. 7, Stanford School of Education, Stanford, Calif., 1971.

Davis, A., and Dollard, J. *Children of Bondage.* Washington, D.C.: American Council on Education, 1940.

Douglas, J. *The Home and the School: A Study of Ability and Attainment in the Primary School.* London: MacGibbon and Kee, 1964.

Doyle, W.; Hancock, G.; and Kifer, E. "Teachers' Perceptions: Do They Make a Difference?" Paper presented at the annual meeting of the American Educational Research Association, 1971.

Emmer, E.; Good, T.; and Oakland, T. "Pupil Effects on Teachers." Research Report No. 63. Research and Development Center for Teacher Education, University of Texas at Austin, 1971.

Feshbach, N. "Student Teacher Preferences for Elementary School Pupils Varying in Personality Characteristics." *Journal of Educational Psychology* 60 (1969): 126–132.

Fleming, E., and Anttonen, R. "Teacher Expectancy or My Fair Lady." *American Educational Research Journal* 8 (1971): 241–252.

Fuchs, E. "How Teachers Help Children Fail." *Trans-Action* 5 (1968): 45–49.

Good, T. "Which Pupils Do Teachers Call On?" *Elementary School Journal* 70 (1970): 190–198.

Good, T., and Brophy, J. "Behavioral Expression of Teacher Attitudes." *Journal of Educational Psychology* 63 (1972a): 617–624.

Good, T., and Brophy, J. "Changing Teacher Behavior: An Empirical Investigation." Unpublished manuscript, 1972b.

Good, T., and Brophy, J. *Looking in Classrooms.* New York: Harper and Row, 1972c.

Good, T., and Dembo, M. "Teacher Expectations: Self Report Data." Unpublished manuscript (mimeographed), 1972.

Good, T., and Grouws, D. "Male and Female Pre-service Teachers' Reactions to Descriptions of Students' Classroom Behavior." Unpublished manuscript, 1972.

Good, T.; Schmidt, L.; Peck, R.; and Williams, D. "Listening to Teachers." Report Series No. 34, Research and Development Center for Teacher Education, University of Texas at Austin, 1969.

Good, T.; Sikes, J.; and Brophy, J. "Classroom Interactions of Male and Female Teachers: Does Teacher Sex Make Any Difference?" Unpublished manuscript, 1972.

Hadley, S. "A School Mark—Fact or Fancy?" *Educational Administration and Supervision* 40 (1954): 305–312.

Horn, E. *Distribution of Opportunity for Participation Among the Various Pupils in Classroom Recitations.* New York: Teachers' College, Columbia University, 1914.

Jackson, P., and Lahaderne, H. "Inequalities of Teacher–Pupil Contacts." *Psychology in the Schools* 4 (1967): 204–208.

Jenkins, J., and Deno, S. "Influence of Student Behavior on Teacher's Self Evaluation." *Journal of Educational Psychology* 60 (1969): 439–442.

Jones, V. "The Influence of Teacher–Student Introversion, Achievement, and Similarity on Teacher–Student Dyadic Classroom Interactions." Unpublished doctoral dissertation, University of Texas at Austin, 1971.

Klein, S. "Student Influence on Teacher Behavior." *American Educational Research Journal* 8 (1971): 403–421.

Kleinfield, J. "Instructional Style and Intellectual Performance of Indian and Eskimo Students." Final report project No. 1-J-027, U.S. Department of Health, Education, and Welfare, Office of Education, Washington, D.C. 1972.

Klinger, R., and Dollar, B. Personal communication, 1972.

Kranz, P.; Weber, W.; and Fishell, K. "The Relationships Between Teacher Perception of Pupils and Teacher Behavior Towards Those Pupils." Paper delivered at the annual meeting of the American Educational Research Association, Minneapolis, Minn., 1970.

Mackler, B. "Grouping in the Ghetto." *Education and Urban Society* 2 (1969): 80–95.

Martin, R. "Student Sex and Behavior As Determinants of the Type and Frequency of Teacher–Student Contacts." *Journal of School Psychology* 10 (1972): 339–347.

Mendoza, S.; Good, T.; and Brophy, J. "Who Talks in Junior High Classrooms?" Report Series No. 68, Research and Development Center for Teacher Education, 1971.

Oppenlander, L. "The Relative Influence of the Group of Pupils and of the Teacher As Determinants of Classroom Interaction." Paper presented at the annual meeting of the American Educational Research Association, 1969.

Palardy, J. "What Teachers Believe—What Children Achieve." *Elementary School Journal* 69 (1969): 370–374.

Quirk, T. "An Experimental Investigation of the Teacher's Attribution of the Locus of Causality of Student Performance." *Dissertation Abstracts* 28 (1967) 256SA.

Rist, R. "Student Social Class and Teacher Expectations: The Self-fulfilling Prophecy in Ghetto Education." *Harvard Educational Review* 40 (1970): 411–451.

Rosenthal, R., and Jacobson, L. *Pygmalion in the Classroom: Teacher Expectation and Pupils' Intellectual Development.* New York: Holt, Rinehart, and Winston, 1968.

Rowe, M. "Science, Silence, and Sanctions." *Science and Children* 6 (1969): 11–13.

Schrank, W. "The Labeling Effect of Ability Grouping." *Journal of Educational Research* 62 (1968): 51–52.

Schrank, W. "A Further Study of the Labeling Effect of Ability Grouping." *The Journal of Educational Research* 63 (1970): 358–360.

Silberman, Melvin L. "Behavioral Expression of Teachers' Attitudes Toward Elementary School Students." *Journal of Educational Psychology* 69 (1969): 402–407.

Snow, R. "Unfinished Pygmalion." *Contemporary Psychology* 14 (1969): 197–199.

Taylor, C. "The Expectations of Pygmalion's Creators." *Educational Leadership* 28 (1970): 161–164.

Thomas, J. "Tutoring Strategies and Effectiveness: A Comparison of Elementary Age Tutors and College Tutors." Unpublished doctoral dissertation, University of Texas at Austin, 1970.

4 · Behavior analysis in the classroom

BARBARA H. WASIK
University of North Carolina
at Chapel Hill

KEY CONCEPTS

Delineation of Goal Behaviors

Measurement of Behavior

Analysis of Setting and Materials

Positive and Negative Consequences
of Behavior

Evaluation of Procedures

Rick, now in the sixth grade, was described by various teachers as having "poor motivation" and "a master of shifting blame for his failures to someone else." "I believe that Rick is capable of doing schoolwork. . . . I cannot capture or hold his attention." "Rick has a poor self concept in school but sees himself as king of the hill when he is in the streets." "He is a born troublemaker." What can his teacher do to alleviate this problem behavior and facilitate the occurrence of appropriate behavior? Should he (1) take away recess, (2) ignore the student, (3) send him to the principal's office, (4) send a note home to his parents, (5) assign extra work, (6) change the classroom seating arrangement, (7) give him easier assignments, (8) send him back a grade, (9) suspend him until he is mature enough to come to school. It would seem that with our teaching experience, we would have immediate and definite solutions to such problems. Yet we have just begun to carefully analyze alternative approaches to such problems and to determine if our strategies are working.

In the past ten years much attention has been directed toward analyzing human behavior, and in the process several behavioral principles have been established. When these principles are applied to actual problems, they are referred to as *behavior modification*, or applied behavior analysis.

Applied behavior analysis, or behavior modification, refers to those studies of human behavior that are conducted because they are important to man and to society (Baer, Wolf, and Risley, 1968). Concerns focus on the presence or absence of appropriate or inappropriate behaviors as defined by one's culture. Areas of study are selected because of their current importance and not because of their relationship to a theory of learning. The topics of study are pragmatic and immediate, called to attention by concerned people who deal with behavioral problems on a day-to-day basis. This approach has two other distinguishing characteristics: (1) an emphasis on what a person actually does rather than a report of what he can do and (2) an attempt to demonstrate control over those events that bring about a change in behavior (Baer et al., 1968).

Although this approach to teacher–student interactions involves systematic procedures based on demonstrated principles, no rigid formulas exist to tell teachers what to arrange for a particular student. The arrangement of programs requires exact information about the behavior of the student and the environmental events effective in altering his behavior.

This approach emphasizes the needs of individuals, an assessment of their behaviors, and a study of the positive and aversive consequences that follow these behaviors. It focuses on the here-and-now life of the student by pinpointing the problem behavior and selecting effective intervention procedures. It requires that teachers be sensitive not only to the needs but also to the likes and dislikes of individual students and that they try various procedures until one is found that is effective for the individual student. Some procedures described in this chapter will be familiar as common teaching practices, practices that can be more effective when used consistently and systematically.

CLASSICAL CONDITIONING

Applied behavior analysis has relied primarily on two basic types of conditioning: classical conditioning and operant conditioning. *Classical conditioning* is exemplified by Pavlov's experiments in which his dogs learned to salivate to the sound of a bell before food was presented. Thus a stimulus is presented that elicits an involuntary response or reflex. When the unconditioned stimulus (food) is repeatedly paired with a second conditioned stimulus (bell), the subject will respond to the conditioned stimulus. In other words, the dog learns to salivate when the bell is sounded, even when food is not present. Many phobic and anxiety responses are learned through classical conditioning.

The principles of classical conditioning can be used to decrease as well as increase behavior. In the 1950s Joseph Wolpe developed a process called *systematic desensitization* for using the principles of classical conditioning to eliminate anxiety responses and phobic reactions; his specific technique is called *reciprocal inhibition*. Under his technique a person is helped to develop a list of objects or events that elicit a fear reaction, and these items are ordered according to the degree of fear reaction they produce. Then the least fearful item, the one the person has only a slight reaction to, is selected and presented to the person repeatedly—until he is no longer afraid. Then the next item is selected, and the technique repeated. Thus the responses that had originally occurred in fear-producing settings are extinguished, and other incompatible responses are increased.

Fear responses can bring about an avoidance of activities that are important in the development of many social skills. A child may avoid social responses that are not fear producing per se, but that have occurred in the presence of other stimuli that did produce fear responses.

School phobia is often dealt with by this process. If a child refuses to go to school and becomes more and more upset the closer he gets to school, one could arrange a procedure that would gradually bring the child in closer and closer contact with the school. The first step might be as simple as seeing that the child gets out of bed and dresses. The next day eating breakfast might be added. Following steps might be walking to the school bus, waiting for the bus, riding the bus, entering the school grounds, and entering the school building. A new step is not added until the preceding step is performed without anxiety. Sometimes the person carrying out this procedure may reward the child for making appropriate responses at each step. Desensitization in this manner is often difficult to separate from shaping and fading, two procedures used in operant conditioning.

OPERANT CONDITIONING

In *operant conditioning* voluntary behavior is modified by environmental consequences following the behavior. Operant conditioning principles seek to facilitate the occurrence of a new behavior and increase or decrease behavioral frequencies. Once a behavior occurs, the probability of its recurrence is a function of the consequences that follow. When a response on our part is followed by positive consequences, the probability is increased that we will repeat the same response again.

When a given response does not exist in a person's repertoire of behaviors, one of several procedures can be used to establish the response: shaping, prompting, or modeling. Sometimes all three may be used. First, one can successively reinforce existing behaviors that approximate the desired behavior, a procedure called *shaping*. By effectively arranging materials and events, one can increase the probability that the desired behavior will occur. One makes paper and pencil available when teaching writing skills. When an approximation of the desired behavior occurs, this behavior can be immediately reinforced; that is, the behavior will be followed by positive consequences that will increase the probability that the behavior will recur. Then gradually reinforcement will be given only for those behaviors that are increasingly *more* like the desired behavior. One may first praise a child for picking up and holding a pencil, later for making marks on a page, and still later, require precise markings that closely resemble letters and numbers before praising his work.

Fading is a related procedure in which the stimuli required for a person to make a response are gradually removed. Teachers often use this procedure in teaching children to write letters. First, a child may trace letters printed on a sheet. Arrows may also be used as part of the stimuli to show in what direction the pencil marks should go. A child may then be presented a sheet with dots marking the outline of a letter. As these steps are mastered, the stimuli are gradually removed, so that ultimately the child makes the responses in the absence of such aids.

A second way of facilitating the occurrence of behavior is by physical or verbal *prompting*. New words can be learned by physical prompting. The employment of prompts, such as forming the mouth of the child in such a way as to facilitate the occurrence of desired sounds, has been found to be effective with children in whom language acquisition is very slow (Lovaas, Freitag, Nelson, and Whalen, 1967). A child who does not spend time in outdoor play activities can be prompted to do so by placing him on play equipment and then reinforcing him for staying on it (Harris, 1967). The teachers at Knightcrest School can prompt the quiet and shy Linda Grey to contribute to the class activities. They may start by working with Linda individually, prompting and reinforcing her verbalizations. She may be asked to describe events that have recently occurred and then be given social attention as she responds. Later, the teacher may bring one or two other children to participate with herself and Linda. As Linda begins to respond with the teacher and with one or two other children, the teacher can place Linda in larger groups. Also, Linda's participation in class can be increased by specifically calling on her for an answer and responding positively to her responses. As she progresses, she may be asked to help another child or to be a group leader. Thus this example of prompting also demonstrates reinforcing successive approximations of the final goal.

Another method that may be used to increase the probability that a response will occur is to model the desired behavior. An adult may say, "Listen to me while I pronounce this word for you." *Modeling* a response can have the effect of developing new response patterns that did not exist previously and are, therefore, novel to the student. A student might observe a short acrobatic performance and then imitate the entire performance. Modeling can also increase or decrease responses that exist in the student's behavioral patterns. Thus a child may observe a teacher or peer perform in a new setting a response the child was already capable of making. The teacher may call attention to his role as model by saying, "Watch how I do this," or he may designate a particular student to serve as a model. Many teachers use this as an effective way of gaining the attention of some children. Nancy Carter might say, "Linda Grey is paying attention so nicely," and the other children would see Linda receiving social praise for her behavior.

You may have wondered about the example I gave for shaping a child to pick up a pencil. Although it is possible to get the response this way, one could probably get the response more quickly by verbally prompting the child to pick it up. Also, providing a young child with peer models or adult models who are using pencils will probably cause an initial response of the child's picking up the pencil.

Bandura (1969) sees modeling as particularly advantageous in the acquisition of responses when one is concerned with large segments of behavior and with language development. The extent of the student's attention is one of the most important variables in determining whether or not modeling will occur, and a number of variables determine whether or not an observer will pay attention to a model. Among these are the characteristics of the model. People who are seen as having high status will be more likely to get attention and have their performance modeled than people who do not have this characteristic. Recently, interest has been focused on the pairing of two students to work together, one as a model or tutor for the other. These pairings can be used advantageously to teach desired behaviors in the latter student. But haphazard pairings will not bring this about. A teacher needs to be sure not only that the desired behaviors are demonstrated by the "model" student, but also that this model is one the second student will attend to and who is viewed positively by the second student.

Another variable determining whether or not the observed behavior will be imitated is the reinforcement provided for the person modeling the behavior. Occasionally, a behavior that has been observed but not imitated will be performed when an incentive for doing so becomes available. Thus a response may become part of a person's repertoire of behaviors, but may not occur unless incentives are provided.

O'Conner (1969) used a symbolic modeling procedure with children who displayed extreme social withdrawal in a nursery school setting. The children viewed a film in which other children were shown interacting socially. The degree of participation of the children in the film gradually increased, and positive consequences followed each of their social interaction sequences. O'Conner then compared two groups of children who exhibited withdrawal behaviors; one group had seen the film, and the other group had not. Observation of the children's behavior in a nursery school setting showed that those who viewed the film increased their social interaction to a level where it was no longer of concern. Increases did not occur for the children who had not viewed the films.

BEHAVIORAL CONSEQUENCES

Once a desired behavior is performed, careful note must be taken of those consequences that follow the behavior. *Positive* or *rewarding consequences* alter behavior differently from *aversive* or *painful consequences.*

Table 4–1 shows the categories into which consequences can be divided. Consequences can be presented or removed, and they can increase or decrease behavior. The *procedures* are defined by the effect of the consequences of the behavior: *Positive reinforcement* is an *increase* in behavior as a result of presenting certain consequences; negative reinforcement is an increase in behavior brought about by the removal of certain consequences.

There are two ways to *decrease* behavior, both of which may be referred to as punishment. Thus *punishment* is a *decrease* in behavior brought about by the presentation of an aversive consequence or by the removal of a positive reinforcer.

The arrows in Table 4–1 indicate reciprocal relationships. Hence behavior that is increased by the presentation of a positive consequence will decrease when that consequence is removed. Behavior that is decreased by the presentation of an aversive consequence will increase when that aversive consequence is removed.

TABLE 4-1 The Relationship Between the Consequences of a Behavior—Positive or Aversive, Present or Withheld—and the Occurrence of the Behavior

	Positive	Aversive
Present	Result: increase in the occurrence of behavior Procedure: positive ↕ reinforcement	Result: decrease in the occurrence of behavior Procedure: punishment ↕
Withheld	Result: decrease in the occurrence of behavior Procedure: punishment	Result: increase in the occurrence of behavior Procedure: negative reinforcement

Presenting positive consequences

The most important principle in increasing the rate of a behavior is positive reinforcement. To recall the preceding definition, positive reinforcement occurs only when an event or consequence following a behavior increases the frequency of the behavior in that situation. If a teacher's attention is rewarding to a student and she praises him for studying, he will study more in her classroom.

Teacher attention is only one of several reinforcers available within classrooms; another reinforcer is *food*. Candy reinforcers were used in a kindergarten setting when the investigators tried to establish social attention as a reinforcer. The children in this kindergarten were from low-income families, and for most this was their first school experience. One goal was to establish adult attention as a reinforcer. On the first two days of the program, whenever the children made any approach toward participation in one of the provided activities, they were immediately given a candy, raisins, or cereal. These food items were paired with social attention: "That's fine." "You are doing so well." Check marks on a card were also given at the same time. The same procedure was carried out whenever a child followed directions. After the first two days the food reinforcers were dropped out; social reinforcement continued; and the check marks became exchangeable for trinkets and prizes. The food helped establish adult attention and check marks as reinforcers (Wasik and Sibley, 1969). *Tangible* reinforcers such as trinkets are often positive reinforcers for young children. Among the variety of items made available in this study were marbles, jack stones, crayons, coloring books, toy cars, balloons, and whistles.

Social attention includes all the verbal and nonverbal interactions of peers, parents, or teachers. Teacher attention has been used very effectively in nursery school settings in altering such maladaptive responses as isolate behavior (Allen, Hart, Buell, Harris, and Wolf, 1964), crawling (Harris, Johnston, Kelley, and Wolf, 1964), and crying (Hart, Reynolds, Baer, Brawley, and Harris, 1968).

Madsen, Becker, and Thomas have demonstrated how effective a teacher's attention and praise are in managing classroom behavior (Becker, Madsen, Arnold, and Thomas, 1967; Madsen, Becker, and Thomas, 1968). Madsen and his colleagues attempted to compare several conditions in controlling a classroom in which elementary school children spent a lot of time behaving inappropriately. A three-phase procedure was arranged in which the teacher first specified the rules of conduct that the students were to follow. Later, the teacher added a second factor—ignoring the children's inappropriate behaviors. In a third phase the variable of teacher praise for appropriate behavior was added. The biggest decrease in the children's inappropriate behaviors occurred when the teacher praised appropriate behaviors.

Time to engage in preferred activities has been used as a reinforcer. Its use is based on a principle of reinforcement postulated by David Premack (1965), which states that for any two responses, A and B, when A is more probable than B, making the availability of A contingent on the prior occurrence of B will increase the frequency of response B. Thus if working in workbooks is lower in probability than painting with watercolors, the frequency of working in workbooks will increase if performance of the behavior is required for a set amount of time (such as 10 minutes) before access to painting with watercolors is given. This principle of behavior has been referred to as Grandma's Law (Homme, Csanyi, Gonzales, and Rechs, 1969): "When you finish washing the dishes, you may play tennis." "When you complete your assignment, you may go outside." For this procedure to be effective, one must be able to control access to the rewarding activities. If these activities remain freely available to the student when one sets up a relationship between two responses, the student's rate of performing the less probable response will not increase.

Response preferences could be used effectively to alleviate some of the problems at Knightcrest Middle School. In this school the children are already working independently on "contracts" arranged at the beginning of a day. The student plays a major role in setting up this contract. One of the students, Marvin Blake, has been described as one who "should be working at a higher level," "is a very lazy student," and "doesn't always seem to use his abilities." Let us accept the teacher's description that Marvin is not performing at an acceptable level. Also, notice that Marvin has several favorite hobbies; among them are reading and playing the trumpet. A relationship between certain activities Marvin does not do well or does not attempt to do and those he does enjoy can be arranged and made a part of the contract. The teacher and Marvin can agree on a set amount of work to be completed, with free-choice time to follow the work. If, during the work period, Marvin completes an arithmetic assignment with over 90 percent accuracy, then, he can be rewarded with 20 minutes of free time to read from a book of his choice. His parents could become part of the contract arrangement and take Marvin to see a marching band or give him trumpet lessons based on the completion of a certain number of assignments on his contract. A study of contingency contracting with school-age children is described by Cantrell, Cantrell, Huddleston, and Wooldridge (1969). They present major questions that must be answered in arranging a contingency contract and describe a way of keeping records on a student's current progress.

Token reinforcers are those that derive their reinforcing power from being paired with another reinforcer such as one of the ones already described. Tokens, which are always exchangeable for other reinforcers, can be such things as colorful chips, slugs, stars, or check marks on a slip of paper. A child could be given a token while he is working on an assignment, and the token could be spent later.

There are several advantages to using a token system. First, tokens can be provided immediately after the demonstration of an appropriate behavior; there is no lag between performance of the desired behavior and the recognition of the behavior. Second, ongoing behavior need not be disrupted when a token is given, whereas a piece of candy may result in a child's stopping work to eat the candy. Third, it is easy to use such a system with a large number of students at one time. A teacher can give tokens immediately for good work, but need not be concerned with a specific reinforcer. Later, each student may select from among several alternative reinforcers.

An early use of a token system with elementary age children was conducted by Birnbrauer, Wolf, Kidder, and Tague (1965) with educable retarded children. One of their goals was to develop programmed instruction materials for these children. Tokens were given when the children behaved acceptably and answered questions appropriately. The tokens were exchangeable for such items as money (for example, nickels) and toys (for example, airplane models). The results indicated that disruptive behaviors were eliminated and the children's rate of working increased.

The effectiveness of a token system depends on the selection of desirable backup events. One way to assure that there are reinforcing events is to provide a reinforcement menu (Addison and Homme, 1966) composed of many events from which students can choose. A student's preferences can vary from day to day, and students can vary from each other in what appeals to them; the menu would provide an ample number of choices for each student.

Removing an aversive consequence

Responses sometimes occur at a low frequency or not at all because their occurrence results in aversive consequences. In a given setting, a person performs alternative behaviors to avoid the aversive consequences, a situation described as *avoidance behavior*. Removing the aversive consequences brings about an increase in the previously low-frequency behaviors. In the classroom one arranges a situation such that as long as an appropriate response from the student occurs, aversive consequences are avoided. A student may be threatened with a paddling if he does not complete an assignment. By completing the assignment, the student avoids the paddling. This results in an increase in the behavior that allows the student to avoid the aversive consequences. Thus one hears teachers saying, "If you do not complete your assignments, I will send a note home." Students can behave in ways that will avoid their having to take a note home. If a teacher uses sarcasm when students blunder, the students may decrease their class participation to avoid the possibility of being the object of such sarcasm.

I am not an advocate of this procedure—that is, the removal of aversive consequences—believing that more socially desirable ways of bringing about change are available. Nevertheless, you should recognize that the technique is used and can be effective. My own experiences in observing classrooms and working with teachers indicate that using threats of aversive consequences in order to accomplish certain objectives is used most often by teachers who do not know effective alternative procedures.

Removing a positive reinforcer

Two procedures for decreasing behaviors are the converse of those for increasing behaviors. To decrease behavior, one can remove a positive reinforcer or present an aversive consequence. Let us look first at the procedure of removing positive reinforcers. Teacher attention is generally a positive reinforcer for many children. When it is systematically withheld for inappropriate behaviors, the behaviors will decrease in frequency.

A variation of removing a specific positive reinforcer for an inappropriate behavior is to remove the student for a short period of time from a reinforcing setting. This procedure, referred to as *time-out*, was one of several variables used to increase appropriate behaviors and decrease aggressive and resistive behaviors in two children in a demonstration school for the culturally disadvantaged (Wasik, Senn, Welch, and Cooper, 1969). Time-out from the ongoing classroom activities was used when either of the two girls were involved in disruptive and aggressive behaviors, such as hitting or kicking teachers or peers or throwing objects. Whenever a child engaged in such an activity, she was warned that she was not supposed to be doing so, was redirected to a new activity, and told if she did not change, she would have to go to the "quiet room." "The teacher then turned from the child for fifteen seconds to allow her to make a change. At the end of the fifteen seconds, the child was taken to isolation only if she had not made any definite move to begin the structured activity and to terminate the unacceptable one" (1969, pp. 184–185). After 5 minutes the child was returned to the classroom, and the teachers immediately had her engaged in ongoing classroom activities.

This process is effective only with children who would rather be in the classroom than in a time-out room, the hall, or the principal's office. As an illustration, in their classroom for educable retarded children Birnbrauer, Wolf, Kidder, and Tague (1965) found that a time-out procedure was more effective during times when children could earn tokens in the classroom than during times when it was not possible to earn tokens. In a study with several colleagues (Wasik, Senn, Mason, and Anastasiou, 1968) I decided specifically not to use a time-out procedure with three second grade boys who already showed a high frequency of not interacting with other children or materials in the classroom.

Another variation of the removal of positive reinforcement in order to decrease the occurrence of a behavior is to introduce a cost factor. A student is charged a portion of something he has as a fine for performing a certain undesirable behavior. This tactic is frequently used in society and may be incorporated into a token economy system. It is used as part of a token economy system developed for use in a residential treatment facility for adolescent boys who have shown delinquent behaviors. The boys may earn points by performing a number of tasks, but they may also lose points for such behaviors as fighting, name calling, and destroying property (Phillips, 1968; Wasik, 1973).

Presenting an aversive consequence

Punishment is presenting aversive consequences following a behavior and results in a decrease in the occurrence of that behavior. Punishment has the advantage of being effective in stopping the behavior. Thus the use of punishment is often reinforcing to the person who applies it, because the undesired behavior stops. Nevertheless, several disadvantages must be recognized. If punishment is applied without reinforcement for appropriate behaviors, the student may not learn those behaviors that are appropriate for the setting. Thus although the student may not perform the punished behavior, he may be just as likely to perform other unacceptable behaviors as he is to perform appropriate behaviors. Consequently, *whenever a teacher uses a program designed to decrease undesirable behavior, he should include a program for increasing appropriate behaviors.*

Albert Bandura has described other potential problems resulting from the use of punishment. The following discussion demonstrates problems that should be of concern to those involved in investigating and using such procedures. First, the effects may not be limited to the undesirable behavior, but may also cause a reduction in other desirable behaviors. This happens when the student cannot discriminate between those situations that result in aversive contingencies and those that do not. Second, in learning to avoid certain behaviors, the student may also learn to avoid certain people and settings associated with the punishment. These two negative outcomes can be prevented by ensuring that the student is reinforced for appropriate behaviors and that the person who administers the punishment also administers reinforcers. Actions that cause the punishing agent to become a model of the kinds of behaviors he is trying to decrease should not be utilized. The potential problems involved in yelling at a child to be quiet or in spanking a child for fighting with a peer are apparent.

SPECIFIC EFFECTS OF TEACHER ATTENTION

As with other consequences, a teacher's behavior may increase, decrease, or have no effect on a child's behavior. Research studies have indicated that in the preschool and elementary grades the teacher's attention is a very effective positive consequence and, therefore, increases the behavior that precedes it. Hence it is usually referred to as a positive consequence. Although peer attention and other events may become reinforcers as children grow, adult attention remains an effective behavior modifier for many.

Let us look at a suggested procedure for maximizing the effectiveness of teacher attention. Table 4–2 presents the times a teacher would interact with a student and the times he would withhold interactions.

TABLE 4-2

Children's Behavior	Teacher's Behavior	Expected Change in Child's Behavior
Appropriate	1. Give teacher attention (praise, instruct, listen, explain) 2. Give food rewards 3. Give tangible rewards 4. Give privileges 5. Give free-choice time 6. Give tokens	Increase
Inappropriate for time and place	Redirect child to appropriate behavior	Decrease
Inappropriate attention-getting	Ignore	Decrease
Aggressive-resistive	1. Withhold attention 2. Withhold privileges 3. Subtract tokens 4. Use time-out procedures	Decrease

One needs to remember that if teacher attention is a positive consequence, attention to inappropriate behaviors will result in their increase.
Thus the teacher should restrict his major interactions to those students
performing behaviors that he wishes to increase or maintain at a high
rate. He should redirect behaviors that are inappropriate for the time
and place, taking care not to give prolonged attention for the inappropriate behaviors. He should ignore those behaviors that are inappropriate
attention-getting behaviors and seem to be maintained by his attention.
For attention-getting behaviors and aggressive-resistive behaviors that
interfere with the privileges of the other students, additional contingencies may have to be instituted. Many teachers use negative reactions
to stop these behaviors. Often, however, the teacher finds that the student's undesirable behavior does not decrease when he spends time
repeating negative statements. Although a negative reaction may have
the effect of immediately suppressing the student's problem behavior, it
may eventually have the effect of increasing the student's behavior. The
increase can occur when teacher attention, regardless of the content,
is reinforcing and especially if the only time this student receives
social attention is when he is misbehaving. Other ways of managing
these undesirable behaviors have been discussed earlier and are listed
here: withhold teacher attention, withhold privileges, subtract tokens
under a token economy system, use a time-out procedure.

EARLY STUDIES IN APPLIED SETTINGS

The early work in the investigation of operant conditioning principles
in applied settings took several different routes. Arthur Staats and his
colleagues worked out an effective incentive system for use with young
children and adolescents. Staats (1968) conducted a longitudinal study
of his daughter that included the teaching of reading, writing, and arithmetic skills, sensory–motor skill learning, and social behavior learning.
The incentives were tokens given for correct responses. They were exchanged first for tangibles such as candy and trinkets and later for
other appropriate reinforcers.

Staats demonstrated the effectiveness of this approach in a series of
laboratory studies designed to investigate the process of learning to
read in preschool and school-age children. As an example of the use of a
token economy system, Staats and his associates presented programmed
material to preschool children requiring them first to read words individually and then to combine the words into short sentences. When
the children were given praise for their correct responses, they became
bored and restless, and after 15 to 20 minutes began asking to leave.
When this point was reached, the children were offered reinforcers

such as candy, trinkets, or tokens exchangeable for toys, each dependent on correct reading responses. Under this condition the children were quite willing to remain with the reading task for as long as 45 minutes and to participate in additional sessions.

Staats then worked with the children who were having problems in reading. In one study he worked with a boy who had never passed a course in school and was also a behavior problem. After $4\frac{1}{2}$ months in a training program using a token reinforcement system, the student passed all of his courses, and his deviant behaviors decreased (Staats and Butterfield, 1965). (Note that the student's undesirable behavior decreased even though no special procedures were implemented. You should be aware that such positive outcomes may occur even though the events responsible for the change are not identified.)

With these results as background, Staats made plans to test his findings with different students and experiments. In one test of his procedures Staats worked with thirteen culturally deprived 4-year-old children. The results showed support for the methods and principles involved in a token reinforcement system as the children learned writing, number concepts, and reading (Staats, 1968).

Other early research was conducted with autistic children, again in noneducational settings. Wolf, Risley, and Mees (1964) used behavior principles to get a $3\frac{1}{2}$-year-old boy to wear glasses. Operant conditioning has also been used with children with speech deficiencies. Lovaas pioneered in training autistic children to use imitative language by using principles of shaping, reinforcement, and punishment (Lovaas et al., 1967; Lovaas and Simmons, 1968).

STUDIES OF PRESCHOOL AND ELEMENTARY CHILDREN

Early in the 1960s preschool and kindergarten settings were used for a series of studies that indicated the importance of adult social attention on children's behavior; early studies were carried out by investigators at the University of Washington. One of the first problems studied by these investigators was that of "operant crying," exhibited by Bill, a 4-year-old whose crying episodes during nursery school increased as the weeks went by. The teachers observed that crying was set off by minor incidents, that Bill was rarely hurt, that his cries became increasingly louder the longer no one paid attention to him, and that one, and sometimes all three, teachers hurried to assist him. Over a period of 10 days the teachers counted the frequency of crying episodes and found that they averaged eight per morning. A program was instituted that called for ignoring Bill's cries completely and giving him attention when he tried to solve his own problems. The crying episodes decreased to one per day during the first 5 days and only one on the succeeding 5 days. The procedures were then reversed to test their effectiveness. That is, when Bill cried, he was given immediate attention, and his constructive efforts were ignored. While these reversal procedures were in effect, Bill's crying increased to six per day, demonstrating the effect of social attention on this behavior. When the teachers returned to the program of ignoring cries, the crying stopped almost immediately and did not recur during the school year (Hart, Allen, Buell, Harris, and Wolf, 1964).

In another study behavior modification techniques were used to increase the activities of a 3-year-old boy whose passivity was so severe that it seemed to be hampering his motor, social, and intellectual development. A program was initiated that called for giving social attention whenever he touched or played on a climbing frame. Because his beginning response level was zero, the teachers had to shape climbing behavior by socially reinforcing small steps toward the goal behavior. First, he received teacher attention when he walked near the climbing frame, then for pausing near it, touching it, and finally for climbing on it.

After he began playing on the climbing frame 60 percent of the play period, the relationship between his behavior and the teacher's behavior was changed, so that attention was *not* given for being on the frame. Over the next several days his activity on the climbing frame decreased to almost zero; however, he began to spend time on other play equipment. This change gave support to the fact that social attention was establishing and maintaining his climbing behavior. Social reinforcement for climbing on the frame was reinstated, and this activity increased. His teachers then began to give him attention for other activities and gradually decreased attention for climbing on the frame. Similar studies followed involving a variety of problems such as isolate play (Allen et al., 1964) and crawling (Harris et al., 1964).

EXCEPTIONAL CHILDREN

Much of the initial work in behavior modification was done in classrooms for exceptional children. Assignment to these special classrooms typically has been based on one of several diagnostic categories: retarded, emotionally disturbed, learning disabilities, culturally deprived, or delinquent. Before describing some of these studies, note that *a behavioral approach to such children would discourage the use of labels.* Traditionally, a person's behavior has been explained by such statements as : "He just has a bad personality." "That's what you can expect from an emotionally disturbed child." "She is retarded, so don't expect too much." "All delinquent boys act that way." These labels, then, begin to take on explanatory qualities, and the causes of the problems are seen as internal ones.

A behavior analysis offers an alternative and more effective method for approaching a person's problems. This method relies on overt measurable descriptions of a person's problems and emphasizes that problem behaviors can be altered by changing the consequences that follow the behavior. This approach recognizes that we do not call a boy delinquent until behaviors such as truancy or theft occur, and it focuses on changing such behaviors.

Although children are assigned to special classrooms after they have been characterized as disturbed, retarded, and so forth, they are removed when the behaviors that were a problem to society have been changed. The behaviors that have been studied most often in these special classrooms are disruptive behaviors, poor academic achievement, and hyperactivity. Similar behaviors are of concern in regular classrooms, but the behaviors are usually less severe in nature (Hanley, 1971).

In a school of children from deprived backgrounds, Sibley, Abbot, and Cooper (1969) planned a program for a kindergarten boy who had many aggressive and resistive behaviors. They implemented a program based on operant conditioning techniques after the more traditional approaches had proved ineffective in altering his behavior. To decrease his deviant behaviors, the teacher was to give positive social attention for his desirable behavior and to ignore his inappropriate and unacceptable behaviors. When these last behaviors became intolerable, the boy was warned of the possibility of social isolation. If he persisted, he was isolated from the class activities for 5 minutes. During this phase the boy's desirable behavior in free play, discussion, and rest activities increased. When the aggressive and disruptive behavior decreased in frequency, a second phase was introduced. During this phase a time-out procedure was used for milder problem behaviors, and the data show that these behaviors also began to decrease.

Another study involved two second grade girls in a classroom for the culturally deprived (Wasik, Senn, Welch, and Cooper, 1969). Each girl had demonstrated aggressive and resistive behaviors during the first several weeks of class, causing the teachers to request assistance in managing the girls' inappropriate behaviors. After behavioral observations were recorded for a 2-week period, a modification program was arranged for each child. The teachers were to praise all appropriate behaviors, ignore inappropriate attention-getting behaviors, redirect behaviors engaged in at the wrong time or in the wrong place, and remove the child from the classroom for several minutes for aggressive and resistive behaviors. When the modification program was in effect, the inappropriate and aggressive behaviors sharply decreased, and the appropriate behaviors increased. Concurrent measures of the teachers' interactions showed that the teachers' positive interactions increased and their negative and redirecting behaviors decreased during the modification condition. An analysis of the teachers' behavior as it affected the girls' behaviors showed that the teachers were restricting their attention to times when the girls' behaviors were appropriate and ignoring inappropriate attention-getting behaviors.

Several investigators have looked at ways of arranging programs for a larger number of children. O'Leary and Becker (1967) arranged a token reinforcement program for seventeen 9-year-old children described as emotionally disturbed. The program was planned to decrease their deviant behaviors, which included temper tantrums, fighting, and crying. A list of instructions was written on the blackboard (in seat, face front, raise hand, work, pay attention, and desk clear). The children were given points based on ratings from one to ten according to how well they followed the instructions. The teacher's social attention was also dependent on appropriate behavior. Deviant behaviors were ignored. The authors sampled the behavior of eight of the seventeen children and found that the amount of deviant behaviors dropped from an average of 76 percent before the beginning of the program to 10 percent during the program.

Another person who has worked to develop an effective procedure for working with emotionally disturbed children is Frank Hewett (1970). Hewett's design involves an engineered classroom with specific methods and goals. He used behavior modification procedures and a set of goals that he called a developmental sequence of educational goals. These are described as follows. For a child to learn successfully, he must, first, *pay attention*, second, make a *response*, third, develop *order* in his attending and responding, and fourth engage in multisensory *exploratory* behavior. At the fifth goal level, ways to gain social *approval* are the major concern, although it is recognized that social attention has been a part of the previous levels. Sixth, the child must acquire *mastery* of basic intellectual and adaptive skills and acquire a foundation of information about the environment. The seventh and highest goal is *achievement*, where self-motivation for learning and the continual pursuit of new skills is developed.

Hewett has an educational task for problems at each level, and he has made recommendations for the type of student reward or reinforcer and for the amount of teacher structuring. Using this set of educational goals, a teacher can begin to identify problem areas (for example, the inattentiveness of a child) and plan programs to correct the behavior. During the day the child receives check marks for working on tasks and for exhibiting behaviors related to goals in the developmental sequence. Check marks are initially exchangeable for tangible reinforcers. As the child progresses, the check marks become exchangeable for a variety of self-selection activities. Finally, the child advances to graphing his own check marks. Later these check marks can be translated into grades.

Sequencing of educational goals and use of an incentive system could be helpful in planning for William Baker at Midview Elementary School. His problems center on the first four goal levels, and these problem areas need to be considered for him. His teacher needs to look very carefully at the level of work required of him and the reinforcers that are available. The curriculum could be too difficult. Planning for appropriate content materials and reinforcing consequences needs to be carried out.

STUDIES WITH GROUPS OF CHILDREN

Several investigators have studied procedures for working with larger groups of children. One of the studies conducted was with a class of twenty-two second grade children in a school for the culturally disadvantaged (Wasik, 1970). The children in this classroom were described as spending a large amount of time in inappropriate activities, and the teachers wanted to increase the children's appropriate academic behaviors. A free-choice activity time was introduced into the classroom, and items that the children had chosen (for example, puzzles, weaving sets, trucks, play doh, and books) were made available. Access to this time was dependent on desirable behaviors.

Before the items were brought into the classroom, a coding system was used to collect base-line data on every child for 2 days. (*Base-line data* indicate the behavioral occurrence before a specific intervention program is implemented.) The data showed that the mean amount of time spent in appropriate behavior for the class was between 40 and 60 percent. Then a *modification,* or *intervention, program* was implemented in which access to two 15-minute free-choice activity times was made contingent on appropriate social behavior and the completion of assignments. The first activity time was at midmorning, and access to this time was contingent on the immediately preceding morning work. The second activity time was at the end of the school day and was contingent on the late morning and early afternoon work. Thus the positive consequences were scheduled to closely follow the appropriate behaviors. Under this condition the mean percent of time spent in appropriate behaviors increased by 20 percent.

To demonstrate the effectiveness of this procedure, the experimenter removed the toys, books, and crafts available in the free-choice time for several days, then put them back. In the absence of the contingency condition, appropriate behaviors decreased to base-line levels, but they increased again when the free-choice activity time was again made contingent on appropriate behaviors. Although a similar procedure was in effect for all children, opportunity to participate in free time was awarded on the basis of individual performance.

In one first grade classroom rewards were made available as a result of the behavior of small groups of children (Wasik and Simmons, 1971). In this classroom, composed of children in a follow-through program, the children rotated in small groups among five 30-minute instruction centers every day. The main teacher worked with the children in the reading center, and a teacher aide rotated among the other four groups. The instructional model was not working smoothly, because the children frequently left their centers, started fights, and interrupted the teacher, the teacher aide, and the other children. There were three objectives in this study: first, to decrease out-of-center behavior; second, to increase the amount of time the students spent in appropriate behaviors; and third, to increase the amount of time the teachers spent teaching.

Base-line data indicated that children were leaving their centers for inappropriate activities as many as twenty times per center and one hundred times per day. A modification program was arranged in which each group of five children was allowed 30 minutes of special activity time every afternoon, provided no one in the group had left the center inappropriately. A chairman was appointed for each group, and the others had to ask him for permission to leave the group. Under these procedures out-of-center behaviors decreased dramatically, occurring no more often than once per day. When the special activity times were withdrawn, the frequency of out-of-center behavior began to increase and did not decrease until the group contingencies were introduced again. While the procedure for out-of-center behavior was in effect, the overall increase in the children's appropriate behaviors and in the teachers' instructional activities was sufficient so that no further procedures were considered necessary.

Group contingencies affecting all children within a classroom were studied in kindergarten, third, fifth, and sixth grades by Packard (1970). He focused on procedures for helping a teacher control the attention of the whole class. In each classroom the teacher decided whether or not everyone was attending. If they were attending, she operated a timer–lighter device which illuminated a light to indicate to the children that they were behaving appropriately. Reinforcers were made available to the group as a whole, dependent on reaching previously set criteria of attending behavior. In the kindergarten class the children received a play activity; in the other three classrooms tokens were given to the class as a whole but could be exchanged for individual choice privileges and activities (for example, using a typewriter, spending time in the gym or in the fun room, which was furnished with several reinforcing items). In all classrooms the group time spent attending to tasks increased.

Other investigators have also looked at procedures that would be applicable to a large number of children. Hall, Panyan, Rabon, and Broden (1968) trained new teachers to manage an entire classroom by making their attention, a classroom game, and participation in a between-period break all dependent on appropriate classroom behaviors. Bushell, Wrobel, and Michaelis (1968) used group contingencies in a preschool classroom to increase study behaviors. These behaviors increased when special events were made dependent on the prior occurrence of the desired behaviors. Using the "good behavior game," Barrish, Saunders, and Wolf (1969) arranged individual contingencies for group consequences.

Several characteristics distinguish these studies from a more traditional approach to maladaptive behavior. One difference, *deemphasis of labeling,* has already been discussed. A second is that the problem *behavior itself is focused on,* and attention is directed toward changing the behavior (that is, the behavior is not considered a symptom of an underlying cause). A third difference is that it is assumed that the *behavior can be altered by planning appropriate environmental events.* A fourth is that the people (for example, teachers, nurses, and parents) *who work on a daily basis with the child who has the maladaptive behavior can become modifiers.* These people are given major responsibility for decreasing the maladaptive behaviors and increasing adaptive, appropriate behaviors.

BEHAVIOR ANALYSIS IN THE CLASSROOM

To implement a behavioral analysis of classroom problems, several steps must be followed. The model in Figure 4-1 is suggested as a convenient guide for facilitating the students' acquisition of desired behaviors. However, one may first ask how to decide which behaviors to teach. A guide for selecting behaviors is given by Ayllon and Azrin (1969) in the statement: "Teach only those behaviors that will continue to be reinforced after training" (p. 49). Teaching skills that will facilitate a student's adaptability to his environment should be the objective. A student's current environment may not maintain basic skills taught by traditional procedures. If these skills are ultimately important for the

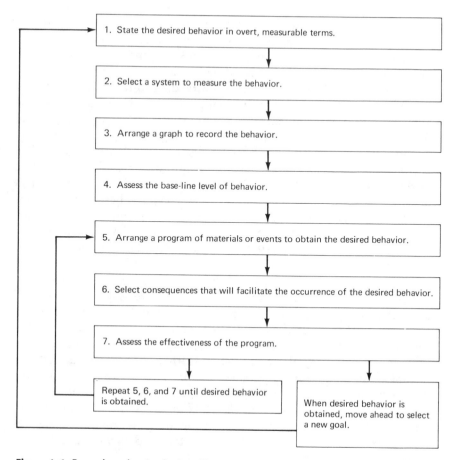

1. State the desired behavior in overt, measurable terms.

2. Select a system to measure the behavior.

3. Arrange a graph to record the behavior.

4. Assess the base-line level of behavior.

5. Arrange a program of materials or events to obtain the desired behavior.

6. Select consequences that will facilitate the occurrence of the desired behavior.

7. Assess the effectiveness of the program.

Repeat 5, 6, and 7 until desired behavior is obtained.

When desired behavior is obtained, move ahead to select a new goal.

Figure 4–1. Procedure for Analyzing Classroom Behavior

student to succeed, then they must be presented by methods that will ensure that the initial new skills will receive reinforcement.

1. Stating the desired behavior in measurable terms

Stating the desired goals in behavioral terms that are explicit, observable, and measurable is an essential first step. To say that you wish a child to "learn more in arithmetic" is not explicit. Explicitly stated objectives usually differ from implicit statements in the choice of verb. Action verbs like *list, spell, compute* and *solve* specify behaviors to be conducted, in contrast to words like *know, understand,* and *appreciate.* A global goal such as "achieve" in arithmetic could be divided into specific behaviors such as "solve these eight problems correctly," or "obtain 90 percent mastery of workbook 5, as measured by the skills test."

2. Selecting a system to measure the behavior

As soon as the desired outcome has been described in overt, measurable terms, a system for measuring the behavior must be found. The simplest method to measure a behavior is to take a *frequency count* of the number of occurrences of that behavior. When a frequency count is taken over a period of time, and stated as so many occurrences for a specified time interval (hour, day), you have a measure of the rate of occurrence. Behaviors are rarely problems in themselves but become so because of either a very low or a very high rate of occurrence. One may take a frequency count of one behavior for one hour during the day. For example, one may count the number of times Michael hits another child in the classroom. This information is obtained by observing Michael during that hour. Frequency counts can also be made on product, or outcome, behavior. For example, one can count the number of problems solved in arithmetic during an hour. In each situation it is very easy to determine whether or not the behavior has occurred and to record its occurrence with a high degree of reliability. (The degree of reliability expresses the amount of agreement between two people that a behavior had occurred.)

Information may be needed not only about the frequency of an event, but also about its duration. This becomes important when study or attending behavior is to be observed. To obtain data on the duration of an event, the use of a stopwatch or clock is necessary. Because of the attention this requires, it is often impossible for a teacher to obtain the data; therefore, an observer has to be in the classroom.

Another method of collecting data is time sampling, which requires that the observer decide at regular intervals whether or not the behavior is occurring. For example, for a 10-minute period he could note at the end of every 15 seconds if a child is studying; this would give forty possible occasions to record attending behavior.

The time-sampling procedure can be used to code the occurrence of not only one but of several classroom behaviors by use of a comprehensive classification system. Two examples of such systems are the Flander's Scale of Interaction Analysis in the Classroom and Spaulding's scale, Coping Analysis Schedule for Educational Settings (CASES) (Simon and Boyer, 1967). When these systems are used, a trained observer, who is not involved in the instructional process, records the occurrences of behavior. These systems typically involve the recording of data by making an entry on a coding sheet at 3-, 5-, 10-, 15-, or 20-second intervals. Each system yields information on several categories of behavior. For example, Spaulding's CASES has thirteen categories covering such classifications of behavior as aggressive, resistive, self-directed, social interaction, and withdrawal. This scale has been used in several studies to give a comprehensive picture of the changes in a child's behavior. When a recording of a child's classroom behavior is indicated, people such as resource personnel, teacher aides, student teachers, and volunteers can be taught to observe and code data. Teachers themselves may take turns and collect such information for each other.

The teacher can also provide the means for the student to record information on his own performance. Once a teacher knows procedures for collecting data, he can teach the student and allow him to keep charts on his own performance. This gives the student immediate feedback and should help him to participate in the decisions about his own classroom goals.

For the remainder of our discussion, I will return to the use of a simple frequency count, a procedure that does not require special resources and is appropriate for recording most classroom events.

3. Arranging a graph to record the behavior

Once the measurement of the behavior has been determined, a way to record the occurrence of the behavior should be arranged. Such information is best summarized on graph paper. Time is plotted along the horizontal axis, and frequency is plotted along the vertical axis. The resulting figure yields information on the rate of occurrence of the behavior in question.

Plotting data on graph paper should be done as soon as possible after the data are collected. This will provide you with an immediate visual comparison of the changes that occur from day to day and will help you to recognize trends or changes in the behavior. Bijou and his colleagues have written a description of ways to interpret data on graphs. Their article is an excellent source to refer to for help in interpreting the data on your graphs (Bijou, Peterson, Harris, Allen, and Johnston, 1969).

4. Assessing the base-line level of the behavior

As indicated earlier, data collected prior to introducing a new procedure is called the base-line data. Once base-line data have been collected, the teacher will compare the data with the statement of desired outcome. Sometimes the act of taking data can bring about a change in the occurrence of the target behavior by bringing into prominence some variables that may not have been noticeable before. You may try counting one of your own behaviors to see if simply counting the behavior will bring about a change in the frequency of its occurrence. If the actual occurrence of the behavior during the collecting of baseline data is different from what was originally expected, one may have to change the description of the desired outcome behavior.

5. Arranging a program of materials or events to obtain the desired behavior

Decisions can now be made about any materials that might be necessary for the behavior to occur. You may select one method for teaching reading to one student and a second method for another student. If one is attempting to increase an academic behavior by arranging a system of behavior management, all materials must be planned for.

The importance of selecting appropriate materials cannot be overemphasized. In my own experience I have seen students referred for aggressive and resistive behaviors or withdrawal behaviors who were being expected to sit quietly and work on assignments that were one, two, or more grade levels above their current performance level. You can readily imagine why such children begin to twist and turn in their seats, disrupt others, throw books across the room, refuse to turn in written work, sit with their head on their desks, or remain silent when asked to respond to a question. Sometimes changing to appropriate materials will be sufficient to bring about the desired change in the student's behavior.

6. Arranging consequences that will increase the occurrence of the desired behavior

When the introduction of new materials is not sufficient to bring about the desired change, one must decide what events might be used as reinforcers for the desired behavior. If the desired behavior does not occur, it may be established within the student's repertoire by shaping, prompting, or modeling procedures. If the desired behavior occurs, one must then decide on ways to increase the behavior. In selecting consequences, one needs to determine what is reinforcing for any one student. A number of behavioral consequences were described earlier. When selecting consequences for a particular student, one must determine what is reinforcing for that student. A helpful aid in selecting reinforcers is to ask the student what he likes. A second procedure is to observe what the student selects when he is given a choice. After selecting the consequences, one can arrange them for the desired behavior, the undesired behavior, or both. For example, if the problem behavior is the child's wandering around the room, one could reinforce sitting quietly or punish wandering around behavior, or one could arrange contingencies for both behaviors.

7. Assessing the effectiveness of the program

Once procedures for changing behavior have been adopted, it is necessary to evaluate their effectiveness. This assessment is a continual process that helps to answer the question of whether the behavior has changed in the desired direction and whether it has reached the desired level. Another question is whether the change is due to the particular procedures that are implemented. This latter question concerns a verification of the procedures and will be discussed in the following section.

The first question is directly related to the statement of the desired behavior. The goal may be academic, such as solving every problem in a group of ten correctly from a base-line level of one correct in ten. Social behaviors, such as decreasing temper tantrums to none per day, may be the desired goal. In each situation it is easy to ascertain whether or not the goal behavior has been achieved. It is not as easy to determine how rapidly one is progressing toward the goal. There are ups and downs as the behavior changes in frequency. Rarely will one obtain the outcome behavior on the first day of a program. A series of decisions must be made to answer the following questions: How long should one implement the program? When has the outcome been reached? Does one need to alter the program? When can one introduce a new outcome behavior?

By plotting the behavior on graph paper and systematically recording the data on a day-by-day or session-by-session basis, one can monitor changes. The necessity of a daily analysis of the behavior cannot be overemphasized. By carefully observing the changes, one can make decisions as to the advisability of continuing with the same program or attempting some other approach. The length of time a procedure is tried before providing definitive data will vary as a function of the frequency of the behavior and of the recording procedures.

If the records are minute-by-minute, the rate high, and the program is being administered uniformily, then increases or decreases (depending on whether the aim is to accelerate or decelerate behavior) should be observed in a few hours. The procedures should be changed if the data show no increase (decrease) in that time. If the unit of recording is a day or class period and the behavior occurs regularly, then five to ten days (periods) will suffice. Similarly, five to ten weeks or months will be necessary if the behavior occurs once a week or once per month. The deciding factor is the number of times in succession that the subject actually experiences the intervention procedure and not the period of time the program is in effect.

It follows that one can make only an approximate prediction of how long he should adhere to a program [Birnbrauer, Burchard, and Burchard, 1970, p. 63].

8. Repeating 5, 6, and 7 until desired behavior is reached

If a continual assessment of the data indicates that the program is not working, the teacher should select different materials or consequences for the student. Once the program is effective, one can proceed with selecting new goal behaviors.

How long to implement the program

If the outcome behavior is obtained, one may ask how long to continue with the program. In most situations the answer is obvious. The teacher has found a program that works, and he remains with it. Some reinforcers, those not usually found in a classroom setting but introduced to bring about a desired change in behavior, are described as extrinsic. Tokens, candy, and trinkets usually fall into this category. Teacher or peer attention and time to engage in preferred activities are often referred to as intrinsic or natural reinforcers. Teachers are often referred to as intrinsic or natural reinforcers. Teachers are often interested in removing extrinsic reinforcers, while maintaining the desired level of behavior. I believe this is an appropriate goal, provided one keeps in mind the primary goal of maintaining the desired behavior at an acceptable level.

Two methods are available to a teacher for removing components of a specific program. The first method is that of fading out parts of the program so slowly that the rate of the desired behavior is not altered. Thus a teacher may first back up tokens with candy or trinkets. Later she may substitute 10 minutes of free time in exchange for a token. Related to this method is the procedure of changing the schedule of the delivery of reinforcement. Thus one may have given a child social attention for each occurrence of social behavior during a specific program. When social behavior begins occurring frequently, the teacher may switch to a fixed-ratio schedule in which he reinforces every second or every third occurrence of appropriate behavior. Later, he may reinforce on a variable schedule with an average of every fifth occurrence. His goal may be to maintain the student's desired behavior with the same frequency of teacher attention received by other students in the class.

Another method of determining if the program is necessary to maintain the desired behavior is to withdraw the program procedures and return to the original base-line conditions (base-line 2). O'Leary and

Becker (1967) describe this as a necessary condition for learning whether or not to continue with the original program. If the desired behaviors persist, one knows it is not necessary to continue with the program. If the desired behaviors are not maintained, one must again use the original program. Then it may be possible to introduce the method described for slowly removing the program.

The method of returning to the original base-line conditions is synonymous with an experimental design for determining if the variables in the program were responsible for a change in behavior. From a research viewpoint, if you introduce a new procedure and the behavior changes, you cannot unquestionably state that your procedure was responsible for the change. Unknown variables could be bringing about the change. Let me illustrate. When I was working in a demonstration school for the disadvantaged, a second grade boy was referred to me because of his aggressiveness toward peers, his failure to complete assignments, and his verbal and physical resistance to teachers' requests. We collected observational data on the boy and because there was a lot of interest in him, held a staff conference with the teacher, social worker, observer, consulting psychologist, and several students. During this meeting we arranged a program in which social attention was made dependent on his desirable behavior and inappropriate attention-getting behavior was ignored. The student's appropriate behavior began to increase, even more quickly than anticipated. Some detective work revealed that his teacher had called the boy's guardian the day of the conference. The guardian had a subsequent talk with the boy, and there was a marked and sustained change in his behavior the following day. Thus all my data showed was that when the program was in effect, there was a correlated change in behavior, but it was not necessarily a result of the program. As a teacher, you do not have to demonstrate just what brought about the desired behavior. But let's say that you are interested in pursuing the question. One thing you could do is remove the program. If the behavior remains the same, you now have added information. It is no longer necessary to keep the program in effect. The student's behavior is under the control of other variables, either ones beginning during the program or ones that are developing in its absence. I have seen teachers withdraw their own social attention, only to have a student's peers take on the role of social reinforcers and maintain a student's behavior. At this point, you know you do not need to reintroduce the program to maintain the desired behavior.

Let us assume that when you removed the program, the behavior decreased to the base-line level. This result would suggest that your program was bringing about the change. The target behavior was absent in base-line 1, present in the program, and absent in base-line 2. In a classroom setting you would then reintroduce your program. At this point you would have carried out a design referred to as ABAB, a basic approach in behavior analysis for investigating whether one behavior or response varies as a result of another event.

There may be instances when an ABAB design would not be used. If one is concerned about eliminating a particularly deviant behavior, one might have reservations about removing a procedure if the removal would restore this behavior. Also, there are some behaviors that come under the control of strong natural contingencies, such as peer reinforcement, once they are established. In such a case, unusual procedures would have to be implemented in order to demonstrate a reversal of the procedures.

When such conditions are in operation, one can consider alternative ways to test the effectiveness of the procedures. When appropriate, the teacher can use the procedures with the same child to help obtain a second desired behavior. For example, if a student's study behavior increases with attention from the teacher, he may also use teacher attention to increase social behaviors.

These procedures offer an added dimension for those who want to use them. In a classroom setting a teacher's primary goal would be to select appropriate outcome behavior for students and to arrange events to produce such behavior. You are accountable for whether or not learning or behavioral change occurred. But you may also be interested in finding out what brought about the change.

MR. BELLAMY'S SIXTH GRADE

Let us look now at Mr. Bellamy's classroom at Bridges Elementary School, where the students have been described as inattentive, not interested in learning, irresponsible, rarely having pencils, notebooks or books, doing little unless threatened, disliking schools and teachers, frequently tardy, hypochondriacal before tests, and considering themselves to be picked on by teachers and other school administrators.

How can one carry out a behavior analysis of this classroom? Returning to the guide suggested earlier, one must first define the desired behaviors in overt, measurable terms. This information is not available. Some behavioral descriptions of problems have been given (for example, rarely having pencils or notebooks), and other programs are described in nonspecific terms (for example, irresponsible). But one must now determine some appropriate goal behaviors. How many desired behaviors can you write for this classroom? You may find that stating the problems in this classroom in behavioral, measurable terms is not an easy task. Later, reread the descriptions of the other two classrooms, and see how many problems are stated behaviorally.

Goals in this classroom can be looked at from two different standpoints. General goals for the class can be considered first, but then each goal will have to be considered for its appropriateness for any one student.

Let us look at one academic concern—arithmetic ability. This may be broken down into two specific computational skills—multiplication and division. An assessment of the students' performance in each area will be necessary. For students who perform very poorly, it will be necessary to assess skills of counting, simple addition, or performance on multiplication tables. The purpose is to determine each student's current level of performing. Only when this is specifically known can appropriate outcome behaviors be stated for each student.

In keeping with the guide described earlier, each desired behavior will have to be stated in overt terms, and a way of measuring and recording the behavior arranged. Can you come up with several hypothetical examples of where the students' level of performance might be and ways to measure and record future changes in behavior? As one example, a count could be taken of how many one-digit numbers a student can correctly multiply by a second one-digit number. The total number would be a base rate. The student himself could keep a record of progress as the total frequency increases.

Now materials and consequences need to be arranged. What might you use to help the children master the multiplication tables? A teacher may come up with some improvised, innovative ideas; he may get some ideas by talking with other teachers and checking published materials. The teacher should also arrange for a positive event to follow occurrences of the desired behaviors. If a week goes by and the records indicate no progress, the teacher will need to reevaluate the materials and consequences.

What we have done so far is to take a general goal of increasing arithmetic ability, divide it into some of its component parts, assess performance, and develop specific programs based on the student's base rate of performance. This implies that possibly no two students will begin a program at the same level. Thus inherent in this approach is the acceptance of individualized instruction; progress for each student is measured against his own base rate, not against national normative data. It will probably help the children achieve the desired goals if a strong program of positive reinforcers is introduced. How do you go about selecting reinforcers for this group? Can you come up with at least three procedures to help?

First, you could ask the students what they want to do or what they would like to have. This procedure was followed in the previously reported study to increase the appropriate behaviors of second grade students, and it is as appropriate with older students. A class meeting could be held in which the students are given an opportunity not only to describe reinforcers, but also to take part in planning goal behaviors. Second, you could observe what the students do when they are given free time. Third, you could list those reinforcers that are usually selected by this age group.

Since no one event is likely to be a reinforcer for all the students, it might be advantageous to develop a token economy system for the class. Under this system the students would receive points whenever they reached a goal behavior. A list of all reinforcers with a point exchange value assigned to each would be available. Each student could then exchange his points for whatever item on the list he wanted that day.

A social skill may also be selected as a goal behavior. Since tardiness has been listed as a problem behavior at Bridges, let us look at coming to school on time as the desired behavior. Mr. Bellamy has already been measuring and recording this behavior, because he has to turn in a daily list of students who are late and the time they arrive. Can you come up with a program to obtain the desired behavior? If you do not want to reinforce coming to school on time, because the students are frustrated with the work when they get there, then remember that part of your planning requires you to see that the ongoing activities are appropriate for the students. It is important to ask if the students are avoiding an unpleasant situation by coming in late. If so, part of the program will be to change the curriculum. Letting each student work at his own level in arithmetic and plot his own progress may possibly lead to a decrease in tardiness.

What can be done to facilitate checking on the progress of each student? One option is to divide the class into groups of five to seven children. Let each group have a leader or manager who is responsible for recording whether each person in his group has completed his assignment. Special reinforcers may be made available if all the students in a group complete their assignments. The group leader could be given positive reinforcers for carrying out his duties, and the opportunity to be the leader could rotate among the group members. A manager system has been used effectively with a group of boys in a residential treatment facility for boys with delinquent and undisciplined behaviors (Phillips, 1968).

Certainly, the two goal behaviors thus far described only begin to encompass the problems in this classroom. The reader can go on to state other goal behaviors and to design programs to promote such behaviors. The token economy system can be expanded to cover a number of these problems.

As stated earlier, behavior analysis of a classroom does not offer easy or simple answers. Rather it asks that one take an objective look at what is going on, set appropriate goals, and measure progress toward those goals. When the goals aren't reached the first time around, one must try again, believing that students learn and that changes are made when the environment is appropriately arranged.

HIGH SCHOOL SETTINGS

The studies and illustrations described so far have been conspicuous in their emphasis on preschool and primary age students. This results primarily from the emphasis investigators have given to the younger age groups, although a few studies have been reported in junior high school settings (for example, Broden, Hall, and Mitts, 1971; Browen, Hall, Dunlap, and Clark, 1970; Kirby and Shields, 1972). At least two factors account for this emphasis. First, many people believe that it is best to use intervention procedures with the younger student. Second, it appears to be more difficult to arrange procedures for older students.

Let's look at the first factor. Young children are learning many new behaviors. Those who develop many inappropriate and maladaptive behaviors find themselves left out of many activities. If one could effectively intervene at an earlier age, the probability is higher that a child could benefit more from his current and future environment. Related to this is the belief that working with the younger student is a preventive measure. As an illustration, students who can be diverted from a series of academic failures may not become potential dropouts. Students who can receive support and recognition within schools may not engage in socially deviant behaviors outside school. The question here is not which age group is more important. Rather, when time and resources have been scarce, many have elected to work with the younger student.

A second factor contributing to the scarcity of data on the older student is the question of the ability to gain sufficient control to implement procedures. Given many existing school settings, those responsible for the actions of the students often have little control over reinforcing events in the students' lives.

The deficit of work with older students is *not* related to the range and depth of problems. College students in a class I taught, made up of undergraduate students and public school teachers, spent time discussing the extent of problems in high school settings. Their discussions led them to list these problems: skipping class, truancy from school, inattentiveness, sarcasm, not completing assignments, drugs, smoking, alcoholism, vandalism, boy–girl relations, sex, clothes, integration. When they finished, they were surprised to see the number of "behavior" problems. Only after these and other problems were discussed did they also list the inappropriateness and irrelevance of many things required of students, both academic and social. Their discussions led them to consider that many problems associated with students could in fact be resolved by a systematic approach on the part of the administration, the faculty, and the students.

The procedures, not the principles, will differ from those used with younger students. One of the key issues my students considered is that the students themselves must be a vital part of the planning of any new program, helping to set up the goals and procedures for accomplishing these goals, and, equally important, taking responsibility for seeing that goals are reached. The students in this class tried writing programs and procedures for helping schools solve some of these problems. Their paper solutions offered many alternatives, but as of yet they are not tried. You, the reader, could now take these problems, consider the principles of behavior change, and see what procedures you would recommend.

SOME SUGGESTED ACTIVITIES

I. The procedures for this activity are subsumed under the steps for analyzing and modifying classroom behavior. Carry out steps 1 through 6 for a behavior selected from your own repertoire of behaviors.

A. 1. From your own repertoire of behaviors, select one that occurs several times a day.
   2. Define the behavior in measurable terms.
   3. Select an appropriate interval for recording the occurrence of the behavior.
   4. Count the behavior for several time intervals.
   5. Plot the behavior on graph paper.
   6. Determine if recording alone brought about a change in the occurrence of the behavior.
B. If the behavior in A is one whose frequency you want to increase or decrease, proceed with a plan to do so. If you are not interested in changing the frequency of this behavior, select another behavior that you would like to modify (for example, eating too much, obtaining low grades) and plan a procedure to reach your goal.

II. Define a behavior in a classroom setting that is a source of concern. Then refer to the steps in Figure 4-1 and, beginning with stating the desired behavior in measurable terms, proceed with the steps listed in the figure. Carry out these procedures for each of the following problem situations:

A. An inappropriate social behavior that occurs at a high frequency.
B. A social behavior of concern because of its low frequency.
C. An academic behavior of concern because of its low rate of occurrence.
D. An academic behavior of concern because of the errors in performance.

REFERENCES

Addison, R. M., and Homme, L. E. "The Reinforcing Event (RE) Menu." *National Society for Programmed Instruction* (1) (1966): 4.
Allen, K. E.; Hart, B. M.; Buell, J. W.; Harris, F. R.; and Wolf, M. M. "Effects of Social Reinforcement on Isolated Behavior of a Nursery School Child." *Child Development* 35 (1964): 511–518.
Ayllon, T., and Azrin, N. H. *Token Economy: A Motivational System for Therapy and Rehabilitation.* New York: Appleton-Century-Crofts, 1969.
Baer, D.; Wolf, M.; and Risley, T. "Some Current Dimensions of Applied Behavior Analysis." *Journal of Applied Behavior Analysis* 1 (1968): 91–97.
Bandura, A. *Principles of Behavior Modification.* New York: Holt, Rinehart, and Winston, 1969.
Barrish, H. H.; Saunders, M.; and Wolf, M. M. "Good Behavior Game: Effects of Individual Contingencies for Group Consequences on Disruptive Behavior in a Classroom." *Journal of Applied Behavior Analysis* 2 (1969): 119–124.
Becker, W. C.; Madsen, C. H., Jr.; Arnold, C. R.; and Thomas, D. R. "The Contingent Use of Teacher Attention and Praise in Reducing Classroom Behavior Problems." *Journal of Special Education* 1 (1967): 287–301.
Bijou, S. W.; Peterson, R. F.; Harris, F. R.; Allen, K. E.; and Johnston, M. "Methodology for Experimental Studies of Young Children in Natural Settings." *The Psychological Record* 19 (1969): 177–210.
Birnbrauer, J. S.; Burchard, J. D.; and Burchard, S. N. "Wanted: Behavior Analysis." In *Behavior Modification: The Human Effect,* edited by R. Bradfield, pp. 19–76. San Rafael, Calif.: Dimensions, 1970.
Birnbrauer, J. S.; Wolf, M. M.; Kidder, J. D.; and Tague, C. E. "Classroom Behavior of Retarded Pupils with Token Reinforcement." *Journal of Experimental Child Psychology* 2 (1965): 219–235.
Broden, M.; Hall, R. V.; Dunlap, A.; and Clark, R. "Effects of Teacher Attention and a Token Reinforcement System in a Junior High School Education Class." *Exceptional Children* (1970): 341–349.
Broden, M.; Hall, R. V.; and Mitts, B. "The Effect of Self-recording on the Classroom Behavior of Two Eighth Grade Students." *Journal of Applied Behavior Analysis* 4 (1971): 191–199.
Bushell, D., Jr.; Wrobel, P. A.; and Michaelis, M. D. "Applying Group Contingencies to the Classroom Study Behavior of Preshool Children." *Journal of Applied Behavior Analysis* 1 (1968): 55–61.
Cantrell, R. P.; Cantrell, M. L.; Huddleston, C. M.; and Wooldridge, R. L. "Contingency Contracting with School Problems." *Journal of Applied Behavior Analysis* 2 (1969): 215–220.
Hall, R. V.; Panyan, M.; Rabon, D.; and Broden, M. "Instructing Beginning

Teachers in Reinforcement Procedures Which Improve Classroom Control." *Journal of Applied Behavior Analysis* 1 (1968): 315–322.

Hanley, E. M. "Review of Research Involving Applied Behavior Analysis in the Classroom." *Reviews of Educational Research* (1971): 597–625.

Harris, F. R. "Field Studies of Social Reinforcement in a Preschool." Education Improvement Program, Duke University, Durham, North Carolina, 1967.

Harris, F. R.; Johnston, M. K.; Kelley, C. S.; and Wolf, M. M. "Effects of Positive Social Reinforcement on Regressed Crawling of a Nursery School Child." *Journal of Educational Psychology* 55 (1964): 35–41.

Hart, B. M.; Allen, K. E.; Buell, J. S.; Harris, F. R.; and Wolf, M. M. "Effects of Social Reinforcement on Operant Crying." *Journal of Experimental Child Psychology* 1 (1964): 145–152.

Hart, B. M.; Reynolds, N. J.; Baer, D. M.; Brawley, E. R.; and Harris, F. R. "Effects of Contingent and Noncontingent Social Reinforcement on the Cooperative Play of Preschool Child." *Journal of Applied Behavior Analysis* 1 (1968): 63–76.

Hewett, F. M. *The Emotionally Disturbed Child in the Classroom*, Boston: Allyn and Bacon, 1970.

Homme, L.; Csanyi, A. P.; Gonzales, M. A.; and Rechs, J. R. *How to Use Contingency Contracting in the Classroom*. Champaign, Ill.: Research Press, 1969.

Kirby, F. D., and Shields, F. "Modification of Arithmetic Response Rate and Attending Behavior in a Seventh-grade Student." *Journal of Applied Behavior Analysis* 5 (1972): 79–84.

Lovaas, O. I.; Freitag, L.; Nelson, K.; and Whalen, C. "The Establishment of Imitation and Its Use for the Development of Complex Behavior in Schizophrenic Children." *Behavior Research and Therapy* 5 (1967): 171–181.

Lovaas, O. I., and Simmons, J. Q. "Manipulation of Self-destruction in Three Retarded Children." *Journal of Applied Behavior Analysis* (1969): 143–157.

Madsen, D. H.; Becker, W. C.; and Thomas, D. R. "Rules, Praise, and Ignoring: Elements of Elementary Classroom Control." *Journal of Applied Behavior Analysis* 1 (1968): 139–150.

O'Connor, R. D. "Modification of Social Withdrawal Through Symbolic Modeling." *Journal of Applied Behavior Analysis* 2 (1969): 15–22.

O'Leary, K. D., and Becker, W. "Behavior Modification of an Adjustment Class: A Token Reinforcement Program." *Exceptional Children* 33 (1967): 637–642.

Packard, R. G. "The Control of Classroom Attention: A Group Contingency for Complex Behavior." *Journal of Applied Behavior Analysis* 3 (1970): 13–28.

Phillips, E. L. "Achievement Place: Token Reinforcement Procedures in a Home-style Rehabilitation Setting for Pre-delinquent Boys." *Journal of Applied Behavior Analysis* 1 (1968): 213–223.

Premack, D. "Reinforcement Theory." In *Nebraska Symposium on Motivation*, edited by D. Levine. Lincoln: University of Nebraska Press, 1965.

Sibley, S. A.; Abbott, M. S.; and Cooper, B. P. "Modification of the Classroom Behavior of a Disadvantaged Boy by Social Reinforcement and Isolation." *Journal of Experimental Child Psychology* 7 (1969): 203–219.

Simon, A., and Boyer, E. G., eds. *Mirrors for Behavior*. Phila.: Research for Better Schools, 1967.

Simmons, J. T., and Wasik, B. H. "Small Group Contingencies and Special

Activity Times Used to Manage Behavior in a First Grade Classroom." *Journal of School Psychology* (1973, In press).

Staats, A. W. *Learning, Language and Cognition.* New York: Holt, Rinehart, and Winston, 1968.

Staats, A. W., and Butterfield, W. H. "Treatment of Nonreading in a Culturally Deprived Juvenile Delinquent: An Application of Reinforcement Principles." *Child Development* 36 (1965): 925–942.

Wasik, B. H. "The Application of Premack's Generalization on Reinforcement to the Management of Classroom Behavior." *Journal of Experimental Child Psychology* 10 (1970): 33–43.

Wasik, B. H. "Janus House for Delinquents: An Alternative to Training Schools." Presented at Workshop on New Treatment Approaches to Juvenile Delinquency. Memphis, Tennessee, 1973. (In press.)

Wasik, B. H.; Senn, K.; Mason, J.; and Anastasiou, N. "Behavior Modification: The Contingent Use of Teacher Attention and Choice Activity Time." Unpublished manuscript. 1968.

Wasik, B. H.; Senn, K.; Welch, R.; and Cooper, B. "Behavior Modification with Culturally Deprived School Children: Two Case Studies." *Journal of Applied Behavior Analysis* 2 (1969): 181–194.

Wasik, B. H., and Sibley, S. A. "An Experimental Summer Kindergarten for Culturally Deprived Children." Education Improvement Program, Duke University, Durham, North Carolina, 1969.

Wolf, M.; Risley, T.; and Mees, H. "Application of Operant Conditioning Procedures to the Behavior Problems of an Autistic Child." *Behavior Research and Therapy* 1 (1964): 305–312.

5 · Locus of control in the classroom

DANIEL SOLOMON
Montgomery County Schools
Rockville, Maryland

MARK I. OBERLANDER
Institute for Juvenile Research
Chicago, Illinois

KEY CONCEPTS

locus of control

internal control

external control

instigation

outcome

expectancy

reinforcement

Before you proceed very far with this chapter, we would like you to think for a moment about what you are doing. You have turned to this page and have started to read. But how have you come to the point of reading a chapter on locus of control? Are you reading it because it is a course requirement, because someone told you to read it, or because it is on a topic that you have decided on your own that you would like to read about? And if, after reading the chapter, you find that you can remember and understand its major points, will this be because of your own ability, the way we wrote it, or some combination of the two? If you find the chapter incomprehensible, whose fault will that be, ours or yours?

The topic of this chapter, *locus of control,* refers to just such decisions and beliefs about the origins of behavior and the assignment of credit or blame for its results.

The question of how much control man has over his own behavior (that is, determinism versus free will) has long occupied theologians and philosophers. Although the question as phrased historically may well be unanswerable, the study of the effects of peoples' *beliefs* about it, and of the characteristics of situations that make one or the other seem more plausible, has become a major concern of psychologists and social psychologists within the past decade. Indeed, the basic postulate in a recent general theory of motivation is that "man's primary motivational propensity is to be effective in producing changes in his environment" (De Charms, 1968, p. 269). In this chapter we will summarize some of the research and theorizing relating to perceptions of and beliefs about control. We will describe some of the most important studies in some detail and will attempt to draw out some of the implications for education.

INTERNAL VERSUS EXTERNAL ORIGINS AND OUTCOMES OF BEHAVIOR

Control can be exerted over two aspects of behavior. One aspect determines whether or not a behavior will be performed, or *instigated*. An individual may consciously choose to take a certain action and do it (read this chapter, for example); on the other hand, he may take an action only because he is coerced to do so. The chosen behavior can be considered to reflect *autonomy*, and the coerced behavior, *conformity*. The second aspect over which control can be exerted is the *outcome* of an act. Some situations are such that the outcome is entirely determined by the individual's skill, ability, and effort; in others good or bad results may be determined by chance or the actions of others, and they may be completely unrelated to the individual's own behavior. The former can be considered instances of *personal*, or *internal*, *control*, the latter, of *external control*. Individuals may also differ in the degree to which they *believe* that people in general, and they themselves in particular, are more internally or externally controlled.

Situations may represent various combinations of control over the instigation and control over the outcomes of behavior. An individual may take a self-initiated, or *autonomous*, action in a situation in which the outcomes (winning and losing) are dependent on his own behavior, or are *internally controlled* (playing a game of darts or checkers, for example); or he may take an autonomous action in a situation in which the outcomes are determined by chance, or are *externally controlled* (shooting dice, or playing blackjack, for example). Similarly, he may be coerced, or feel it necessary to *conform*, in a situation in which the outcomes depend on his own skill, effort, and ability, or are internally controlled (taking a test in school, for example), or he may conform in a situation in which the outcomes do not depend on his behavior but are externally controlled (participating in the draft lottery, for example).

These examples of internal–external instigation of action and internal–external control of outcomes are relatively extreme. Each of these two dimensions should be considered to represent a continuum. Many situations would fall at intermediate points, representing some combination of internal and external control. A child's homework performance, for example, may be instigated partly by his own interest in a topic and partly by the expected fulfillment of class requirements. For an expert poker player, the outcome of a game is substantially influenced by his skill as well as by the chance distribution of cards.

PERCEPTION OF INTERNAL VERSUS
EXTERNAL INSTIGATION OF BEHAVIOR

Because many situations fall at intermediate points, perception of the relative importance of internal versus external factors to the instigation and outcomes of behaviors is not always clear-cut. Brehm and Cohen (1962) have analyzed some of the factors that lead people to judge that behavior (either their own behavior or that of others) is voluntary (self-instigated). If a person remains in a situation even though he does not have to, he is seen as remaining voluntarily. Voluntary instigation of behavior is also seen in situations in which one complies even though compliance is not strongly pressured, one alternative is selected from among several equally attractive alternatives, an individual makes a choice even though there is little pressure to do so, one complies to a strong *illegitimate* force (assuming that one would not do so unless he wanted to perform the act anyway), or a decision is made and acted on only after much thought and the experience of much uncertainty and conflict. All of these factors appear to be means by which the possible effect of situational factors can be minimized. If it seems unlikely that behavior has been compelled by the situation, it is assumed that the behavior must have been internally instigated.

The meaning and importance that one attaches to one's own behavior or to that of others depends heavily on whether one sees that behavior as voluntary or involuntary. One is much more likely to accept responsibility for an act of his own if he believes it was voluntary, or self-instigated. A common defense used by the Nuremberg trial defendants, Adolf Eichmann, and some of those involved in the My Lai massacre has been that the acts in question were ordered by individuals higher in the chain of command, that the defendants were essentially coerced to comply with such orders, and that they were, therefore, not responsible for the acts and their consequences. A person who believes that his own actions or statements were voluntary is more likely to consider them as representing his "true" feelings, beliefs, desires, opinions, and so on. For example, certain subjects in some psychological experiments were asked to argue for positions that were opposed to their actual beliefs. Some of the subjects were influenced to do this so subtly that they felt they had voluntarily chosen to make such arguments. Subjects who had strong reasons to believe that the choice was voluntary changed their opinions to accord with the position that they argued more than subjects who believed that they were simply responding to strong external pressures (such as the offer of a very large monetary reward).

It seems plausible to assume that individuals who believe their participation in educational activities is voluntary should similarly be more strongly motivated, learn more, and have better retention for what is learned than those who see their participation as involuntary or coerced. The voluntary participants are more personally committed to the activity; it is therefore more central to their self concepts, more salient, more attended to, and more deliberately directed. Similar points about the values of "self-directed" learning have been made by Dewey and Dewey (1915), Montessori (1964), Neill (1960), and many others, including current proponents of "open" education. But short of such radical solutions as "deschooling" (see Illich, 1971) or providing the equivalent of the noncredit courses offered in many adult programs throughout the range of grade levels, how can such voluntary educational participation be made possible in an education system that is in essence compulsory? Although some educators, following Neill (1960), have experimented with noncompulsory attendance with apparently favorable results, wide extension of such practices does not seem likely to occur. But even within this constraint, many things can be done to increase the degree to which students' day-to-day and minute-to-minute activities are selected voluntarily. The extreme option would be to give the children complete freedom to select activities with no externally imposed limits and no preselected sets of alternatives. This, of course, would require a different approach to curriculum than is currently in effect in most educational systems. A more limited approach, which could still give students a substantial degree of voluntary control over school events, would be to provide alternative plans (the students could participate in developing such plans) from which to select day-to-day activities. (Note the similarity of this approach to some of the suggestions for improving self concept and self-esteem made by Coopersmith and Feldman in Chapter 7.) Or students could participate in setting up a curriculum for a school year or part of it, with each individual or the class as a whole deciding on the sequence with which to cover the curriculum. Whether such approaches would be effective with individuals who see their educational activities *in general* as coerced, involuntary, and meaningless is a question that has not as yet been answered, however.

One's perception of *others'* behavior as voluntary or involuntary can also have implications for education. Just as with judgments of one's own behavior, an individual is likely to consider statements or actions of another that he considers to be made voluntarily to represent that person's true feelings, beliefs, and opinions, while those that he sees as involuntary, coerced, conforming to norms, expectations, role requirements, and so on, are not considered to reveal the speaker's, or actor's true feelings, beliefs, and opinions. Thus if a teacher makes consistently positive (or negative) comments to the children in her class, with little differentiation in the responses to different productions, the children are likely to conclude that this is the teacher's behavioral response to a role requirement (or to the teacher's perception of the role requirement) and that it therefore tells nothing about the teacher's true opinions of the various productions. On the other hand, a teacher may see a child who is quiet, conforming, and compliant and who performs all required classroom activities with equal efficiency as responding to externally imposed behavioral standards, and therefore the teacher may believe that the child's actions reveal nothing about his own interest in the classroom activities. Since both teachers and students depend on what they can consider genuine feedback from the other party regarding the adequacy of their own efforts in the educational situation (teachers for judging their effectiveness and altering their methods and approaches; students for evaluating their success in mastering the various skills, abilities, and bodies of information), it is important that teachers attempt, along with their students, to develop classroom atmospheres in which statements and actions are voluntary, in actuality as well as appearance, and reflect the true opinions of the parties involved. Students who see a teacher's comments as attempting to conform to a theory or as reflecting an underlying prejudice or hang-up (a behavior perceived as being coerced by an irresistible internal motive can be considered as involuntary as an externally coerced one) will pay little serious attention to such comments.

INTERNAL–EXTERNAL CONTROL OF OUTCOMES

A large amount of research and theorizing has been devoted to the second aspect of control mentioned at the beginning of this chapter, that concerned with the ability to influence the *outcomes* of one's behavior. Most of the work related to this aspect of control has developed out of the social learning theory of Julian Rotter (1954, 1966). In brief, this theory states that the likelihood that an individual will perform a given behavior in a given situation depends on the individual's *expectancy* (or subjective probability) that the behavior will result in a favorable outcome (or positive reinforcement) and the value or importance of that outcome to the individual (reinforcement value). If an individual sees an available goal or reward in a given situation but does not think that his getting it or not getting it depends on the adequacy of his own behavior, then he might be described as having an "external control" perception of that situation. He sees no contingency between his behaviors and the attainment of desirable (or undesirable) outcomes. If, on the other hand, the individual believes that he can produce behaviors in the situation that will be directly responsible for his either getting or not getting the desired outcomes, he can be described as having an "internal control" perception of the situation. Several studies have applied these notions to the prediction of people's behavior in "skill" and in "chance" situations. These studies start by assuming that when a situation or task is such that the outcome is dependent solely on the skill of the performer, the outcome will be seen by the performer as being under his internal control, whereas a situation in which the outcome is determined solely by chance will be seen as being under external control. It was expected that in a skill situation the individual would pay attention to the relationship between his behavior and the outcome and apply what he learned to similar situations in the future, whereas in a chance situation there would be no perceived relationship between the individual's behavior and the outcome, so there would be nothing for the individual to learn and apply to future situations.

The first study that attempted to test this hypothesis was conducted by Phares (1957). He devised two experimental tasks that were sufficiently ambiguous so that by changing the instructions he could get his subjects to believe the outcomes were determined by either skill or chance. His subjects were college girls taking an introductory psychology course. For each task the subject was asked to match an example with a standard comparison. The first task involved judgments of colors. Ten small sample paint patches of different shades of gray were mounted on different colored sheets of construction paper and placed on a large drawing board. The subjects were given smaller patches with the same colors, each mounted on a white filing card. There were thirteen such cards (with none of the standard colors repeated more than twice). The subjects' task was to take their cards one at a time and tell the experimenter which of the patches on the drawing board corresponded to the color on each card. The second task was somewhat similar. In this case judgments of line lengths were involved. Ten narrow strips of black construction paper, varying in $\frac{1}{8}$-inch steps from 1 inch to $2\frac{1}{8}$ inches in length, were each mounted, at varying angles, on filing cards. All ten cards were then mounted, also at varying angles, on a large drawing board. Each subject was given thirteen small cards, each with a strip of construction paper identical to one on the display drawing board. The subjects' task was to match the line on each of their cards with one of those on the drawing board.

All subjects performed both tasks, but were led to believe that different conditions determined outcomes. "Skill" and "chance" instructions were developed for the study, and in every case a subject who received skill instructions for her first task would receive chance instructions for her second and vice versa. Subjects getting the skill instructions were told that the tasks were difficult, but that the score reflected ability, that correct matchings were possible, and that some people did well and some poorly, depending on skill. The chance instructions, on the other hand, described the tasks as being so difficult that no subject had made consistently correct matchings, and success was therefore a matter of luck only. The subjects were given information about their "success" or "failure" after each matching attempt, but in fact the sequences of successes and failures were predetermined and unrelated to performance. Each subject "succeeded" on seven trials and "failed" on six. The subjects' spontaneous comments led the experimenter to conclude that they believed the success and failure reports. The subjects' expectancies concerning the connection between their matching attempts and the outcomes were measured by asking them to make a bet before each attempt as to whether that attempt would be successful. From one to ten chips could be bet each time.

The bets provided the main data to test the hypothesis. The results showed quite clearly that the number of chips bet was more likely to increase after success and decrease after failure in skill than in chance tasks (as defined for the subjects in the instructions). There was also a somewhat greater tendency to make "unusual" shifts in the bets (down after success, up after failure) in chance than in skill situations. The author concluded:

> The findings thus support the view that categorizing a situation as skill leads (the subject) to use the results of his past performance in formulating expectancies for future performances. In chance situations, on the other hand, past performance does not provide a basis for generalization to future trials since (the subject) is not the effective agent in obtaining reinforcements (Phares, 1957, p. 341).

Other studies using different procedures and tasks have shown comparable results. In one study, for example, subjects were given identical instructions with tasks that were constructed to appear to represent skill or chance situations (although in fact identical "success" sequences were used in both). One of these tasks involved physical steadiness (skill), the other ESP "guessing" (chance). Again, increases and decreases in expectancy following success and failure were greater in skill than in chance conditions (Rotter, Liverant, and Crowne, 1961).

Rotter (1966) summarized these and other studies as indicating that "when a subject perceives the task as controlled by the experimenter, chance, or random conditions, past experience is relied upon less. Consequently, it may be said that he learns less, and under such conditions, he may indeed learn the wrong things" (p. 8).

Some other research evidence (summarized by De Charms, 1968) has shown that when students feel that they are able to exert effective influence in controlling the educational situation they are in, they are more likely to have positive feelings toward the teacher and to be willing to work for him than when they feel that they have no effective say in the procedures. A group of subjects listened to a tape-recorded lecture and were asked both to learn the material and to evaluate the lecturer, who, they were told, was behind a one-way screen. They were later told that they were not performing well and were asked for suggestions that the lecturer might use to help them improve their performance. The subjects asked for a summary of the lecture. The lecturer immediately accepted this suggestion with some of the groups and immediately rejected it with others. He then gave another short lecture with a summary at the end for some groups but not for others. The students evaluated the lecturer with a questionnaire at the end of the session. When he had complied with the request, he was liked better than when he had failed to do so. The students were also willing to work harder for the lecturer on a later, unrelated, "odious task" if he had complied with their suggestion than if he had not. Thus students who felt they had been effective in influencing this classroom-like situation, and had not been merely responding to external demands, felt more favorable toward the teacher, more secure, and more motivated to work in the situation.

There are many ways in which benefits such as these can be realized in ordinary classroom situations. Virtually all aspects of classroom procedure and policy can be made to reflect at least partially the desires and opinions of students. If attempts to move in this direction are made, it seems important however, that the influence and power sharing be *genuine*. A teacher who attempts to give students the feeling of effective participation, but subtly attempts to influence the outcomes of their decisions or is unwilling to accept certain decisions, is likely to evoke feelings of frustration and betrayal, and ultimately, a perception on the part of the students that they have even less effective control in the classroom than they would otherwise.

For educational practices the major implications of these experimental findings concern the student's opportunity to see a connection between his actions and their effects. If a student believes that grades, test scores, favorable or unfavorable comments from teachers, classroom practices, and the like are unrelated or only slightly related to his own efforts (that is, are externally controlled), there will be little reason for him to attempt to improve or adjust his efforts. The more clearly and closely related his efforts are to outcomes important to him, the more effort and attention he is likely to expend on them, because he sees the outcomes as internally controlled.

SITUATIONAL DETERMINANTS OF PERCEPTIONS OF OUTCOME CONTROL

Factors *leading* to the view that the outcomes of a task are internally controlled have also been the subject of some investigation. People are likely to see tasks such as that used by Phares (1957) as relating to their own skill if the number of successes or failures in a right–wrong situation is significantly far from 50 percent, if clear patterns of reinforcements seem to emerge, or if long sequences with a single, repeated outcome occur. Such perceptions may, of course, be inaccurate. (See Kelley, 1967.) An external situation may appear to be responsive to an individual's efforts when in fact it is not. A possible example of this is increasing business profits during a period of increasing inflation. An individual businessman may erroneously think that his profits are the result of changes or increased efforts he has made, when actually they are rising because of the total economic situation and would do so no matter what he did. There is also some evidence that people tend to attribute good outcomes to their own efforts and bad outcomes to external causes. In a study by Johnson, Feigenbaum, and Weiby (1964), for example, subjects taught fictitious students arithmetic materials. After the subjects "taught" the first batch of material, they were told that their students had done poorly. They were then given a second batch of materials to teach. Following this, some subjects were told that their students had done well; others were told that their students had done badly. Those subjects whose students showed no improvement tended to put the blame for this on the students; those whose students improved tended to take the credit themselves and judged their second presentations as being better than their first. It is, of course, probable that all subjects had changed their teaching behavior, attempting to improve it for the second batch. Only the subjects with the "improved" students had any evidence that seemed to validate whatever new methods had been attempted, however.

How do teachers' comments influence children's perceptions of behavior–outcome contingencies in classrooms? This may vary somewhat from child to child, but some likely factors can be mentioned. If a teacher's comments to a child, evaluating his work, are at odds with the child's own self-evaluations a significant portion of the time, it seems unlikely that he will feel he is able to evoke favorable comments with his own, deliberate efforts. In such a case the child will feel unable to predict what behaviors will lead to favorable responses from the teacher. If a teacher's comments are consistently favorable (or unfavorable) to one child or group of children, the comments will not be useful to the child for evaluating and directing his educational efforts. Even if a child's work is consistently good (or bad), it is probably necessary for him to receive feedback that reflects even very small variations in the work in order to help him identify and follow up on such variations. Behavioral consistency is also probably very important. If a teacher responds differently on different occasions to work that appears to the child to be of equal quality, or if the teacher gives similar responses to work that the child feels to be of unequal quality, the child will be unable to see a clear and predictable relationship between his work and its outcome, at least as far as the teacher's reactions are concerned. A similar effect may be produced by a teacher who responds differently to similar work done by students of similar ability in a class.

The degree to which the teacher feels that the children's classroom behavior and learning are related to his own efforts probably has important implications for his morale and satisfaction also. A teacher who feels that children show little significant learning no matter what his efforts, or one who feels that the children's learning is determined by factors independent of the classroom and his own efforts, is unlikely to be very content as a teacher.

DIFFERENCES BETWEEN PEOPLE IN BELIEFS ABOUT CONTROL OF OUTCOMES

A large number of studies have been done that treat internal–external control of reinforcement as a personality variable. These studies assume that each individual has a general tendency to consider his successes and failures as being either under his own control or simply the result of chance, fate, or powerful others. It is assumed that individuals differ in this tendency, some tending to see their outcomes as internally controlled, others as externally controlled, others as some combination of the two. Rotter (1966) suggested that learning about the causal connection between one's own behavior and its effects begins in infancy, and that subsequent experiences may influence the development of the control orientation. For some, the early environment may be structured in such a way that behaviors lead to outcomes clearly, quickly, and consistently. For others, the connection may be slower, less reliable, and less clear. If such differences are maintained over long periods of time, it seems likely that an individual from the first type of environment will develop a general expectancy that his own behaviors lead to predictable effects, and one from the second type of environment will be more likely to expect that occurrences that affect him are not under his own, deliberate control, but respond to more distant and less predictable forces.

Several instruments have been developed to measure this variable. The most widely used one was developed by Rotter and some of his associates, and is called the I–E (internal–external) Scale. This scale consists of twenty-nine items, each presenting the subject with two alternatives from which he is asked to select the one closer to his own belief. The items on the scale refer to events in general and in a variety of areas. Thus the scale is considered to represent a *general* belief, cutting across specific areas. In addition, the authors took care to word the items and instructions so as to elicit individuals' *beliefs* about control of reinforcements rather than their *preferences* for internally or externally controlled situations. Some of the items in this scale follow:

1. a. Many of the unhappy things in people's lives are partly due to bad luck.
   b. People's misfortunes result from the mistakes they make.
2. a. The idea that teachers are unfair to students is nonsense.
   b. Most students don't realize the extent to which their grades are influenced by accidental happenings.
3. a. I have often found that what is going to happen will happen.
   b. Trusting to fate has never turned out as well for me as making a decision to take a definite course of action.
4. a. Becoming a success is a matter of hard work; luck has little or nothing to do with it.
   b. Getting a good job depends mainly on being in the right place at the right time.
5. a. The average citizen can have an influence in government decisions.
   b. This world is run by the few people in power, and there is not much the little guy can do about it.
6. a. It is hard to know whether or not a person really likes you.
   b. How many friends you have depends upon how nice a person you are.
7. a. Sometimes I can't understand how teachers arrive at the grades they give.
   b. There is a direct connection between how hard I study and the grades I get.
8. a. What happens to me is my own doing.
   b. Sometimes I feel I don't have enough control over the direction my life is taking.

Some of the earliest studies that measured individual beliefs in internal–external control investigated behavior with some of the same learning and performance tasks described earlier, in which the effects of skill and chance instructions were explored. When given ambiguous instructions that allowed for the possibility of either skill or chance perceptions, people who scored at the internal end of the scale behaved on these tasks in ways similar to people given skill instructions, and those who scored at the external end behaved similarly to people given chance instructions (that is, there were smaller expectancy shifts after success and failure, more "unusual" shifts, and so on).

A number of studies have shown that individuals with internal orientations were more likely to try to influence their life situation than those with external orientations. For example, Seeman (1963) found that internals knew or learned more control-relevant material than did externals. This was shown in one study of the knowledge tuberculosis patients had of health information and in another of the information reformatory inmates had concerning parole regulations. Internals and externals did not differ with regard to their knowledge of "neutral" information, however.

Other research has shown that internals are more likely to resist attempts to influence them. In one study Ritchie and Phares (1969) found that internals were especially prone to react against covert or subtle influence attempts, and externals were more likely to conform. In another study Biondo and MacDonald (1971) found that when internals were subjected to overt influence attempts in situations where they could clearly see that they were being manipulated, they responded with *reactance* (that is, with behaviors opposite to what was being urged). Externals, on the other hand, tended to conform both to subtle and to overt influence attempts. Some additional research has shown that externals are more likely to conform to social norms.

Individual internal–external control scores have also been found to be related to one's relative standing in the social environment. Lower-class people typically score more toward the external end of the scale than do middle-class people, and blacks score more external than whites. These scores probably represent fairly accurate reflections of the barriers that in fact stand in the way of disadvantaged and minority-group individuals, preventing them from realizing significant effects from their efforts to influence their environments. The more often one has found that important happenings in his life have originated from sources that he is unable to control, the more likely he should be to develop an external orientation. Conversely, if one has found the environment responsive to his actions a good portion of the time, he should be more likely to develop an internal orientation.

Similar reasoning concerning the origin of internal and external orientations has led some researchers to try to see whether different kinds of child-rearing practices might cause the development of these different orientations in children. In several studies (for example, Katkovsky, Crandall, and Good, 1967; Davis and Phares, 1969), some of which got their information about child rearing from interviews with parents and some from actual observations of parent–child interactions, it was found that parents who are warm, encouraging, flexible, approving, consistent, and who expect children to be independent at an early age produce children with more internal orientations than those who are hostile, rejecting, punitive, and dominating. (Also note the similarity between these factors, which lead to an internal orientation, and the factors discussed in Chapter 7 by Coopersmith and Feldman, which lead to the development of positive self concepts and high self-esteem.) Parents of the first type give their children chances to exert influence over their environment and themselves, and see to it that many of these efforts meet with success (defined by their own expressions of approval and praise). In addition, the parents' "flexibility" indicates that they are willing to make changes in plans, rules, and so on, in response to exertions of influence from their children. Children who learn that their demands and suggestions are treated seriously and have significant effect at home may come to believe that similar efforts will have similar effects in a variety of other situations. Parents of the second type, however, restrict and dominate the child's environment. The child's efforts to influence the environment are less likely to be encouraged, praised, or responded to, and therefore are less likely to be effective. The child, generalizing from such ineffectiveness, is likely to develop the belief that his efforts to exert influence are likely to be ineffective in other situations as well.

A number of studies have related individuals' internal–external control orientations to other personality characteristics. Externals have been found to score higher than internals on measures of such factors as anxiety, dogmatism, suspiciousness of others, and hostility, all of these possibly reactions to feelings of frustration engendered by a sense of powerlessness. Internals, on the other hand, typically feel themselves to be effective, industrious, powerful, assertive, independent, and trusting of others. Some of the most interesting personality-related investigations, from the standpoint of education, however, concern differences between internals and externals in their reactions to threat, particularly failure. The general prediction made in such studies is that externals, having an acceptable and non-ego-involved explanation ready-made for situations of threat and failure (that is, they are due to external and uncontrollable forces), should find such situations *less* disturbing than internals, who are oriented toward taking the responsibility for such outcomes on their own shoulders. In a study by Efran (1964) it was found that externals were more likely to remember their own failures than internals. Phares, Wilson, and Klyver (1971) induced failure in their subjects in two different conditions in an experiment. One was a "distraction" condition (the two experimenters carried on an audible, private discussion while the subjects were trying to work on an anagrams task), the other, a "nondistraction" condition (the same task, but without the distraction). When asked indirectly about reasons for their failure, externals were more likely than internals to assign blame outwardly in the nondistraction condition, but blame assignment was similar between externals and internals in the distraction condition. It appears that the external situational effect was so clear in the distracting condition that differences in orientation between subjects did not become relevant for the attribution of blame. It was only in the situation that in itself did not provide any clear and compelling reason to assign blame inwardly or outwardly that the participants' internal orientations or predispositions had an effect on the way they assigned blame for failure. These results are consistent with the idea that internals are less likely to recognize their own failures because they feel more responsible for them and therefore find the recognition more threatening and unpleasant than do externals. This study also suggests that this effect only occurs when there is some ambiguity about the reason for failure.

INTERNAL–EXTERNAL CONTROL OF OUTCOMES AND SCHOOL ACHIEVEMENT

If people with internal and external orientations differ in the ways just mentioned, it follows logically that they should also differ in their achievement striving and achievement motivation. Research investigating such differences has generally supported such an expectation. In a study of high school students Franklin (1963) found internals more likely than externals to show evidence of achievement motivation. For example, the internals reported making earlier attempts to investigate colleges, were more likely to plan to go to college, and spent more time doing homework. Other studies have shown internals to get higher grades and higher achievement test scores than externals; such findings have been true for "deprived" as well as "nondeprived" children, but have been obtained more often with boys than with girls.

White and Howard (1970) reported an interesting study that investigated the compatibility between different control orientations in students and each of two educational conditions, in a residential school for underachieving students. This study attempted to relate locus of control orientation to the effectiveness of two instructional methods in a general science course. The subjects were seventh grade boys, who were of average to above average ability, but who were achieving two or more grade levels below age norms. The subjects were divided into a group of internals and a group of externals, and half of each group was subjected to one of two instructional methods. The first treatment, "role assumption," consisted of student-directed learning. It involved instructions for the students to assume the role of scientist and to make their own selections of materials to study. The teacher's role was that of a resource person, who could aid the student in finding information and materials for experimentation and exploration. The teacher gave no reinforcements. The second instructional treatment involved teacher-directed procedures that were geared toward experiments, reading assignments, and in general gave the impression that the teacher was the expert who was in control. Teachers provided reinforcements "when they were justified." In neither group were the students given grades. The results, based on the students' scores on a standardized science achievement test at the end of the school term, were as follows: Internal students learned the same under both teaching conditions; however, those students who were characterized as externals learned considerably more under the role-assumption teaching condition. Presumably externals, seeing little connection between their efforts and reinforcements, perform better in a setting without reinforcement; whereas internals, who do see such connections, may perform well in the setting with reinforcements, because this corresponds with their orientation, but may perform equally well in the self-directed setting, possibly because they provide their own reinforcements. White and Howard concluded from their study that it is possible to design learning climates that correspond to particular I–E types and thereby improve achievement and learning. The results of this study are of particular importance due to the fact that the subjects were underachieving students, a group that is currently of great concern to many educators.

Although much of the research relating locus of control to achievement has used a measure that assumes that locus of control represents a general orientation that individuals apply to many or all of the situations they encounter, this assumption has been questioned by some investigators. Since a control orientation presumably develops out of a person's experiences in a variety of particular situations, and it is likely that for many individuals these experiences have been very different in different kinds of situations, it is logical to expect that an individual's control orientation in one class of situations may be very different from what it is in another class of situations. A child's parents may have been very responsive to his efforts at reading and writing but indifferent and unresponsive to his athletic or artistic endeavors. If such reactions (or nonreactions) were repeated sufficiently often, it might be expected that such a child could develop an internal orientation for reading and writing activities and an external orientation with regard to art and athletics. One implication of this point would be that measures of internal–external control that refer to a single kind of activity and do not try to generalize across different kinds of activities should be developed.

Researchers at Fels Institute in Yellow Springs, Ohio, have been conducting a series of investigations of children's achievement, adapting Rotter's general theory to this particular area. They began with the assumption that an individual's control orientation may be different for different kinds of situations and therefore developed a measure of internal–external control orientation that was limited to academic-intellectual achievement situations, because it was in such situations that they wished to be able to predict children's school achievement and striving behavior. They also developed items that would make the instrument suitable for children from early grade school age (third grade) through high school. In addition, they developed items that asked about the child's acceptance of responsibility for *successes* as well as *failures*. The instrument that they developed is called the Intellectual Achievement Responsibility (IAR) Questionnaire. Three scores are derived from it: a total score (based on thirty-four items), a score reflecting the child's *internal* acceptance of responsibility for positive outcomes or successes (I+), based on seventeen items, and a score reflecting the child's acceptance of responsibility for negative outcomes, or failures (I—), also based on seventeen items. In each of these items a positive or negative outcome is described, and the child is asked to select one of two possible causes of that outcome, an internal cause or an external cause. Following are some of the items in this instrument (from Crandall, Katkovsky, and Crandall, 1965).

1. If a teacher passes you to the next grade, would it probably be
   a. because she liked you, or
   b. because of the work you did?
2. When you have trouble understanding something in school, is it usually
   a. because the teacher didn't explain it clearly, or
   b. because you didn't listen carefully?
3. If you solve a puzzle quickly, is it
   a. because it wasn't a very hard puzzle, or
   b. because you worked on it carefully?
4. When you forget something you heard in class, is it
   a. because the teacher didn't explain it very well, or
   b. because you didn't try very hard to remember?
5. If people think you're bright or clever, is it
   a. because they happen to like you, or
   b. because you usually act that way?
6. Suppose you didn't do as well as usual in a subject at school. Would this probably happen
   a. because you weren't as careful as usual, or
   b. because somebody bothered you and kept you from working?
7. Suppose you became a famous teacher, scientist, or doctor. Do you think this would happen
   a. because other people helped you when you needed it, or
   b. because you worked very hard?
8. If a teacher says to you, "Try to do better," would it be
   a. because this is something she might say to get pupils to try harder, or

b. because your work wasn't as good as usual?

With this instrument it has been found that boys (but not girls) who attributed achievement responsibility to themselves spent more time in intellectual free-play activities, showed more intense strivings in such activities, and scored higher on reading and arithmetic tests (Crandall, Katkovsky, and Preston, 1962).

The IAR instrument has been used in many other studies of children's achievement. In one of these (Solomon, Houlihan, Busse, and Parelius, 1971) behavior of parents toward their child was observed after the child had been given a series of problem-solving tasks and the parents had been asked to help the child as much as they liked. One set of findings seemed to indicate that the development of a tendency in children to accept credit for successes may have quite different origins from the tendency to accept blame for failures. Mothers who tended to disagree with or reject their sons' comments had sons with low I+ scores (that is, who tended to *reject* responsibility for their successes). On the other hand, mothers who tended to agree with and accept their sons' comments had sons with low I— scores (that is, who tended to reject responsibility for their *failures*). These results were interpreted as showing boys' reactions to *unexpected* successes and failures. If a boy's achievement efforts typically produce negative reactions from his mother, he may come to believe that this is the effect to be expected from his own efforts and therefore assume that when he receives a positive reaction, it must be due to something other than his own efforts. In the same way, if his efforts typically get positive reactions from his mother, he may believe that this is what is to be expected from his own efforts, and therefore assign the unexpected negative reactions or failures to external causes. Some similar results were obtained in a study by Katkovsky, Crandall, and Good (1967), but in this case the *fathers'* behavior was related to their *daughters'* I + and I— scores.

Work on the meaning of I— and I+ scores, following reasoning quite similar to that in the last paragraph, has been done in a series of studies by Weiner and Kukla (1970). They suggest that persons with strong motivation for achievement (who have presumably come to expect success) consider successes or positive outcomes to be generally the result of their own efforts, and failures (presumably unexpected) to be caused by external factors. At the same time, persons with weak achievement motivation (those who presumably expect failures) consider failures generally to result from their own efforts and to be their own responsibility, and they assign the cause for the (unexpected) successes they encounter to external factors. In one study these researchers gave children the IAR scale and a measure of achievement motivation. Boys who scored high on the achievement motivation measure had higher I+ scores than those who scored low on achievement motivation; that is, those who were motivated to achieve were more likely to consider successes to be the result of their own efforts than those who were not motivated to achieve. Male grade school children with low achievement motivation were more likely to assume responsibility for their failures than were those with high achievement motivation (that is, the former had higher I— scores), but this was a weaker effect. Also, these differences did not occur with the sample of girls in this study.

In another experiment the researchers looked at the same relationships with more direct behavioral measures of the acceptance of responsibility for successes and failures. Subjects were asked to perform an ambiguous task (predicting the occurrence of each in a series of Os and Is) that was actually determined by chance but was accompanied by instructions that made it appear as if both skill and chance were involved in producing the outcomes. At the end of the experiment the subjects were asked, after they had added up their scores, how many points of their total were due to "skill rather than lucky guessing." They were also asked to estimate how they would do if they tried a similar task again and to state how hard they had tried on the task. Subjects with high achievement motivation ascribed more "skill points" to their total if they had gotten relatively high scores on the task (succeeded) than if they had gotten relatively low scores on the task. Subjects with low achievement motivation showed little difference in skill points regardless of whether they had succeeded or failed. In addition, subjects with high achievement motivation believed that they had tried harder when they had succeeded than when they had failed, and subjects with low achievement motivation showed no such difference. Subjects with high achievement motivation were more likely to expect to do better with another attempt than those with low achievement motivation. These results were considered to show again that those with high levels of achievement motivation consider success to result from their own skill, and failure from luck or other external causes; the results for those with low achievement motivation, though less clear, gave some support to the notion that they accepted responsibility for failures but not successes.

In a final experiment done by Weiner and Kukla (1970), subjects were asked to judge the degree to which performance was "due to ability or effort of the person" for a series of hypothetical tasks; the subjects were given information about the "success" or "failure" of an individual and the difficulty of the task (defined in terms of the percentage of "the group" that succeeded at the task). The more difficult the described tasks were, the more likely subjects were to charge success to ability or effort (that is, to internal causes); conversely, the easier the tasks were, the more likely subjects were to charge *failure* to internal causes. Success at a task that anyone can do is seen as being due to the easiness of the task rather than the skill of the person; success at a task that few can do is seen as being related to skill. Failure at a task that few can do is seen as being caused primarily by the difficulty of the task, and failure at a task that most can do is seen as reflecting a low level of skill or motivation.

FURTHER DISTINCTIONS
WITHIN LOCUS OF CONTROL

An additional refinement of the concept and measurement of internal–external control has recently been made by Gurin, Gurin, Lao, and Beattie (1969). They pointed out that some of the items on the I–E scale refer to the degree to which *people in general* are responsible for their successes and failures, and other items refer only to *one's own experience* and the causes of his own successes and failures. They suggest that the meaning of an internal orientation that applies to all people may be very different from one that applies only to oneself, and therefore that such distinctions should be included in measures of the concept. They also suggest that the possible causal agents named in the I–E instrument cover several categories, which should also be distinguished. Some items consider fate or chance as causal agents, and others attribute causation to powerful others. For people whose efforts to exert effective influence are hindered by environmental barriers, the distinction between these different external agents, when assigning blame for frustrations, may be quite important. There are many elements in life for people in low-income groups that are out of their own control, but are not due to chance. Among these are such things as discrimination, scarcity of educational opportunities, low incomes, job unavailability, and so on. It would be realistic for a person in such circumstances to assign blame for many of his difficulties to the operation of the social-economic system, an external cause, rather than to chance or fate (another external cause). Acceptance of internal responsibility for difficulties related to such factors would be unrealistic and possibly even pathological (indicating intropunitiveness, for example). These researchers, therefore, developed an instrument that included many of the items from the I–E scale, but also included a number of additional items designed to get at some of these other elements, many with particular reference to the attribution of blame or credit for blacks' successes or failures with respect to civil rights.

They gave this questionnaire to black college students and found that the answers to these questions formed *clusters* (or "factors") that did seem to reflect these various subcategories of internal and external control. Some of the students responded similarly to all or most of the items that referred to their *general control ideology*, that is, their beliefs concerning whether events in general are controlled by internal or external forces; responses to these items also tended to be different from those to items concerned with the students' beliefs about *personal control*, that is, beliefs about whether one's own successes and failures are internally or externally caused. With respect to the items about civil rights barriers, it was found that the students could be differentiated according to whether they assigned blame to the affected *individuals* or to the *system*. Those who selected items assigning *individual blame* attributed blacks' failures to their own lack of skill, ability, training, effort, or proper behavior; those selecting items that assigned *system blame* attributed these failures to racial discrimination and a lack of available opportunities. As with previous studies of internal–external control, scores from the personal control items were found to relate to motivation and performance, expectancy of success, self-confidence, and level of job aspirations. But the scores from the control ideology items did not relate to any of these things. The authors concluded from these results that it is only the personal control items that relate to personal motivation, at least for these students. The ideology items, although they may indicate the way the person feels about the world in general, tell nothing about how he relates this feeling to his own personal experience and how he translates it into motivation and performance.

With the measure of *individual versus system blame*, however, a different pattern of findings was obtained. This measure did not relate to any of the above motivational variables or to traditional achievement variables. It was, however, related to a measure of "nontraditionality of aspiration" (aspirations for jobs in areas traditionally closed to blacks); those who attributed blame to "the system" were *more likely* to state such nontraditional aspirations. System blamers were also more likely to state a belief in the use of group action to overcome discrimination and reported a greater degree of participation in civil rights activities. The personal control measure did not relate to these beliefs and activities, and was actually negatively related to a measure of racial militancy. Thus it was found that personal control students tended to be personally achievement oriented, committed to working within the rules of the system toward the goal of their own personal advancement. Students with an orientation toward blaming the system tended to be less motivated toward the goals of personal achievement, defined in traditional terms, and less likely to accept the rules of a system that they saw as being largely responsible for their difficulties. These students were more likely to have goals of *group* advancement. In the words of the authors,

> When internal–external control refers to Negroes' conceptions of the causes of their condition as Negroes, and these conceptions are related to more innovative, coping criteria, it is the external rather than the internal orientation that is associated with the more effective behaviors. When an internal orientation implies self-blame as a Negro, it also seems to involve a readiness to accept traditional restraints on Negroes' behavior [Gurin et al., 1969, p. 47].

LOCUS OF CONTROL AND THE EDUCATION OF DISADVANTAGED CHILDREN

We have discussed the effects of individuals' locus of control orientations on school achievement and on civil rights beliefs and activities. We have also discussed some environmental factors that may help such orientations to develop or change. It has been suggested that people who experience increases in the effectiveness of their attempts to influence their environment should also increase their sense of personal control (particularly those in deprived social statuses, who are typically subject to external control). Therefore, it has been predicted that participants in recent and current social movements oriented toward the extension of power and control (such as black power, red power, women's lib, and community control of schools) should, as a result of that participation, become more internal in their locus of control orientations. Although little research has been done to date to test this notion, there is some evidence that children in integrated schools have more internal orientations than those in segregated schools (Coleman, Campbell, Hobson, McParland, Mood, Weinfeld, and York, 1966; White, 1971). The prediction is not quite as clear here, because the children *participate* in desegregation but generally have no part in bringing it about; some contradictory results have also been reported, showing that the social class composition of a school is more important than its racial composition to the children's control orientation (St. John, 1971).

If it is true that "deprived" children generally tend to have external control orientations, and their "nondeprived," usually middle-class teachers are more likely to have internal control orientations, there may well be differences in related expectations and assumptions that could lead to serious difficulties in the classroom. If a teacher, believing reasonable effort leads to predictable outcomes, assigns work to a student who believes his effort has no bearing on the outcome and therefore does the work in a detached and minimal fashion, the teacher is likely to become annoyed and scold the child. The child may see no reason for the scolding, because he is not inclined to relate it to his previous behavior, or if he does relate it to his own behavior, he is likely to conclude that his efforts lead only to failure and therefore may try to avoid such efforts even more in the future. In such situations teachers should avoid the use of punishment or scolding (because these can lead to inhibition and avoidance). Rather they should help the children to learn to differentiate between different degrees of reward and praise and point out, explicitly and verbally, the causal relationship between different degrees of effort and different degrees of success. The kind of program most likely to promote the learning of this relationship would probably be one in which the student's success and failure are defined relative to his own prior performance rather than to that of other class members. Many nonindividualized class situations may actually promote externality, by making it possible for bright and well-informed students to succeed with little effort and dull or ignorant students to fail with much effort.

There is some reason to believe, however, that the students' externality may not be universal in ghetto schools. The research showing class and race differences in locus of control (for example, Lessing, 1969; Lefcourt and Ladwig, 1965) has used the global, undifferentiated measures. In at least one study using the more situation-specific IAR measure (Solomon, Houlihan, and Parelius, 1969), no significant race or class differences were found in control orientation. Since this measure refers to achievement situations, it may be that even though children differ in their beliefs about how much control people have over their environment in the world outside, they are able to perceive relatively accurately the relationship between their behaviors and the successes and failures they experience in the particular classroom situation. To us, this seems a rather hopeful finding, because it implies that control orientations may be shaped by what occurs in particular situations and that a person need not be permanently limited to the orientation that has been most consistent with his previous experiences.

EDUCATIONAL SITUATIONS AND LOCUS OF CONTROL

We have discussed a substantial amount of research concerning several measures of individual internal–external control orientations. What are the educational implications of this research? It seems plausible to approach this question from two perspectives: First, how can educational situations be structured to help children to develop or enhance the optimal locus of control orientation? Second, can educational situations be set up that allow children to make the best use of whatever orientations they have to begin with? We will consider each of these.

Concerning the first question, the results of the Gurin et al. research raise serious questions about what kind of an orientation with respect to internal–external control should be considered "optimal." Although an internal orientation is apparently most consistent with traditional personal achievement goals, an external orientation may be more suited for other goals that are equally valid, if less widely held. In our view, the most reasonable solution to this problem is to suggest that the optimal and most effective style of attributing blame and credit is the one that is most accurate. If one lives in an environment in which one's own behavior has reliable and predictable effects, it is rational and accurate for him to believe in internal control, and it would be irrational for him to believe that all outcomes are externally determined. If, on the other hand, one lives in an unresponsive environment, in which effects do in fact depend on external causes, an external orientation would be the most likely to be adaptive and effective and an internal one would be harmful. It does seem, however, that an environment in which an internal control orientation is an accurate reflection of reality would be the kind of environment that most people would find satisfying and fulfilling. Therefore, we would recommend that educational situations should be developed that strive for two objectives with respect to locus of control. In the first place, they should be responsive, nondominative environments in which children's efforts do lead to predictable effects and in which, therefore, an internal attribution of causation is a true one. In the second place, children should be helped to develop *accuracy* in their attribution of blame and credit for failures and successes, so that in educational situations and in others as well they will be able to act realistically. Some suggestions for ways to help children increase accuracy in their attribution of causation are suggested by Katz (1967). These include helping them to become sensitive to their own internal processes and feelings, so that they can, for example, recognize the amount of effort they exert on tasks and become able to relate differences in effort expended to differences in outcomes. Perhaps explorations with situations in which the degree of internal or external causation is deliberately manipulated and the children are given an opportunity to learn to see identifiable cues indicating differences in this characteristic would be a valuable way to help them to develop accuracy in internal–external attribution of blame and praise.

The best procedures for developing classroom situations in which internal orientations are realistic and adaptive and, at the same time, children are helped to develop or enhance internal orientations would probably turn out to be those that parallel the kinds of environments and environmental experiences that produce internal orientations in children to begin with. Thus we would suggest that teachers try to develop classroom environments in which children have an effective say in the development of rules and procedures, and that teachers react to children's performance in class with consistent, but discriminating, approval. It would also seem useful in helping children develop such orientations for teachers to give them as much independence as possible and to be flexible and responsive to children's suggestions. Paradoxically, it seems likely that great sensitivity on the part of the teachers could, if teachers act too quickly, limit the development of internal orientations in children. If a teacher senses or understands a child's need and responds to it before the child has had a chance to formulate a request or demand, an effect has been produced without any preceding overt act on the part of the child. The cause of such an outcome is to a large degree external to the child. If such quick responses occur regularly in a child's experience, it would be reasonable and accurate for him to develop a belief in external control, as far as his own experience is concerned. This is not to say that teachers should avoid developing their own sensitivity to the needs of the children in their classes, but that they should avoid acting to fulfill children's needs before they have made an effort to express their needs relatively directly. Of course, some children will be unable to do this; for them the development of an internal control orientation may not be the most pressing concern, and the teacher should act in order to promote needs that he feels are more important for the particular child (such as security and comfort).

Is it possible to create educational situations in which children are able to make maximum use of the control orientation they already have, be it internal, external, or neutral? The study by White and Howard (1970) is probably the clearest example of an attempt to investigate this question in an educational setting, and it produced results that showed that it is possible to create situations in which both internals and externals can function well. Some earlier research (summarized in Joe, 1971) showed that internals perform better in skill situations, and externals perform better in chance-determined situations. Most classroom situations, however, are defined in terms of developing or using skill, and it is not easy to see how one might adapt chance-determined tasks to the promotion of learning goals. However, external control includes other determinants besides chance, and some of these could easily be brought into learning situations. When a child works in a group, for example, the degree to which he is personally responsible for the quality of the group's product is less than it would be for a project that he did independently. If a child finds internal attribution threatening, he might well be more comfortable working on group projects, where he need take only a share of the responsibility for the outcome. If there are other students in the same class who prefer to produce effects for which they consider themselves the prime cause, independent projects might well be to their liking. Classes can be organized so that children can take their choice and work on either group or individual projects. Similar reasoning can be applied to the use of tutors in classes. Some students might like to have tutors, primarily because it allows them to attribute the cause of their learning to an external source. Others, with the same level of educational need, might object to tutors, because they prefer being able to attribute cause internally. Similar points can be made about control over the instigation of learning activities. Although the measurement techniques have not yet been developed, it is reasonable to suppose that individuals also differ in their relative preferences (or orientations) for internally and externally instigated activities, and that these differences also have implications for fitting students to educational situations.

LOCUS OF CONTROL
AND THE SCHOOL SCENARIOS

We will conclude this chapter with an attempt to relate locus of control to the school situations set out in the scenarios.

The possibility that middle-class (presumably relatively internal) teachers may be likely to react in negative ways to lower-class children, who are (or are seen as being) external in their locus of control orientation, was discussed earlier. The teachers' comments that Mr. Bellamy of Bridges School found in the cumulative folder suggest that previous teachers were indeed concerned with locus of control issues at Bridges. For example, a comment made about Rick Washington, a problem student, is: "Rick is a master of shifting blame for his failures to someone else." In other words, the teacher may be saying "this boy is external; he does not accept responsibility for his failures." Yet the teacher may be engaging in some externalizing behavior himself; he may be putting all the blame on Rick in order to avoid recognizing the possibility that he may also bear a share of the responsibility for Rick's failures. We saw earlier (in the study by Johnson et al. 1964) that there is a general tendency for people to be internal with respect to their successes, but external with respect to their failures. External teacher behavior in attributing blame for student failures, even among teachers who are generally internal and who expect their students to be internal, is probably the rule rather than the exception.

That the Bridges' teachers see external blame attribution as a general characteristic of the students at that school is suggested by their description of the students as, among other things, considering themselves "picked on by teachers and other school administrators." Although research using general locus of control measures has shown that lower-class students are on the whole more external than middle-class students, there is also considerable variation within each of these groups. It seems probable that the teachers at Bridges, in making such a blanket characterization, are overgeneralizing and not attending to differences between students that are almost certain to exist, as they do in most other groups.

We have discussed the notion that an individual's locus of control may be different in different situations, depending on the kinds of experiences he has had in previous similar situations. Another of the teachers' comments about Rick is a possible illustration of this point. The teacher noted, "Rick has a poor self concept in school but sees himself as king of the hill when he is in the streets." This remark could imply that Rick feels that he has more control of outcomes in one situation than he does in another. He may perceive life outside of school, life with peers on the streets, as offering greater opportunities for self-initiated, self-maintained, and predictably successful behavior. The school apparently has not structured the learning environment in such a way as to make it possible for Rick either to feel that he has control of outcomes or, if he does feel that outcomes are responsive to his efforts, to feel that they will be successful a reasonable portion of the time.

The students' locus of control may also be influenced by the institutionalized learning climate of the school and the expectations sometimes conveyed by school policy. Let us examine one extreme example of school policy that reflects the more generalized orientation that the school imparts to its students. Bridges School has "a policy of automatic promotion," the effect of which in terms of locus of control seems likely to be the inhibition of internality and fostering of externality. The failing student must very quickly come to realize that his own efforts bear little relationship to school progress, and furthermore, the successful student must also come to understand very rapidly that differential expenditure of effort does not lead to differing reinforcements, at least as far as this index is concerned. This does not mean that a rigid grading-passing-flunking system is very much better for the development of internality. A system in which poor students fail in spite of the best efforts is also likely to promote externality, at least for those students. The system most likely to promote internality in *all* students, as suggested earlier, is one in which an individual's outcomes are clearly tied to his efforts, regardless of how his work compares to that of his classmates.

Such a system appears to be in effect at Knightcrest Middle School, which employs a "continuous progress system," a framework within which individual attention can be exercised and a student, to some measure, can progress at his own rate. The mere fact that the school has moved away from rigid age placement suggests that students may see the situation as providing some options. The school has also established a curriculum that emphasizes "independent study or 'contract' work, with the pupil taking a major responsibility for selecting the subject matter he pursues and the method he uses to pursue it." Such a program, if well carried out, could promote the development of internal control, but also seems well suited for optimal utilization of whatever control orientations students come with. Let us for a moment refer back to the study by White and Howard, where it was found that self-directed learning was most effective for external students, bringing their level of achievement up to that of the internals. It seems likely that the structure of learning that Knightcrest wishes to establish will serve as a flexible setting where both internals and externals can learn. Students in this setting will also probably have relatively great control over the *instigation* of their school activities, a factor that, as we have seen, should serve to increase motivation and feelings of commitment.

The description of Knightcrest suggests that options are created for the individual student; now let us examine their effects on one person. Marvin Blake is presented as an individual who uses realistic differential perception in gearing his behavior toward situations where he can maximize his success. He apparently does have an internal control orientation; that is, he considers success and failure as depending on his own efforts. He shows an interest in musical matters and develops his musical talents (where he believes he can be successful), while shying away from athletic activities (where he expects failure). It appears that Marvin is realistic in his assessment of what his efforts in different areas are likely to produce, and he is fortunate to find himself in a school setting where such choices are possible. We noted previously that Rick Washington of Bridges could not find a niche for himself within the school setting where he could initiate behavior in areas of interest to him. Rick was forced to seek situations outside of school in order to be reinforced for his efforts, because, apparently, satisfactory options did not exist in school.

A closer examination of Marvin's cumulative record from grades one to five (before he came to Knightcrest) seems to show a change in him; he seems to have been transformed from an inquisitive student, who showed initiative and, we would assume, functioned with an internal locus of control orientation, to a student who began to show signs of overdependence (grade two), impulsivity (grade three), laziness, and a need for prodding and close supervision (grade four). What led to this transformation in Marvin? These changes could reflect a shift from an internal stance in relationship to academic matters to an external orientation. Marvin's experience in elementary school may very likely have been radically different from what Knightcrest has to offer. It is possible that Marvin was reacting to a graded school setting, an insensitive teacher, or a situation that was simply inhibiting to an inquisitive and self-directed child. The comments made about Marvin in third, fourth, and fifth grades also point to a discrepancy between his high ability and his moderate academic achievement. We also note that teachers are apparently disturbed by this ability–achievement discrepancy and tend to assign the blame for it to Marvin. Apparently, in the more flexible and individually directed setting at Knightcrest, Marvin's control orientation has once again shifted in a more internal direction.

The other student from Knightcrest, Linda Grey, is described as being very quiet, yet rather sure of herself, and as being slow to respond to questions, especially if there is a possibility of equally correct answers available. These factors suggest a very strong internal orientation. Her long deliberations may indicate an intense desire to be right and an equally intense desire to avoid being wrong. It was mentioned earlier that failure may be especially threatening to internal individuals, because they take full responsibility for it on themselves. Thus Linda may be especially slow and careful in her academic activities because she feels such a strong degree of responsibility for their outcomes. A very high level of internal control can lead to great tension and anxiety in this way; students showing such high levels may actually be unrealistically internal, and might perhaps be helped to recognize situational factors that are out of their control and also influence outcomes.

Midview Elementary School is characterized by features that are quite distinct from those we have considered at the two previous schools. Unlike the homogeneously lower-class Bridges and homogeneously middle-class Knightcrest, Midview represents a heterogeneous cross section of students. There are students at Midview who come from upper-class families, as well as some from middle- and lower-class families. Also, Midview is an integrated school. Some research has suggested that minority group students in integrated schools have more of an internal orientation than those in segregated schools. Although this is a general possibility, which a teacher in such a school should bear in mind, it does not tell anything about the actual orientation of any particular student. For that, there is no substitute for paying close attention to the behavior and needs of the individual student. In a school with such a varied population, students have many opportunities for comparing themselves with one another and learning from one another. The internality of some students may increase as a result of their watching other, more internal, students act and produce predictable outcomes.

Now let us look at some of the individual students in this school. Katherine Fowler's description of her student Mary Cairns is another clear example of the tendency that many teachers apparently have of looking for external factors to explain a student's poor performance (Mary's homelife and I.Q. in this case) and of failing to consider the possibility that they (the teachers) may bear a share of the responsibility for this outcome.

Another failing Midview student is William Baker, whose principal area of deficit is reading. William's I.Q. is reported as being 91, but other data suggest that his potential level of intelligence is considerably higher than this would indicate. William works effectively in groups. We have suggested elsewhere in the chapter that one way in which a teacher can respond to the unique requirements of each student's learning pattern is by attempting to give him the opportunity to learn in situations that make optimal use of his level of locus of control. It is possible that William prefers groups because he finds it difficult to assume full responsibility for either the instigation or the outcome of individual learning experiences. Yet within the safety of a small group setting, he functions in an alert, good-humored, and interested fashion. In this setting, where he does not have to take full responsibility for outcomes, William apparently can benefit from school activities.

In the Midview scenario we are also introduced to a student who seems to be functioning with somewhat greater success than the two other students described, but whose adaptation to school is still apparently somewhat limited by a conflict between her control orientation and the school setting. Sheila Smith is described as someone who "enjoys doing schoolwork that interests her but has to be prodded to do work she doesn't enjoy." It may be that the factors that led this student to enjoy one type of activity over another relate to her perception of who instigates her behavior and whether she can clearly formulate the relationship between her own efforts and the resultant reaction from the teacher. Increasing the number of school activities that allow her to exercise both types of control (particularly control over the instigation of behavior) would probably be a reasonable way to promote Sheila's satisfaction with school and her learning as well. It seems likely that for students such as these three at Midview a teacher concerned with the development of realistic and adaptive control orientations can make it possible for children's school behavior to be altered, and for them to approach more closely their optimal learning potential within the context of a school environment that allows for some variety in the settings and procedures employed.

SOME SUGGESTED ACTIVITIES

1. Observe or set up classroom situations, some of which give students much opportunity to select the activities they engage in and some of which give students very little such opportunity (instigation of action). See whether you notice any differences between these situations in terms of students' interest, motivation, and commitment. Do there seem to be differences between individual students in their relative preferences for one or the other of these kinds of situations? If so, how do these differences show themselves?

2. Observe individual children in class, paying particular attention to their actions (including verbal statements) and the responses they evoke from the teacher or other students. Do some children seem to get more consistent and predictable responses than others? Do the responses correspond to the effort expended more with some children than with others? Do these differences seem to have any effect on the children's subsequent behavior? Do different children show any behaviors that might lead you to think that they differ in their expectation or belief as to whether outcomes follow predictably from their own actions?

3. Think about your own behavior in various situations. Have you been in situations in which you had no control over the instigation of your behavior? How did it feel? Did you like it? What effects did it have on your behavior? What about situations in which you felt you had complete control over the instigation of your behavior? And situations in which you felt that the outcomes or responses you received either were or were not directly related to your own efforts?

4. Think about your tendencies in somewhat ambiguous situations. Do you think you are more likely to assume responsibility for being in the situation and for its outcomes or to assign responsibility to agents outside yourself? Do your tendencies in this regard differ according to whether it is a pleasant or unpleasant situation, or whether the outcomes are good or bad? Think about these questions with regard to classroom situations and your relationships with students.

REFERENCES

Biondo, J., and MacDonald, A. P. "Internal–External Locus of Control and Response to Influence Attempts." *Journal of Personality* 39 (1971): 407–419.

Brehm, J. W., and Cohen, A. R. *Explorations in Cognitive Dissonance.* New York: Wiley, 1962.

Coleman, J. S.; Campbell, E. Q.; Hobson, C. J.; McParland, J.; Mood, A. M.; Weinfeld, F. D.; and York, R. L. *Equality of Educational Opportunity.* Washington, D. C.: Department of Health, Education, and Welfare, Office of Education, 1966.

Crandall, V. C.; Katkovsky, W.; and Crandall, V. J. "Children's Beliefs in Their Own Control of Reinforcement in Intellectual-Academic Achievement Situations." *Child Development* 36 (1965): 91–109.

Crandall, V. J.; Katkovsky, W.; and Preston, A. "Motivational and Ability Determinants of Young Children's Intellectual Achievement Behaviors." *Child Development* 33 (1962): 643–661.

Davis, W. L., and Phares, E. J. "Parental Antecedents of Internal–External Control of Reinforcement." *Psychological Reports* 24 (1969): 427–436.

De Charms, R. *Personal Causation.* New York: Academic Press, 1968.

Dewey, J., and Dewey, E. *Schools of Tomorrow.* New York: Dutton, 1915.

Efran, J. S. "Some Personality Determinants of Memory for Success and Failure." *Dissertation Abstracts* 24 (1964): 4793–4794.

Franklin, R. D. "Youth's Expectancies About Internal Versus External Control of Reinforcement Related to N Variables." Unpublished doctoral dissertation, Ohio State University, 1963.

Gurin, P.; Gurin, G.; Lao, R. C.; and Beattie, M. "Internal–External Control in the Motivational Dynamics of Negro Youth." *Journal of Social Issues* 25 (1969): 29–53.

Hersch, P. D., and Scheibe, K. E. "On the Reliability and Validity of Internal–External Control As a Personality Dimension." *Journal of Consulting Psychology* 31 (1967): 609–614.

Illich, I. *Deschooling Society.* New York: Harper and Row, 1971.

Johnson, T. J.; Feigenbaum, R.; and Weiby, M. "Some Determinants and Consequences of the Teacher's Perception of Causation." *Journal of Educational Psychology* 55 (1964): 237–246.

Joe, V. C. "Review of the Internal–External Control Construct As a Personality Variable." *Psychological Reports* 28 (1971): 619–640.

Katkovsky, W.; Crandall, V. C.; and Good, S. "Parental Antecedents of Children's Beliefs in Internal–External Control of Reinforcements in Intellectual Achievement Situations." *Child Development* 38 (1967): 765–776.

Katz, I. "Comments on Dr. Kelley's Paper." In *Nebraska Symposium on Motivation,* edited by D. Levine, pp. 238–240. Lincoln: University of Nebraska Press, 1967.

Kelley, H. H. "Attribution Theory in Social Psychology." In *Nebraska Symposium on Motivation,* edited by D. Levine, pp. 192–238. Lincoln: University of Nebraska Press, 1967.

Lefcourt, H. M., and Ladwig, G. W. "The American Negro: A Problem in Expectancies." *Journal of Personality and Social Psychology* 1 (1965): 377–380.

Lessing, E. E. "Racial Differences in Indices of Ego Functioning Relevant to Academic Achievement." *Journal of Genetic Psychology* 115 (1969): 153–167.

Montessori, M. *The Montessori Method.* New York: Schocken, 1964.

Neill, A. S. *Summerhill.* New York: Hart, 1960.

Phares, E. J. "Expectancy Changes in Skill and Chance Situations." *Journal of Abnormal and Social Psychology* 54 (1957): 339–342.

Phares, E. J.; Wilson, K. G.; and Klyver, N. W. "Internal–External Control and the Attribution of Blame Under Neutral and Distractive Conditions." *Journal of Personality and Social Psychology* 18 (1971): 285–288.

Ritchie, E., and Phares, E. J. "Attitude Change as a Function of Internal–External Control and Communication Status." *Journal of Personality* 37 (1969): 429–443.

Rotter, J. B. *Social Learning and Clinical Psychology.* Englewood Cliffs, N. J.: Prentice-Hall, 1954.

Rotter, J. B. "Generalized Expectancies for Internal Versus External Control of Reinforcement." *Psychological Monographs* 80 (1, Whole No. 609) 1966.

Rotter, J. B.; Liverant, S.; and Crowne, D. P. "The Growth and Extinction of Expectancies in Chance Controlled and Skilled Tasks." *Journal of Psychology* 52 (1961): 161–177.

Seeman, M. "Alienation and Social Learning in a Reformatory." *American Journal of Sociology* 69 (1963): 270–284.

Solomon, D.; Houlihan, K. A.; Busse, T. V.; and Parelius, R. J. "Parent Behavior and Child Academic Achievement, Achievement Striving, and Related Personality Characteristics." *Genetic Psychology Monographs* 83 (1971): 173–273.

Solomon, D.; Houlihan, K. A.; and Parelius, R. J. "Intellectual Achievement Responsibility in Negro and White Children." *Psychological Reports* 24 (1969): 479–483.

St. John, N. "The Elementary Classroom As a Frog Pond: Self-concept, Sense of Control, and Social Context." *Social Forces* 49 (1971): 581–595.

Weiner, B., and Kukla, A. "An Attributional Analysis of Achievement Motivation." *Journal of Personality and Social Psychology* 15 (1970): 1–20.

White, K. "Belief in Reinforcement Control Among Southern Negro Adolescents: The Effects of School Desegregation, Socioeconomic Status, and Sex of Student." *The Journal of Social Psychology* 85 (1971): 149–150.

White, K., and Howard, J. L. "The Relationship of Achievement Responsibility to Instructional Treatments." *The Journal of Experimental Education* 39 (1970): 78–82.

6 · Motivation in the classroom

PATRICIA WALLER
University of North Carolina at Chapel Hill

JOHN GAA
University of North Carolina at Chapel Hill

KEY CONCEPTS

multiple determinants of behavior

need hierarchy

modeling

goal setting

assessment of students' motives

All too often in our schools we are confronted with students who "are not performing up to their potential," or at least not up to the expectations of their teachers and parents. When this happens, we tend to label the child as unmotivated and in many cases treat him as though this were a permanent condition. To proceed in this manner ignores the complexity and potential multiplicity of motives that affect each of us. A student who appears to be unmotivated may in fact be highly motivated, but not in the way the teacher or parent wishes. The student may be motivated to achieve in school, but at the same time be motivated by other forces, for example, peers, not to achieve in school. The number of potential motivators influencing a student at any one time may be great, and in fact, these motivators may suggest a number of alternative behaviors. To complicate matters further, we are not able to measure motivation directly, but can only infer it from observed behavior.

Teachers who have any individual students or perhaps an entire class that appears unmotivated can easily become highly frustrated and feel that there is nothing that they, as teachers, can do. Although in individual cases it may be that an aversion to school or the pull of other forces is so great that it is impossible for the teacher to significantly affect the students' motivation, this is not the case as frequently as many people believe. There are a number of techniques based on psychological principles that the teacher can use to increase the probability that students will be motivated to achieve in school. However, since no two people share the same experiences, the teacher must employ different techniques with individual students by taking

151

into account relevant differences found among human organisms. Teachers may not be able to reach all students, but they certainly ought to be able to motivate a far greater percentage than they currently do. This chapter presents a number of psychological concepts with related educational techniques designed to affect the student's perception of the classroom and thereby increase his motivation to achieve in school. An understanding of the motivational concepts discussed, together with an appropriate selection of the motivational techniques described, should enable teachers to increase the motivation, interest, and participation of students in school.

In choosing to focus on motivational techniques in this chapter, we have not intended that the chapter represent the entire field of motivation. Many of the concepts discussed in other chapters of this book are referenced in this chapter, because they discuss topics that are also related to motivation. Additionally, there are other topics, which are not covered, that a student concerned with motivational theory might wish to investigate.

Although traditionally our school system has stressed the academic achievement of students, there are many other outcomes associated with schooling that are very important. The deliberate encouragement of behaviors such as curiosity, creativity, an enjoyment of learning, and reading may go further toward ensuring future achievement and personal development than emphasizing academic achievement per se. Furthermore, the development of some of these attitudes and behaviors may have more to do with ultimate success and happiness in life than academic knowledge. Certainly, any attempt to motivate students must take into account possible long-term academic and nonacademic consequences. There are a number of techniques that most teachers use to control short-term, day-to-day behavior that, although effective, may have long-term negative effects or, at best, may do nothing to develop long-lasting positive behaviors and values. An example is the use that many teachers make of corporal punishment in the classroom. It may control behavior at a given moment, but the long-term effects may be devastating.

MASLOW'S NEED HIERARCHY

Historically, motivational theories focused on drives, instincts, and basic physiological needs. This focus is changing, with the emphasis shifting to more precise aspects of motivation. One well-known theory of motivation that has demonstrated utility for examining the motivation of students in schools is the hierarchy of needs and motives developed by Maslow (1943, 1970). Maslow identified six basic need

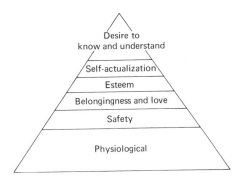

Figure 6–1. The Six Levels
of Maslow's Need Hierarchy

categories: (1) physiological, (2) safety, (3) belonging and love, (4) esteem, (5) self-actualization, and (6) desire to know and understand. (See Figure 6-1.)

Maslow believed that human needs act as important determinants of behavior. He proposed that categories of needs can be ordered in terms of primacy of fulfillment, so that an individual's primary efforts will be directed toward the lowest level needs that are not currently satisfied. It is a rare instance, such as in emergency situations, when we focus *all* our efforts on the satisfaction of a single level of the need hierarchy. However, focusing efforts on a lower level need may significantly reduce the amount of effort, time, and interest available to deal with higher social and intellectual needs.

Physiological needs

Maslow described only the major biological needs, for example, need for food, water, sleep, elimination, and shelter, in his consideration of physiological needs. He suggested that it is virtually impossible, as well as unnecessary, to attempt a definitive listing, because the list might well be infinite, depending on the degree of desired specificity.

If one or more of these basic physiological needs is unsatisfied, the individual may be dominated by the necessity for fulfilling it. The individual's other capacities that are not necessary for the fulfillment of this unsatisfied need may become dormant and, in extreme cases, dissipated. The future may literally be defined in relation to the satisfaction of this particular need. When the need is satisfied, other higher needs emerge to influence the individual.

Maslow pointed out that in our society it is very rarely necessary for the majority of the population to concentrate exclusively on physiological needs. This, however, does not mean that basic physiological needs are not important, or dominant, in given situations. Examples of shifts in a student's orientation toward the fulfillment of physiological needs can be seen in everyday classroom situations. All one must do is to observe the decrease in attention to academic concerns displayed by elementary students who must go to the bathroom or by students when the lunch hour nears. Both situations may be of short duration and easily satisfied; however, they do serve to point up how even a nonchronic, temporary failure to satisfy a need may influence behavior.

In addition, these needs and the behavior associated with them often serve as channels for the fulfillment of other needs as well. That is, the person who believes or acts as though he is hungry may actually be seeking the satisfaction of higher level needs, for example comfort, dependence, or acceptance. People who eat when nervous or emotionally upset provide illustrations of this. Students may occasionally develop psychosomatic ailments in an unconscious attempt to remove themselves from a stress situation (for example, a test). In this instance the student may feel he is physically ill when his primary need is on another level entirely.

Safety needs

The influence of safety needs is most clearly seen in younger children who have not yet learned to inhibit their reactions to threat or danger. The average child and, less overtly, the average adult prefers a safe, orderly, predictable environment. Such things as inconsistency, unfairness, injustice, as well as overt physical dangers may make an individual anxious and fearful. The role of the family in the child's learning to handle fear is vital. Children who are raised in a nonthreatening, loving family situation don't ordinarily react fearfully to nondangerous situations. The support and comfort provided by this type of family situation seem to provide for many of the basic safety and security needs.

As with physiological needs, most adults and children in our society are largely satisfied in relation to safety needs. However, in times of perceived threat or insecurity, these needs and their related behavior may dominate the individual's orientation and greatly lessen the influence of other needs. For example, a student who is physically afraid of another student may be more concerned with avoiding that student and a potentially threatening situation than he is with concentrating on classroom activities.

The belongingness and love needs

The belongingness and love needs have been described as the desire for close, affectionate relationships with others and for a place in a social group such as the family or peer group. As the more basic physiological and safety needs are satisfied, the individual will increase his wish to attain these relationships and may forget that he possibly disregarded these needs when striving to satisfy more basic needs. We often tend to underplay the importance of the social group, the neighborhood, colleagues, classmates, and so on in motivating behavior. However, interactions with others in these situations are crucial to the individual's self-image. (See Chapter 7 by Coopersmith and Feldman.) Anyone who has observed, or experienced, the influence of the peer group in shaping the behavior of its members has seen this concept at work.

In this framework love is not seen as synonymous with sex. Sexual behavior is most often a very complex behavior, representing a combination of sexual needs together with other needs such as love, affection, and esteem.

Esteem needs

Nearly all people in our society have a need for a positive self-image based on a relatively stable, positive self-evaluation, and on the esteem of others. Basically, this need is demonstrated in relation to two sets of desires. The individual may express his need for esteem through a desire for strength, achievement, adequacy, mastery, competence, confidence, independence, and/or freedom. He may additionally seek a positive reputation and prestige (respect or esteem from others), status, fame, glory, dominance, importance, attention, dignity, and/or appreciation, that is, esteem in the form of recognition. (See Chapter 7.)

Satisfaction of self-esteem needs will most often lead to self-confidence and a sense of personal worth and adequacy. Conversely, thwarting of these needs may lead to feelings of inferiority and weakness and in turn to a feeling of basic discouragement. All too often this is the case in school, where many students rarely experience success and eventually drop out.

The need for self-actualization

In spite of success and the fulfillment of the need for esteem, an individual may very well be discontent unless he is doing what he as an individual is "fitted" for. Basically, the need for self-actualization espoused by Maslow is based on man's desire for self-fulfillment and the need to realize his potential. Satisfaction of this need may be expressed in a number of ways and can often be in relation to the individual's selection or rejection of careers. The opportunity to provide for this type of motivation is best available in a school such as

Knightcrest Middle School, where both the encouragement and the facilities are provided for effective individualized work.

The desire to know and to understand

Maslow (1968) believes that there are positive impulses in all people to satisfy curiosity, seek knowledge, seek explanations, and gain understanding. These positive motives are seen as opposed to negative determinants of learning such as anxiety and fear.

In Maslow's view, psychologically healthy people tend to be attracted to the mysterious, the unknown, the chaotic, as well as to an examination of the unorganized and unexplained. These behaviors appear to be natural tendencies and not learned; children do not have to be taught to be curious. Many observers believe that schools today often extinguish the curiosity and information-seeking behavior that children have when they enter school (Holt, 1964, 1967; Kohl, 1963; Herndon, 1968). Certainly, the emphasis in our schools on a single correct response may play an important part in diminishing curiosity.

The aesthetic needs

Although the preceding six categories of needs are the only ones usually associated with Maslow, he has proposed a seventh that seems to greatly influence the behavior of some individuals. He proposes that some individuals have an aesthetic need and that some of their behavior may be interpreted and better understood in light of this need. The aesthetic need can be seen in such things as the need for order, symmetry, closure, and the completion of an act. As Maslow has pointed out, little is known about this topic in a scientific, experimental sense.

Reversals in Maslow's need hierarchy

Although Maslow's hierarchy implies a rigid ordering of needs, and most people do follow the hierarchy, there are numerous examples of exceptions. According to Maslow, perhaps the most common reversal occurs when self-esteem needs assume more importance than love. In many instances such a reversal may involve a redefinition of the situation. For example, the perception that the most loved person is the most powerful and successful may lead to such a reversal. The most dramatic reversals may occur because of adherence to ideals, value systems, and the like. In a similar way, the strength of aesthetic needs, such as creativity, may be so strong that they become more important than any other need. Consider the following case history in which such a need reversal apparently occurred.

A fourth grade teacher had a boy in her class who went home every day for lunch. When it was discovered that when the child went home each noon he was not receiving any lunch, the school principal immediately decided to put him on the free lunch program at school. The boy refused and insisted on continuing to go home and maintain a "front." The principal was adamant until the teacher convinced him to leave the child alone because there was something much more important involved than whether the boy received any lunch. This teacher was speaking of the hierarchy of needs described by Maslow. The child's need for self-esteem was greater than his physiological need for lunch. Such reversals in the need hierarchy are unusual, but the teacher must be sensitive to them when they arise. There is no mold into which all students can be fit.

Since people are often unaware of needs and complete satisfaction of a need is not necessary for other needs to appear, exact labeling of the motivators in any given situation can be quite difficult. In fact, most often there is no single determinant of behavior but rather multiple determinants.

Importance of Maslow's hierarchy for education

Maslow's hierarchy is important not only for its emphasis on the gratification of needs as opposed to an orientation that would deprive people of their needs in order to motivate them, but also for the guidelines it provides for the analysis of behavior. In schools the need hierarchy can provide an effective means for examining the reasons for students' behavior. At the most basic level, a student may seem unmotivated to the teacher when in fact he is hungry, cold, or tired. An example of this might be a student who sleeps in class, not because he is bored, but because he works the night shift at a local factory or his parents permit him to watch the late movie on TV. Many of the students at Bridges and Midview Elementary Schools may soon be working after school and evenings to help their family finances. It is not uncommon to find farm children (like some of the Midview students) who spend long hours working or children from economically deprived environments (like students from Bridges) either assuming major responsibility for running the home or working in order to supplement the family income. In both cases, students may be tired and sleepy in school because of their outside work. Simply familiarizing oneself with the home situation of students may indicate children for whom the satisfaction of physiological needs is a primary motivating factor. Also school practices such as providing breakfast and lunch programs (either free or at reduced cost), free milk, gym classes, and recess take on considerable importance when viewed from this perspective. In North Carolina it has been reported that the free breakfast program increases student attendance at school by as much as 10 percent. No matter how good the educational program is, it is of no benefit to the student who does not attend. A free breakfast program may be a small investment to ensure the presence of some of the students most in need of the school experience. These things are not frills, but are useful in shifting a child's focus to higher levels of motivation. Although teachers are limited in their ability to deal with such problems as hunger and shelter, measures can easily be taken to reduce the importance of factors such as the need for exercise and elimination.

In dealing with safety needs, the teacher is again somewhat limited as far as factors outside the school are concerned. However, there is no reason for the classroom situation itself to become a source of concern for the student in terms of safety. Recently, one of the authors was made aware of a teacher who administered corporal punishment with an automobile fan belt. In this case the teacher himself served as a source of fear; if a child is motivated by avoidance of this type of punishment, there is very little chance of the student's maximizing his learning potential. Certainly, other factors such as fearing the class bully, being afraid to cross busy streets, and tension between peer groups within the school or on the school bus may be directly related to the school experience and to a certain extent can be controlled by school personnel. Fire drills and tornado drills, for example, may serve to reduce general fears as well as providing actual instruction in how to respond to potential emergencies.

Very often schools provide for the esteem needs of only the best students and do not structure activities so that the academically poorer students have a chance for success. An adult who worked for twelve years at a job in which he rarely if ever succeeded might well be viewed as masochistic. Yet, we expect many students to complete twelve years of schooling with few, if any, experiences in which they can gain esteem through success or achievement. Consequently, many of these students turn to nonacademic pursuits, either inside or outside the school, to satisfy their need for esteem. To expect them to do otherwise is simply not reasonable.

The use of individualized instruction, open classrooms, and nongraded schools is designed to provide increased opportunity for meeting the students' self-actualization needs and their need to know and understand (Walberg and Thomas, 1972). By increasing the alternatives available to the students, one increases the likelihood of their being able to explore new areas where success can be achieved. However, a series of studies (Ellis and Miller, 1936; Stouffer, 1956; Wickman, 1928) has indicated that many teachers list inquisitiveness as a behavior problem.

KLAUSMEIER'S MODEL

Maslow's hierarchy of needs is designed to allow for increased understanding of the needs that motivate people. As a tool for the analysis of behavior, it can be quite valuable. The list of needs suggests areas in which the individual may be motivated, but it does not attempt to suggest techniques by which the needs can be met. There has long been a need for the development of techniques that can be realistically implemented to motivate students in classroom situations. Klausmeier and Ripple (1971) have developed a set of research-based principles of motivation, which provide guidelines for the teacher to use in developing techniques to motivate students. Although these guidelines are based on hypotheses that have been tested in school situations, they are not presented as being a definitive list of all motivators that may occur in the classroom. Indeed, Klausmeier recognizes that teachers may generate additional principles and/or guidelines and that as research in the area of motivational theory in school settings progresses, the principles may be modified, changed, and expanded.

Although Klausmeier's principles are not directly derived from Maslow's hierarchy, the hierarchy is reflected in Klausmeier's list of principles and guidelines. Because Klausmeier's model is designed to focus on those areas where the teacher has the most potential influence, not all the needs discussed by Maslow are necessarily considered. For example, Klausmeier does not deal with the physiological and safety needs identified by Maslow.

The principles of motivation and corresponding instructional guides enumerated by Klausmeier appear below. These principles focus on different aspects of the school, the first four on the learning of subject matter, the next two on social behavior, and the last two on both achievement and social behavior.

The following discussion of Klausmeier's model focuses on the instructional guides associated with each principle. Each of these guides suggests practical applications of the motivational principle involved and is therefore of direct interest to the reader, who is concerned with teaching but lacks a sophisticated background in psychology.

Klausmeier's Principles of Motivation

Principle	Instructional Guide
1. Attending to a learning task is essential for initiating a learning sequence.	1. Focus students' attention on desired objectives.
2. Wishing to achieve control over elements of the environment and to experience success is essential to realistic goal setting.	2. Utilize the individual's need to achieve and other positive motives.
3. Setting and attaining goals requires learning tasks at an appropriate difficulty level; feelings of success on current learning tasks heighten motivation for subsequent tasks; feelings of failure lower motivation for subsequent tasks.	3. Help each student to set and attain goals related to the school's educational program.
4. Acquiring information concerning correct or appropriate behaviors and correcting errors are associated with better performance on and more favorable attitudes toward the learning tasks.	4. Provide informative feedback.
5. Observing and imitating a model facilitates the initial acquisition of prosocial behaviors, such as self-control, self-reliance, and persistence.	5. Provide real-life and symbolic models.
6. Verbalizing prosocial values and behaviors and reasoning about them provide a conceptual basis for the development of behaviors.	6. Provide for verbalization and discussion of prosocial values.
7. Expecting to receive a reward for specific behavior or achievement directs and sustains attention and effort toward manifesting the behavior or achievement. Nonreinforcement after a response tends to extinguish the response. Expecting to receive punishment for manifesting undesired behavior may lead to suppression of the behavior, to avoidance or dislike of the situation, or to avoidance and dislike of the punisher.	7. Develop and use a system of rewards as necessary to secure sustained effort and desired conduct. Use punishment as necessary to suppress misconduct.
8. Experiencing high stress and anxiety is associated with low performance, erratic conduct, and personality disorders.	8. Avoid the use of procedures that create temporary high stress or chronic anxiety.

1. Focus students' attention

Because school is only one part of the environment in which the student lives, it is often necessary for the teacher to overcome other interests, which divert the student from the classroom. However, many teachers fail to realize that before this can be done, they must know what it is they wish to focus the students' attention on. In recent years there has been renewed interest in the writing of specific, observable, behavioral objectives to accomplish this (Vargas, 1972; Payne, 1968; Kibler, Barker, and Miles, 1970; Mager, 1962). Whether or not exact instructional objectives in behavioral terms are employed, the teacher must know what the objectives are before they can be communicated to the student. All too often, classroom instruction proves inadequate because neither the students nor the teacher really knows what is to be accomplished in even the most general sense. Several studies (Mager and Clark, 1963; Miles, Kibler, and Pettigrew, 1967) have demonstrated that increased achievement occurs when both students and teachers understand the objectives.

There are a number of ways, in addition to precisely stating the objectives, to focus the students' attention on a specific area of study. Properties of the environment such as change, movement, size, intensity, and repetition can be manipulated. The following examples are cited by Klausmeier and Ripple (1971) and indicate novel ways in which curiosity can be induced.

To get students interested in India, a teacher first held a class discussion, asking each student to tell whatever came first to his mind when he thought of India. Then each student wrote a "pretend" letter to a high school student in India, asking questions about what he most wanted to know. The letters helped the teacher to discover the preconceptions (and some misconceptions) the students had and to evaluate their existing interests.

Intermediate school children were introduced to the study of the "cold lands" in this way: The pupils arrived at school on a cold morning, the first day after the Christmas vacation. Eager to get in from the cold, the children hurried to their classroom. There, to their surprise, they found they were still cold. The teacher had arranged to have the heat in the room left at the low vacation level, with the result that the thermometer registered 55 degrees in the north side of the room. Still wearing their snowsuits, therefore, the children handled the totem pole and the walrus teeth that were displayed and examined photographs of Lapps with reindeer herds, laughing Eskimos on Baffin Island, Aleuts ice fishing, and many other relevant scenes, pinned to the bulletin boards. After spending a few minutes looking at all these things, some of the children began an intent scrutiny of library books that had been placed on tables. One or two others started to search for the cold lands on globes and maps. The novel appearance of the room and its unusual temperature were instrumental in arousing curiosity and directing pupil attention toward the study of the cold lands. (pp. 330–331.)

2. Utilize the individual's need to achieve

The need to achieve success is very closely related to the need to know and understand and the needs for love and belonging, esteem, and self-actualization. As was discussed in the consideration of Maslow, helping to satisfy these needs is a very effective way of developing a high level of motivation.

Many students, who have found school to be unrewarding in terms of achievement, may not spontaneously manifest this need to achieve. It is very important, therefore, that teachers give special attention to those students who do not demonstrate a need to achieve, as well as encourage students with a high need to achieve. The most important point is that the teacher must provide actual conditions in which the student has high probability for success rather than simply providing encouragement in an abstract sense.

Although the ways in which this need develops is a complex matter, the evidence does indicate that the development of the need to achieve is related to child-rearing practices. Parents of children with a high need to achieve provide a warm and accepting environment. In addition to providing this warm, loving parent–child relationship, the parents have high expectations for the child and place high demands on him. Furthermore, parents of children with a high need to achieve allow their children a high degree of independence (McCelland, Atkinson, Clark, and Lowell, 1953). Many of the factors found to be associated with a high need to achieve are also associated with high self-esteem, and indeed the two appear to be closely related. (See Chapter 7 by Coopersmith and Feldman.)

Although success is an important motivator for students, it must be success at a task that is truly challenging. Therefore, the teacher must know the students well enough to know just how well each can perform and then provide each with tasks that will strengthen his abilities. There is a fine line between a challenging task and an overwhelming task. Students should not be given tasks at which they have no chance of success, but they should be given tasks that provide a challenge for them. Success will then mean something. It will not be simply a hollow victory. This is particularly true for individuals with high levels of need achievement. When given a choice of tasks with success probabilities of approximately 100 percent, 50 percent, and 0 percent, individuals characterized as having a high level of need achievement prefer the medium risk task. Children also vary in their response to failure. Students who have met with failure consistently are not ready to be challenged to any great extent. They may need to experience a much larger ratio of success to failure than students who have a longer history of success. Mentally retarded students can tolerate very few consecutive failures before they lose interest in a task. On the other hand, exceptionally bright, highly motivated students become bored with long periods of uninterrupted success (Long, nd.). This points up the need for the individualization of tasks, not only in terms of level of material, but in terms of probability for success.

Because both the need to achieve and the development of high self-esteem appear to be dependent on a strong positive relationship between an adult (parent and/or teacher) and child, an important factor in the classroom is the teacher–student relationship. If the student has positive feelings toward the teacher, the student will more likely do the required work, and the work itself will acquire positive value, because for the student it is associated with the good feelings he has for the teacher. Investigations of how eminent scientists became involved in their fields support this contention. It was usually a particular teacher who encouraged these scientists and inspired them to enter their areas of eventual expertise. Whatever else a strong, warm student–teacher relationship may accomplish, there is good evidence that it is the essential precursor to much of the student's development, academically and otherwise. (See Chapter 2 by Schlechty and Chapter 3 by Good and Brophy for further discussions of this relationship between student and teacher.) This is particulary true for students in schools such as Bridges Elementary, where the environment does not lend itself to the development and maintenance of a high level of need achievement in academic areas. For students such as Rick Washington and Julia Clark of Bridges and William Baker of Midview, the student–teacher relationship may be crucial in their development in both academic and nonacademic areas.

3. Help each student to set and attain goals

By helping a student to set and attain goals, the teacher accomplishes a number of important outcomes. The learning environment is structured for the student, and at the same time a mechanism for providing feedback on achievement and behavior is established. Ultimately, this should help the student understand the relationship between his intentions and actions, and their consequences. (For an extended discussion of this point, see Chapter 5 by Solomon and Oberlander.)

A number of factors related to goal setting have been examined experimentally, primarily in laboratory studies. Four of the most important of these factors—knowledge of results, specificity of goals, difficulty of goals, and the origin of goals—are discussed here.

A. KNOWLEDGE OF RESULTS. Recent studies of knowledge of results have indicated that knowledge of results is primarily related to the shaping of an individual's goals, and these goals, in turn, affect performance. (For an extended discussion of this point, see Chapter 5 by Solomon and Oberlander.) Studies (Locke, 1967; Locke and Bryan, 1966b, 1967a, 1968a, 1969a, 1969b, 1969c; Locke, Cartledge, and Koeppel, 1968; Porat and Haas, 1969) designed to investigate the relationship between goal setting and knowledge of results have been quite consistent in showing that knowledge of results does not result in an automatic gain in performance. Rather it is the type and level of performance goals that are set as a result of the knowledge of results that are important. Although knowledge of results directly affects behaviors such as driving a car or reading a page, some effects that were previously attributed to a knowledge of results are actually due to different levels of motivation produced by various types and levels of goals set by the individual based on a knowledge of results.

Increased information (knowledge of results) results in more accurate levels of goal setting and decision making. Thus the primary role of knowledge of results is in influencing the goal–setting process.

B. SPECIFICITY OF GOALS. A second aspect that must be considered in the development and use of any goal-setting procedure is the degree of specificity of the goals. Typically, two types of goals are used by classroom teachers. The first is the "do your best" type and is probably by far the most commonly used. The teacher simply tells the student to "do your best," leaving the individual free to interpret the goal in any manner he chooses. The second type of goal direction includes specific, quantitative goals—for example, the goal of getting fifteen of twenty spelling words correct on the weekly spelling test.

Mace (1935) reported in an early study that a changing goal based on previous performance is more effective in increasing achievement than instructions to students to "do your best." This technique of comparing "do your best" goals with other types of goals has served as the basis for more recent studies. Bayton (1948) found that, although the use of general goals increased the achievement level of students, as the goals became more specific, the level of performance increased further. It should also be pointed out that the idea of specifying goals is inherent in the consideration of teaching techniques. For example, Harrison (1967) suggests that allowing learners to know what the teacher expects of them will enable them to achieve these intentions more efficiently.

Locke and Bryan (Bryan and Locke, 1967; Locke, 1967; Locke and

Bryan, 1967a, 1967b) also investigated the question of the effect of specific goals versus the effect of "do your best" goals on achievement. In each case the results indicated that specific goals yielded superior performance levels when compared with the "do your best" goals. In one of these studies subjects with low motivation were given specific goals to reach, and subjects with high motivation were told to "do your best." By the end of the second retest, the low-motivation group with the specific goals had "caught" the high-motivation group in relation to both level of performance and attitude toward the task. The results obviously suggest the potency of specific goals in increasing motivation (Locke, 1967).

C. DIFFICULTY OF GOALS. Closely related to the question of the specificity of goals is the question of the maximal level of goal difficulty. Research indicates that in any goal-setting procedure feedback should be provided to ensure an adequately high difficulty level of the goals set. In a number of studies (Bryan and Locke, 1967; Fryer, 1964; Locke, 1966, 1967; Locke and Bryan, 1966b, 1967a, 1968b), most of which also examined the question of specificity, the problem of difficult versus easy goals was examined. The results of all of the experiments support the conclusion that the harder the goal is, the higher the performance level. Of course, if goals are so difficult that they are almost never attained, performance may well decrease with the lack of positive reinforcement. It should be noted that none of these studies were conducted in ongoing classroom situations, and all were short-term tasks, where appropriate goals were apparent to the subject.

D. ORIGINATOR OF GOALS. The question of who sets a specific goal in a teaching situation is also important. The early work by Mace (1935), which focused on the specificity of goals, also compared self-set with experimenter-set goals. His results indicated that self-set goals were superior to experimenter-set goals in terms of the subject's performance level.

Research by Locke (1966) has shown that those subjects who set their own goals performed better than those subjects who received "easy" fixed goals, but less well than those receiving "difficult" fixed goals. Locke, Bryan, and Kendall (1968), in summarizing five related studies, again pointed out that self-set goals are superior to goals assigned by the experimenter, but only if the goals set by subjects are of appropriate difficulty and specificity.

The majority of the research on goal setting has focused on the types of variables discussed here. Although specific conclusions can be drawn as to what form goal setting should take, these conclusions can be misleading, because most research has been conducted in laboratory settings. The transition to a school classroom is often difficult because students are frequently not aware of what constitutes an appropriate goal in a school classroom. Therefore, although it is theoretically best for a student to set goals on his own, it may be necessary for a teacher to indicate potential goals, to provide information about the difficulty of the possible goals, and to encourage the student to select his own goals from among the possibilities provided.

Research on the systematic use of goal setting, using individual goal-setting conferences with students in first, second, third, and fourth grade classrooms, indicates that the goal-setting conferences result in significantly higher levels of achievement as well as changes in goal setting itself (Gaa, 1970). Following this initial field study, the individual goal-setting conference format was further field tested in several schools and the earlier findings replicated (Quilling, Fishbach, Rendfrey, and Frayer, 1971).

The format of individual goal-setting conferences has recently been expanded and adapted for use in secondary schools. A recently completed study indicates that the procedure may be even more effective at the secondary level. Students who participated in the individual goal-setting conferences demonstrated significantly higher levels of academic achievement, significantly higher positive attitudes toward the class, and perhaps most interesting of all, a significant shift toward a belief in a personal responsibility for their achievement (Gaa, 1973). (For an extended discussion of the research on belief in responsibility for achievement, see Chapter 5 by Solomon and Oberlander.)

The individual goal-setting conferences employed in these studies used a technique that can easily be carried out by classroom teachers. A teacher first identifies what tasks the student will be working with during the coming weeks. In addition, any tests, reports, or behavior problems that are relevant are identified. These are organized into a form so that the student can be asked to choose among alternatives and set performance goals in relation to specific activities. For example, students may be informed of an upcoming test and asked to set a goal in terms of a grade or score. The advantage of having a prepared list is that the responses may be recorded and used as the basis for feedback during the next conference.

An entire weekly individual goal-setting conference consists of more than the actual goal setting. The initial section of the conference is devoted to providing the student with feedback on his general classroom performance and achievement and feedback in relation to the goals set during the previous conference. This feedback is vital, both as a source of reinforcement for positive action and as an indicator of the appropriateness of his past goals. Suggestions for modification of behavior and techniques for accomplishing the changes might be discussed at this time. (For a detailed discussion of behavior modification, see Chapter 4 by Wasik.)

Following the feedback the teacher provides the student with an overview of what will be going on in the class in the coming week as well as tests, assignments, and papers that are due. This portion of the conference provides the student with an overview of what will be happening in the class and allows for a better understanding of the goal-setting portion of the conference, which follows.

This individual goal-setting conference procedure may seem to run counter to some of the suggestions based on laboratory studies discussed earlier. For example, students are not free to set any goals they wish, because they are responding to the alternatives available in the class, even if the teacher stresses individualized instruction. However, in the development and testing of the procedure, differences between the laboratory and the ongoing classroom made it necessary to modify and compromise in order to develop a workable technique.

This motivational technique is one that has been shown to be effective in various educational settings and that requires very little additional training of teachers. Also, large sums of money are not required to carry it out. Done weekly with younger children and at least biweekly with secondary students, these conferences provide a simple, workable, technique that allows both the teacher and the student to gain a greater understanding of what is going on in the classroom.

4. Provide informative feedback

The fourth guideline suggested by Klausmeier relates to the need to provide students with informative feedback. Frequently, students are unable to evaluate the quality or the appropriateness of their own work or behavior without the help of others. Evaluative feedback is perhaps the most common type of feedback provided by a teacher. Feedback and knowledge of results have often been associated with direct gains in performance. However, as was previously discussed, a number of recent studies (Locke, 1967; Locke and Bryan, 1966b, 1967a, 1968a, 1969a, 1969c; Locke, Cartledge, and Koeppel, 1968; Porat and Haas, 1969) have indicated that knowledge of results does not result in an automatic improvement in performance, but rather it is the type and level of performance goals that are set using the knowledge of results that are important. Whatever the exact mechanism involved, feedback of various types has been shown to be effective in producing improved achievement in a wide range of classroom settings (Plowman and Stroud, 1942; Page, 1958; Sweet, 1966).

Feedback may be effectively provided in a number of ways and for a number of types of behaviors. As Klausmeier and Ripple (1971) point out:

Receiving information about correct and incorrect responses and also a short comment which indicated the teacher's subjective estimates increased motivation. Feedback also may be given regarding oral contributions, physical actions, and other performances of the student in one-to-one settings, small groups, and large groups. Small group discussions, question and answer sessions, and other group interchanges of information are valuable to the extent that informative feedback is provided to various participants [p. 334].

5. Provide real-life and symbolic models

People are constantly observing and imitating models. In the classroom students are exposed to three types of models: *real-life, symbolic,* and *representational.* Teachers, administrators, and other children are the major real-life models in school. Symbolic models are presented in oral or written material, pictures, or through a combination of verbal and pictorial devices. Models presented on film and on television are representational and are of potentially great importance, although what exactly is the effect of television on attitudes, values, and behavior is far from clear. A number of studies have shown that aggressive behavior seen on television may be modeled by children (Bandura, Ross, and Ross, 1963; Hicks, 1965; Eron, 1963), but the television industry has vigorously denied this effect (Television Information Office Releases SM 15, 1963).

Generally, schools focus on providing models that demostrate behavior that adults consider desirable. However, one of the most potentially influential models is often overlooked: the daily behavior of teachers and parents. Certainly, the ways in which parents and teachers treat each other may have a great effect on a child's behavior. It is no coincidence that we so often hear that old refrain "Do as I say, not as I do." (See Chapter 4 by Wasik.)

On the surface the process of modeling seems to be a simple, straightforward one whereby an individual learns from watching others. Although most people realize that they model and imitate the behavior of others at times, modeling is often overlooked in the consideration of motivation. Perhaps one reason for this is that modeling does not directly involve the use of overt reinforcement, and much recent emphasis in motivation research has been on identifying the variables involved in various reinforcement situations. Modeling seems to provide its own reward, or at the very least the rewards involved are often extremely subtle. During modeling the individual involved often adopts behavior patterns without any visible inducement.

It was stated that on the surface the process of modeling is a straightforward one whereby the individual learns from watching others. This statement is often taken to mean that modeling is simply another name for imitation; such is not the case. Modeling is more inclusive than imitation and is by no means limited to an exact replica of the demonstrated behavior. Not only does modeling include the direct adoption of behavior, but it also refers to the adoption of other behaviors that may be symbolic equivalents of the modeled behavior. For example, subjects exposed to aggression in the form of a knife fight in a motion picture may display a high level of aggression afterward without themselves participating in a similar knife fight (Walters and Thomas, 1963).

Modeling would seem to have a number of advantages over the use of reinforcement in schools. Although many, if not most, forms of behavior modification require one-to-one interaction between the teacher and student to be effective, the use of models allows the teacher to influence the behavior of large numbers of students simultaneously. In addition, with modeling it is not necessary for the teacher to wait for a behavior to appear in order to reinforce it. Indeed, because the modeling process provides a technique for inducing behavior, it may be employed very profitably to elicit the behavior that the teacher desires to reinforce. This is particularly important in that research has demonstrated that acts that are low in the individual's hierarchy of responses may not appear unless elicited by a model (Bandura and McDonald, 1965).

The use of modeling changes behavior in two primary ways, the most overt way relating to inducing the individual to perform a behavior that is new to that individual. For instance, Mr. Bellamy of Bridges Elementary School may well serve as a model in demonstrating appropriate positive attitudes toward learning, which his students may not have previously learned in their environment. It is easy to suppose that because we are dealing with behavior change, all change in behavior would fall in this category. However, this is not the case and in fact the development of totally new behavior patterns may not actually be the most important long-term consequence of the modeling process. Equally, or perhaps more, important is the ability of a model to elicit behavior that already exists in the individual's repertoire. This assumes that an individual has acquired a behavior pattern, but for some reason does not demonstrate it. In this instance modeling involves a restructuring of the individual's hierarchy of response preferences in a given situation. An instance of this type of modeling could conceivably occur in the future for Linda Grey. Many girls who reach puberty early become interested in boys earlier than their peers. The case study of Linda indicates that this may be true for her. If, as many girls do, Linda rejects her academic pursuits in order to gain social status, her performance in school may suffer drastically. An example of modeling that would elicit behavior that exists in the individual's repertoire (but is now dormant) might occur if Linda were assigned to a teacher who combined physical attractiveness and academic excellence. This teacher might well serve as a model who would lead Linda to reassert her previously excellent academic habits. This second consequence of modeling is particularly important when one considers that we all too often assume that a student's failure to perform a given behavior indicates that he has not adequately learned the behavior. In fact, much learning involves a two-step process consisting of acquisition and performance phases. Modeling can potentially influence both phases, but in relation to lasting change and to classroom evaluation, the inducement of the second phase is vital.

Three factors directly affect the probability of the individual's participating in a given modeling situation: the *characteristics of the individual*, the *characteristics of the behavior*, and the *characteristics of the model*.

The individual who is to learn to model the behavior must have the skills, abilities, and attitudes necessary to perceive the behavior and to perform that behavior or related behaviors. As mentioned previously, we often assume that a failure to demonstrate a given behavior indicates a failure to learn what is involved. The individual must not only be able to understand the behavior, but he must also be able to demonstrate it in order to successfully model a given behavior. Not only must an individual have the capabilities to learn and demonstrate a behavior, he must also possess interest in observing and performing the behavior. Although this is simply common sense, it is often overlooked in practice. Individuals will also presumably differ in their susceptibility to the modeling process and in their preference for a given model.

The characteristics of the behavior can make a great difference in whether or not modeling is successful. When the behavior to be modeled is complex, it should be remembered that the learning of complex behavior by modeling is easier if it is broken down into smaller, component parts (Bandura, Grusec, and Menlove, 1966). The model may either demonstrate each of the components separately or demonstrate the entire complex behavior with the component parts clearly identified. In either case, the efficiency of the learning will be enhanced if the component parts are not only identified, but the relationship between one act and the next identified and made clear.

Finally, of great importance in modeling are the characteristics of the model. A number of variables of the model and of the model–subject relationship may be important in any given modeling situation (Bronfenbrenner, 1970).

A. The influence of a model increases as the individual perceives the model as possessing a high degree of competence, status, and control over resources relevant to the situation. This is in essence a power and/or prestige consideration, where the individual attributes more worth to the copying of behavior demonstrated by someone he perceives as being high on this dimension. (See Chapter 2 by Schlechty for a discussion of this phenomenon.)

B. The power of the model increases as the degree of prior nurturance or reward displayed by the model increases. If the model is someone who the individual is familiar with and has a warm, rewarding relationship with, successful modeling is more likely to occur. This is one of the reasons that individuals tend to model those people in their surroundings who are personally important to them.

C. Those individuals who are most likely to serve as models for a child are those people who are central to his life and who are major or primary sources of support and control. This naturally would include parents, but may also include playmates, other peers, older children, and adults who play important roles in his day-to-day activities. Although there has been little research on the relative influence of these various models, instances of each category can be identified for most children.

D. To the extent that an individual perceives the model as being like himself, the model will gain influence. Basically, this is a dimension of the individual's identifying with the model, and has been demonstrated experimentally in a number of studies (Burnstein, Stotland, and Zander, 1961; Stotland, Zander, and Natsoulas, 1962; Rosekrans, 1967).

The importance of this point is reflected in the need for more male teachers in the lower elementary grades. Unfortunately, there are very few males for boys to identify with and model in our present schools and especially in elementary schools. The additional need for teachers from minority groups is also indicated. The students at Bridges Elementary School, especially the boys, are extremely fortunate to have a black male, Mr. Bellamy, as a teacher. As a model he is someone with whom his male students can identify. For black males in many of our schools this is an unfortunately rare experience.

E. The use of several models all exhibiting similar behavior will tend to be more powerful than a single model. Not only will the behavior seem more acceptable in the sense that a number of people are doing it, but the probability of the individual identifying with at least one of the models is greatly increased. This argument has been used in supporting the use of techniques such as team teaching, where the individual student may be exposed to a number of potential academic models, that is, teachers.

F. The influence of a model tends to increase when the behavior exhibited is central to the actions of a group in which the individual is a member or to which he aspires to belong. This influence can probably be seen most dramatically during adolescence, when the influence of the peer group is not only important, but perhaps is at its most overt level.

G. Whether the modeling process can actually induce a performance of (as opposed to simply the acquisition of) a given behavior may well be influenced by the observed consequences for the model when the behavior is demonstrated. Very simply, if the behavior produces consequences that the subject interprets as positive, he is more likely to model the behavior. However, if the model receives what is perceived as a punishment by the subject, the modeling process is likely to lead to an inhibition of the observed behavior.

It is important to remember, however, that in any given situation a number of potential models, as well as previous modeling experiences, may influence the individual. It may be the case that a particular modeling situation will not be successful because the perceived reinforcement or punishment related to the behavior does not outweigh the rewards associated with a separate, incompatible behavior.

The degree to which a child can identify with the model is crucial, and it is therefore the responsibility of the teacher to realize that what serves as a model for one student may not serve as a model for another. Therefore, it may be necessary to provide a wide range of models, depending on the degree to which the class differs on this dimension.

An important point to remember is that individuals are not limited to modeling overt psychomotor skills. Although these skills are often obvious examples of modeling, they probably represent the least important type of modeling in the long run. Attitudes, values, and life-styles are often influenced by modeling.

6. Provide for verbalization and discussion of prosocial values

The sixth guideline outlined by Klausmeier involves the verbalization and discussion of positive social values and behaviors. By having an individual verbalize positive social values, one may accomplish three purposes: *awareness, understanding,* and *acceptance.*

We often assume that an individual who is demonstrating inappropriate behavior does so by choice. This is not always the case. Indeed, in some instances the individual may be unaware of any appropriate alternative behaviors. By having the student verbalize the *positive values* and describe alternative behaviors, the teacher can assure that at least the cognitive realization of the *appropriate behavior* exists. In most cases, however, simply knowing what behavior is appropriate in a given situation is not enough. The question of why a behavior is "right" or "expected" or "good" logically follows the verbalization of what is expected. If verbalization *and* discussion are undertaken, the student is more likely to find answers to this question, which in turn are more likely to affect his behavior. Ideally the processes of stating, discussing, and reasoning will lead to the incorporation of values into the individual's motivational system. Behaviors related to these values would then be independent of adults or other authority. If this sequence is carried through, the individual becomes increasingly self-directive in relation to both school learning and general behavior.

7. Use rewards and punishments as necessary

Whether to use rewards and punishments in the classroom and/or when to use them are two questions that cause a great deal of concern among teachers. Punishment, whether actual or threatened, is widely employed by teachers. Very often it is ineffective, many times producing the opposite results from those desired. Rewards are also often employed; but most often they go to those students who need additional reinforcement the least, while little or no reinforcement is provided for those who most desperately need it.

These extremely important motivational concepts are dealt with in detail in Chapter 4 by Wasik. Her analysis of the area is directly related to the implementation of behavior modification systems, but may be used as the basis for a consideration of the results of using reinforcement or punishment in less specific situations.

8. Avoid the use of stressful procedures

The relationship between stress and performance is relative to both the individual involved and to the given situation. However, for most people low levels of anxiety increase performance, and higher levels, or concentrations, of anxiety tend to diminish performance.

For most students the school environment itself produces an increase in the level of stress. This increase probably is enough to maximize performance for some individuals, but for a few this small increase is enough to interfere with performance. The introduction of additional stress, whether on purpose or accidentally, by the teacher or the school situation will only increase anxiety. This increase, in turn, will probably lead to a decrease in performance rather than the improvement that many teachers expect. Teachers should seek to identify highly anxious children and seek to decrease stress for them. Students who are motivated by the other factors discussed in this chapter do not need artificially induced stress and anxiety to learn.

In their descriptions of what they view as the typical student, the teachers at Bridges Elementary School identified a behavior that is often associated with excessive stress in testing situations, namely hypochondriacal illness before tests. Teachers can frequently observe a phenomenon that is similar in nature; the student who simply cannot perform adequately in a testing situation, even though he may have previously demonstrated his ability to handle the material evaluated.

OTHER CONSIDERATIONS

The frameworks for describing motivation introduced by Maslow and Klausmeier are of vital importance to the teacher in the classroom, because they provide a model in which a number of important concepts are brought together. There are, however, a number of other important concepts that are not described by the Maslow and Klausmeier models that may be important in helping you as a teacher to understand the dynamics of motivation in the classroom. We have selected some of the most important motivational concepts omitted by the Maslow and Klausmeier models and describe them here.

1. Self-esteem

The desire to gain esteem was discussed earlier in relation to Maslow's hierarchy of needs, with the focus being on esteem as a general concept. Of the various types of esteem, perhaps the most important from the standpoint of the teacher in the classroom is self-esteem. Children who are successful both academically and in other areas are characterized by high levels of self-esteem. Certainly, one goal of the school should be to promote and encourage children to value themselves and their accomplishments in a positive way.

High self-esteem is associated with achievement (Purkey, 1970). Yet many children come to school with a low self-esteem. Are there remedial steps that the school can take with such children? The fact is that the school is probably the major hope, if not the only hope, for these children. An accepting teacher coupled with reasonable success in school can make a difference to a child experiencing deprivations in other areas of his life. Unfortunately, all too often schools not only do not enhance the self-esteem of students, but reinforce the existing low self-esteem of these students.

Three major conditions appear to exist for children who possess high self-esteem. First, such children come from homes in which the parents are accepting of the child. Second, the parents of these children provide clearly defined values and behavior limits for their children. Third, within these limits parents permit considerable tolerance of a wide variety of behaviors.

Although these conditions pertain to the parent–child relationship, it can be worthwhile to try them in the classroom. Accordingly, the teacher who would encourage high self-esteem in his students would first communicate to the students his acceptance of them. It is recognized that this is much easier said than done. There are always some student–teacher relationships that are less than optimal, and it is probably best for the teacher to recognize this and make every attempt to deal with the student fairly, even if it is not possible for the teacher to accept the student completely. Second, the teacher should establish clear-cut rules and regulations that provide guidelines, such as for the completion of homework on time or the maintaining of reasonable order in the classroom. Within the major guidelines, which should provide a degree of security to both students and teachers, students would be allowed considerable self-expression, so that there is no feeling of regimentation.

Finally, a necessary condition in developing self-esteem is to provide for the experience of success and achievement upon which self-esteem in school is based. Realizing the extent of the individual differences involved in a typical classroom, the teacher must make many of these success experiences relative to the previous performance of the individual. It is important that the teacher recognize this and provide the reinforcement necessary for the development of positive self-esteem. Too often teachers focus only on outstanding academic achievement when providing reinforcement; in the future teachers must deal with the total person, not simply the academic performance of the individual. (For a detailed discussion of this topic, see Chapter 7 by Coopersmith and Feldman.)

2. Delay of gratification

In school the ability to delay gratification, to wait for a reward, is very important, for most rewards connected with going to school are received long after the task is completed. Some children appear to be able to postpone gratification or reward and consequently to be able to plan for the distant future, to set goals with relative ease, but others appear to need immediate reward for their efforts in order to persist. This ability to delay gratification is related to a number of personal and social characteristics. Intellectual ability and social class are two of the most important personal and social characteristics related to this trait (Mischel and Metzner, 1962; Mischel and Gilligan, 1964). In general, children from lower-class backgrounds are less likely to display the ability to delay gratification. It is likely that the experiences of the lower-class child have taught him that postponement of reward is unlikely to pay off. If his own immediate environment offers no examples of success associated with prolonged effort, there is little reason to expect him to choose such a route. In many cases the economic and social environment may be so hostile that rewards simply cannot be guaranteed on a long-term basis. Additionally, appropriate models may not be available to demonstrate the payoffs associated with prolonged long-term effort. It may also be true that in some environments the reward for prolonged effort and long-term planning in fact does not warrant the effort involved.

Can the school provide conditions that will enable a child to develop this ability to delay gratification? Not only is the development of this orientation an important consideration, but schools must also take into account ways in which normal reward and reinforcement patterns can be modified until the long-term orientation can be developed. Ordinarily, schools provide children relatively little immediate feedback or knowledge of results. Homework is turned in, graded, and returned at some later date. Usually there is a minimum of a 24-hour delay between the time the work is accomplished and the time a grade is received. Often the delay is much longer. If a student has little ability to postpone gratification, then even high marks may not have the desired effect.

For such a student it may be necessary for the teacher to institute procedures that provide more immediate feedback and reward for good performance. Assignments can be shortened and completed during class time with each student bringing his paper to the teacher so that it can be evaluated and help provided immediately. Materials presented in programmed instruction form can also be effective with such students. A deliberate effort can be made to provide feedback and reward, first at relatively short intervals, then with increasing delay. For example, if special privileges, such as early recess, are given to a class or individual for good performance, the reward can initially be given after a relatively short period of the desired performance, with the work period being gradually increased. At first one page in a workbook must be completed accurately before one can be dismissed. Eventually, the assignment may be extended to two, three, four, or more pages.

The important principle for the teacher to remember is that the student's behavior will provide an index of how effective the technique is. If the student is not responding positively, then either the reward is not an effective reward for that student, or the required task is too much for the child to accomplish at this time without some intermediate reward. The task can be reduced and/or simplified to see if the reward begins to show effects. If that does not work, a different reward may be in order. Although we often tend to assume that all students will respond to the same types of rewards, this is certainly not true. For example, some students, particularly those from lower-class backgrounds, may not perceive grades as meaningful and may not respond to good grades as a reinforcer. For these children it is a challenge for the teacher to discover what is meaningful to the student. Some have advocated using money as a reward, arguing that money is the universal reinforcer or reward in our society. Certainly, money maintains much of the behavior of the adult population. Although money has been demonstrated to have a positive effect with children in school, most teachers do not find themselves in a position where they can dispense money as a reward for learning. Teachers are faced with the overwhelming task of instilling knowledge in students while having relatively few reinforcers at their command. Early recess, special privileges such as being allowed to play with puzzles or games, and praise from a teacher who has a good relationship with a student are possible rewards. Many students will also respond to increased responsibility as a reward. The use of token economies based on a systematic earning of rewards for desired behaviors has received considerable attention recently. (For a detailed discussion of this see Chapter 4 by Wasik.)

Once a reward is working, then the requirements placed on the student can gradually be increased to achieve the same or greater rewards. In this way the teacher can use rewards to help the student learn not only the academic content of the school's curriculum but also the ability to delay gratification.

3. Feeling of control over one's destiny

It is part of the nature of childhood to feel inferior in relation to adults. The child is, in fact, inferior to the adult in many important ways. He is smaller and weaker physically; he has less intellectual skill; and by virtue of his comparatively limited experience he is at a disadvantage. Most children are able to traverse the childhood years with no harmful lasting effects from this period of obvious inferiority. Most children exhibit confidence and appear to feel in control of what happens to them, even though in actual fact they may have relatively little real control.

The importance of this feeling of control over one's destiny should not be underestimated. In a nationwide study of integration in the schools and the associated achievement of pupils, it was found that school factors such as physical facilities, course offerings, and library resources had surprisingly little relationship to student achievement (Coleman, 1966). The thing that was associated with achievement more than all the school conditions combined was the degree to which students felt they had control over what happened to them. White students on the whole were more likely than minority groups (except for Oriental Americans) to possess this feeling of control. However, when a minority student did feel that he controlled his destiny, his achievement was higher than that of white students not having this characteristic.

Experiences aimed at allowing the student to express himself and to plan his own activities should encourage this characteristic. The practice of goal setting and contracting, discussed earlier in this chapter, whereby a student negotiates with a teacher to reach an agreement about how much work will be completed in a specified period of time, can help the student feel that he is in control of what he does (Gaa, 1973). Although students vary in their need for structure, the teacher should not provide more structure than is necessary. Furthermore, the encouragement of students to evaluate their own study efforts, to participate in the selection and development of their courses of study, and to generally assume responsibility in the classroom can have desirable results both in achievement (White and Howard, 1970) and in the development of feelings of control (White, K., 1972). (For an extended discussion of this topic, see Chapter 5 by Solomon and Oberlander.)

4. Persistence motivation

Every teacher is familiar with the old adage "If at first you don't succeed, try, try again." Yet there are many students who appear to live by the adage "If at first you don't succeed, give up." So frequently when a student seeks a solution to a problem and his attempt fails, it does not occur to him to try a different approach. This occurs not only with specific academic problems but also with social problems. The adult counterpart of such a student is seen applying for a specific kind of job at a specific place, and if that does not materialize, he may never assess his job potential for other openings in other places. If a student can learn to develop what might be called *persistence motivation*, he will be able to deal with a wide range of problems without the need for outside helping agencies.

To develop persistence motivation, a student must experience failure. Failure is a form of frustration or punishment, and most educators consider punishment and frustration something to be avoided in the learning process. We would hold that this is not necessarily so. This does not mean that teachers should deliberately incorporate failure into a student's program of instruction. Failure is almost sure to occur without such planning on the part of the teacher. However, since all of us are bound to meet with failure many times throughout the course of our lives, perhaps the experience of dealing with it effectively is of educational value. This should not be interpreted as support for the position some teachers take that *constant* failure prepares a student for the real world.

One of the reasons educators object to failure is that it leads to unpredictable results. So long as a student is succeeding, we can reinforce or reward the specific behavior that is desired. However, when a student fails and is consequently punished for a specific kind of behavior, it may not be clear to him exactly what kind of behavior is appropriate. As a result he may engage in a variety of behaviors, and in a sense the teacher has lost control over what is happening. Still, we are proposing that the ability to think of a variety of behaviors in the face of failure is highly desirable in itself. It is just such flexibility that will help a person eventually to arrive at a satisfactory solution. Thus behavior variability per se is something that should be encouraged. Presumably, the reason man has succeeded in the course of evolution is because he possesses such an astounding capacity for a wide variety of behaviors. By the same token, the individual's ultimate survival in society may depend on his ability to generate a wide range of behaviors.

How can a teacher help a student to develop motivation to persist in the face of obstacles? If a student shows a tendency to give up at the first sign of problems, the teacher should *not* provide him with ready alternatives. To do so will only teach the student to come to the teacher for solutions. Rather the student should be encouraged to think of alternative behaviors. He should be asked to consider what other possibilities exist. If necessary, the teacher should provide leading questions to help the student think of what different routes of action exist. The crucial point is that the teacher does not become a source of solutions. The teacher only provides the minimum guidance necessary to enable the student to seek his own solutions. The good teacher, like the good parent, becomes less and less necessary.

It should be pointed out that it is not easy to withhold information from a student and watch him struggle. Yet if the teacher always provides the answers, he has failed to teach the student to rely on his own resources. In the long run that lesson is probably more important than the immediate problem at hand.

The more variability in behavior that the student can produce, the more likely he is to arrive at a solution. When he does arrive at a solution, in addition to solving the immediate problem, he has learned something about persisting in the face of failure. Because what is important is response variability, the teacher should encourage even some fairly inappropriate responses as being one way of attacking the problem, although the teacher may also want to explore with the student what other effects such a response is likely to have.

It should be emphasized that what we are calling persistence motivation does not refer to blind persistence in the face of failure. Rather we are referring to a persistence that incorporates a flexibility in approach. One possible response to failure is to abandon the goal that was sought, and there are times when this is the best behavior available.

The experience of failure can be used to develop persistence motivation, first by generating a large amount of behavior and second by generating a variety of responses. Teachers should observe how well students can handle frustration. If a student becomes able to tolerate more and more frustration, the teacher should wait longer and longer before encouraging or reinforcing the student.

5. Fantasy

Frequently included in lists of defense mechanisms and described as something that may be harmless in small quantities but potentially dangerous in large doses, fantasy has more recently begun to achieve respectability. It may be an essential ingredient in creativity (Torrance, 1960), and it is present in persons of high achievement and notably lacking in underachievers (Gallagher, 1960). Fantasy may be necessary for the delay of gratification. The person who can persist in working toward a distant goal is assisted by the ability to envision or fantasize that goal (White, R., 1964). Apparently, fantasy can provide a person with intermediate rewards on the way to a distant goal (White, R., 1964).

Fantasy may also help in developing interpersonal skills. A person who can imagine the position of another person is better able to respond with sympathy. A student can be encouraged to develop his capacity for fantasy in a number of ways. Certainly, assignments that require originality, whether verbal or otherwise, should contribute to the development of fantasy. Students could even be encouraged to develop ideas about possible long-range goals. For example, the student who expresses an interest in politics could be asked to consider in more detail the possible results of his choice. He could be asked to suggest what kinds of things he should be doing now to prepare himself for such a career. Once he has thought about his present activities in relation to his future goals, he might be encouraged to contact local persons in similar careers to ask them about what they would recommend specifically to him in preparing for such a position. Biographies of persons in various occupations could also be suggested to the student as a source of information. Many children, from lower-class backgrounds particularly, show a marked discrepancy between their stated choices of occupation and the behavior they exhibit. For example, they profess to want to be a physician, but they plan to drop out of high school as soon as they are old enough. Exercises in fantasizing about such goals and their implications should lead to greater agreement between goals and intermediate behavior.

APPLICATION OF MOTIVATION PRINCIPLES TO SCENARIOS

Knightcrest middle school

The students at Knightcrest have, on the whole, probably had experiences both at home and at school that would encourage the development of high self-esteem, the need to achieve, and a sense of control over one's destiny. It is also highly likely that they have developed the ability to delay gratification. The teachers at Knightcrest are working with students who come equipped with much of what a teacher likes to see in pupils. However, in one important way the Knightcrest teacher is handicapped. Like the teacher at Bridges, the Knightcrest teacher does not enjoy the complete respect and appreciation of the parents or the students.

Still, the students who attend Knightcrest are probably, as a group, going to succeed in spite of what the teachers do. It has been frequently noted that students from the upper middle class are destined to succeed. Indeed, the outstanding success of graduates of such institutions as Harvard and Yale may have little to do with their having attended Harvard or Yale. They simply come from families in which success is a given (Jencks et. al., 1972). Nevertheless, even privileged children have problems and can benefit from interaction with a teacher who realizes that these problems are important to the student.

The organizational structure of this school is ideal in terms of utilizing many of the motivational concepts and techniques discussed in this chapter. The individualization, continuous progress, and independent contract systems lend themselves to the type of individual conferences and goal setting considered earlier.

Although Marvin Blake is certainly a success compared to the average sixth grader, he does not seem to be utilizing his intellectual ability to the extent that might be expected. He is small for his age and may suffer by comparison when it comes to physical pursuits. Boys who are small for their age and who mature late have been found to be handicapped socially (Mussen and Jones, 1957). Thus it may be appropriate at this stage in his development for Marvin to focus more heavily on the development of his social skills than on intellectual pursuits. Certainly, the importance of the social aspect of some of his problems should not be overlooked when the belongingness needs described by Maslow are considered.

Still it should be possible to get him to assume more responsibility for his work. Because he is interested in eventually joining the Forensic Society, it may be possible to use his interest in debating to get him more deeply involved in intellectual pursuits. Perhaps initially he could be encouraged to prepare arguments on an issue that he could present in conjunction with another student. As he becomes more interested in a topic and devotes more effort to pursuing it, he is likely to become more spontaneous in his oral presentation of a position. It was mentioned that reading is one of his favorite pastimes. The kind of materials he likes to read can provide suggestions for topics for debate. It would seem particularly appropriate to employ individual conferences with Marvin, which would allow his teachers to investigate his interests in reading and to design feedback and reinforcement procedures to strengthen his self-esteem.

Comments made over the years by his teachers indicate that Marvin has the ability to do much better work if he applied himself to it. His IQ scores, achievement scores, and his home environment are certainly consistent with this evaluation. We are forced to conclude that he has the ability to succeed academically if he wishes. At this stage he is about to embark on what is probably the most difficult period of social adjustment in the school. Marvin is especially handicapped for a male because of his small physique, his glasses, and his shyness. Therefore, the teacher would do well to encourage Marvin's development of interpersonal skills. His security in interpersonal relations is doubtlessly related to his applying himself more adequately in the intellectual sphere.

Linda Grey is in some danger of joining the ranks of the underachiever, at least in comparison with her previous achievement. Early physical development in a girl is frequently accompanied by a loss of interest in academic pursuits (Jones and Mussin, 1958). Still, many girls manage to combine studying with their growing interest in the opposite sex. Linda has in her favor the fact that she is a reticent person. Her history of control, almost bordering on overcontrol, may enable her to navigate the next few years with her academic record intact. If so, her high level of ability, her strong interest in academic subjects, and her long-range ambitions should combine to guarantee her success. In the meantime, anything the teacher can do to understand and assist her in reducing the conflicts Linda will have to deal with in the near future should be of help. For example, until the other girls catch up with Linda physically, she is likely to be lonesome for female companionship and hence thrown more into the company of older boys. Efforts should be made to see that Linda continues to enjoy success in her academic work and to make school as reinforcing as possible, so that Linda will want to continue her academic pursuits.

Bridges elementary school

The environment surrounding Bridges, both physically and attitudinally, is unlikely to be supportive of a high level of academic achievement. Neither the necessary physical attributes, such as books, a wide variety of experiences such as trips and cultural events, and learning games, nor the social support necessary for most individuals to achieve are present. Realistically, it is probable that for most of the students at Bridges whether they eventually succeed or fail in the world will depend on such nonintellective qualities as dependability, honesty, integrity, reliability, and the ability to relate to people in social situations. Because many of these students do not have the necessary background to earn distinction for their intellectual abilities, it is important to encourage and reinforce these other qualities, so that the school will not become so aversive that the students drop out at the first opportunity into a world hostile to the school dropout.

To place a student in a classroom where only traditional academic values are rewarded without taking into account the differences in the backgrounds of the students is to doom many of the students to failure. There are two basic ways of attacking this problem, both of which focus on making school a place of interest and meaningful reward.

The first method is based on the hypothesis that if a student is encouraged and rewarded for socially acceptable behaviors other than, or in addition to, academic achievement, he can experience the satisfaction of success and the consequent development of self-esteem and self-confidence. One obvious way to implement these rewards is to hold individual conferences designed to determine students' interests and values and to encourage prosocial behaviors.

The use of formal or informal individual conferences by no means exhausts the ways in which teachers can seek to develop and reinforce positive behaviors. For example, one of the authors had the experience of attending a rural county school in the South, where by the fifth grade a small group of boys had acquired a reputation for being the "bad guys" in the class. These boys skipped school frequently, hid their cigarettes on the way to school where they could be conveniently located later, and generally expressed declining interest in a school environment that offered them no hope of success. It then happened that a smaller school was established farther out in the country to handle some of the overflow of students. This smaller school included the first through the sixth grades and was housed in portable one-room buildings with one grade in each building. Although equipment and personnel were in short supply, the school had a middle-aged woman as principal who took the group of "bad guys," with all their family and personal problems, and promptly put them in charge of such things as distributing the milk to the classrooms and collecting the money. By giving them responsibilities such as these, she communicated to these children the faith and confidence she had in their abilities, and perhaps most important of all, she let them know that she genuinely loved them and cared about what happened to them. The response of these "bad boys" was incredible to witness. Boys whose only interest in class had been the extent to which they could disrupt it now turned to their books and began to apply themselves. Their absenteeism disappeared, and they began to take more interest in their personal appearance. None turned into a stellar pupil in an academic sense, but they all showed reasonable progress in their work. Unhappily, it was necessary at the end of the sixth grade for these students to return to the original school, where their reputations were already established. Upon reentering the old environment, they fell into their old patterns of behavior.

The important point is that during their enrollment at the newer school they showed dramatic changes in their overall behavior as well as in their academic progress. These changes were primarily the result of one woman's efforts. She had no control over the home environment or the prior history of these boys. They came to her with already established behavior patterns that classified them as difficult, incorrigible, and academically handicapped. Whether it would have been possible for this woman to guide these boys through their adolescence without losing them is a moot question. Yet for a period of 2 years one person in a school system did exert a strong positive influence on them with remarkable effects.

The second way in which a teacher can develop motivation in schools like Bridges Elementary School is to attack the problem directly by structuring the situation so that each student can be successful. This success may only be relative to the student's own past performance, but nevertheless it is a success. If this is to be done, the school must allow for a maximum of individualization and a minimum of the type of interpersonal academic competition that forces poor students to continually be compared with the top students. Unfortunately, it seems that most schools in our inner cities and other poverty areas (like Bridges) do not allow for this individualization. Schools like Knightcrest Middle School would theoretically be ideally suited for working with kids from an economically deprived background such as the students in Bridges School.

The needs of the students at Bridges are legion, and a teacher in such a situation cannot help but feel powerless in the face of the problems confronting both him and his students. Such children are usually characterized by an inability to delay gratification, a lack of persistence in the face of failure, the feeling of little or no control over their destiny, low self-esteem, and a low need to achieve. Additionally, many of the students are not able to consistently satisfy basic physiological needs, and they arrive at school tired, cold, wet, or hungry.

Many of the motivational techniques discussed earlier in this chapter, particularly goal setting and individual conferences, may be quite effective in increasing the student's level of interest in school and in changing his attitude toward the class. These techniques along with others specifically designed to increase the students' feeling of control over their own destiny, such as class participation in determining rules and arriving at reasonable assignments and activities, should also operate to increase their self-esteem. When a teacher includes the students in the classroom planning, he is communicating to them a sense of trust in their ability, which is associated with the development of high self-esteem and a high need to achieve. Perhaps one of the most important skills the students at Bridges need to acquire is persistence motivation. If these students can be taught to continue to respond and try alternative approaches in the face of adversity, they are likely to achieve independence in later life.

For the children at Bridges Elementary School the fact that Mr. Bellamy attended a school similar to Bridges is at the same time an advantage and a disadvantage. Painfully aware of the problems faced by his students, he may despair of any effect he might have, whereas a more naïve teacher might hope to succeed. Still the fact that he went to a school very much like Bridges and is now a schoolteacher should provide a model for the children, showing that it can be done. He should have a particular advantage with a student like Rick Washington. Rick clearly has developed his social assets well beyond his intellectual assets. With no father in his home, Rick might well look to Mr. Bellamy as the primary adult male model in his life, at least for this year. Rick is much more likely to respond to efforts by such a teacher than he is to respond to a teacher from the middle class. Also, our discussion of modeling theory has indicated that since Rick is "the most popular boy in the class," any successes that Mr. Bellamy can achieve with him are likely to make it easier to work with the other students. Rick's leadership qualities and potential as a model should not be lamented by his teachers but rather seen as an opportunity to reach other students through him. In view of the number of students like Rick, it would be well to consider increasing the number of male teachers in elementary schools in the inner city.

Julia appears to be well below average in terms of intellectual potential. Yet she is probably not using what she has. It is important that the school continue to be a pleasant experience for Julia, or she will likely drop out shortly. It may be that the work is becoming progressively too difficult for her, and she does not have a chance to master one level before she is thrust into a higher level. If Julia could have access to simpler materials at which she could experience some success, her time in school would be better spent, even if the materials are not at the grade level in which she is formally enrolled. It would be better for her to be working on third or fourth grade materials and mastering them than to be working on sixth grade materials that leave her lost and foundering. Julia is a good example of a student who needs to experience success in nonintellectual areas, since intellectual pursuits are not her forte. A hint of an area of possible success may be provided in the comment of one of her teachers to the effect that she does beautiful artwork. This should definitely be investigated by Mr. Bellamy.

More than anything else, Mr. Bellamy can offer his students hope. Although it is not frequently the case, strong effective adults *can* develop from a difficult and unhappy childhood (Langner and Michael, 1963). The person who is upwardly mobile often rejects the lower-class values by the time he is in his teens. This may mean that he is alienated from his peers and even from his family during his childhood and adolescence. The authors would argue that it is better to develop behaviors and values that are in conflict with one's primary group in order to achieve a reasonable adulthood rather than accept the values of one's surroundings and limit the future choices available in terms of life-style. Mr. Bellamy should actively discourage his students from adjusting to their situation by accepting it. He should instill in them a dissatisfaction along with the hope for something better. At the same time he should encourage the behavior skills that will enable them to get out of their present situation and into something that will prove more satisfactory in the long run. For many of Mr. Bellamy's students, to adjust is to give up.

Midview elementary school

The students at Midview represent a mixed bag. The wide range of interests, potential, and social backgrounds presents a challenge to the most experienced of teachers. Yet the very variety in Midview offers a golden opportunity for students to teach one another not only through peer tutoring, but in many informal ways as well. In a sense the students at Knightcrest are deprived of any real standards of comparison, so that it is difficult for them to recognize and appreciate the advantages they have. By the same token, they have no real opportunity to develop campassion for persons with much more limited means and endowment. They represent a truly segregated population. Not so at Midview. Here the teacher can capitalize on the variation in the classroom to broaden the horizons of both advantaged and disadvantaged. The needs of the Midview students vary, so that there is ample opportunity for the application of all the measures suggested in connection with the special skills described earlier in this chapter.

Sheila Smith at Midview has expressed an interest in becoming a veterinarian, a profession demanding long years of diligent application. She is active in 4-H and loves to work with animals. Although she may not realize her goal of becoming a veterinarian, she certainly has the necessary intellectual potential. In the meantime her current interest in the profession could be used as the basis for involving her more deeply in her schoolwork. Her teachers should help her to understand the relationships between the subjects she is presently studying and her long-range goals. She could also explore some of the ramifications of her career choice by sending for catalogs from veterinary schools to see what the entrance requirements are and what courses she will have to take to earn her degree. Contact could also be made with any local veterinarians to discuss with them what is involved in obtaining the training. Finally, neither the school nor Sheila's parents should lament her tomboy tendencies. There is evidence that girls who are tomboys are the most likely eventually to attain intellectual achievement (Maccoby, 1963). Additionally, late-developing girls are socially better adjusted in the long run (Jones and Mussen, 1958).

William Baker is in desperate need of remedial reading. Every effort should be made to provide this kind of help for him. Because he scores higher on tasks not requiring reading (the manual dexterity items and the items concerning similarities and differences on the Stanford-Binet and the nonlanguage items on the California Mental Maturity Test), there is a question of whether William suffers from a perceptual handicap such as dyslexia. His problem should be diagnosed, so that appropriate measures can be taken. Without help he will almost certainly show progressively poorer performance in every subject that depends on reading skill, and from now on most of his subjects will rely heavily on reading ability.

With a large number of students in the class the teacher is obviously not able to provide extensive personal attention. Yet there are self-instructional materials available that could be tried with this boy, and some of the individual techniques discussed earlier might prove effective. It would not be appropriate to subject him to lengthy sessions, since it is unlikely that his concentration and interest would be sustained. Yet a brief reading assignment each day, followed by a brief evaluation of comprehension, could be of help. Individual reading conferences provide an ideal technique for implementing this. William has normal intellectual potential and above average athletic and social skills. He should be able to achieve reasonable success if he remains in school. Yet it is unlikely that he will stay long enough to graduate if his reading deficiency is not corrected.

SOME SUGGESTED ACTIVITIES

1. Observe in an ongoing classroom situation. What goals does the teacher communicate to students? What goals do students seem to set for themselves? How often are goals actually overtly stated?
2. Think about Maslow's need hierarchy in relation to the subject and grade level you plan to teach. What things can you as teacher do to provide for student needs at each level. At what levels of the need hierarchy are you most limited and why?
3. Observe in an ongoing classroom situation. What needs in Maslow's hierarchy are provided for? What needs are not provided for? How might the teacher have proceeded differently in order to satisfy more of the students' needs?
4. Think about yourself in your role as a student. Which needs in Maslow's need hierarchy are satisfied for you by learning and by the school environment?
5. Observe in an onging classroom situation. What types of behaviors does the teacher model? What attitudes does the teacher model? How often do other students seem to serve as models?

REFERENCES

Bandura, A., and McDonald, F. J. "The Influence of Social Reinforcement and the Behavior of Models in Shaping Children's Moral Judgments." *Journal of Abnormal and Social Psychology* 2 (1965): 698–705.
Bandura, A.; Grusec, J. E.; and Menlove, F. L. "Observational Learning As a Function of Symbolization and Incentive Set." *Child Development* 37 (1966): 499–506.
Bandura, A.; Ross, D.; and Ross, S. A. "Imitation of Film-Mediated Aggressive Models." *Journal of Abnormal and Social Psychology* 66 (1963): 3–11.
Bayton, J. A. "Performance As a Function of Expressed and Non-Expressed Levels of Aspiration." *American Psychologist* 3 (1948): 274.
Bronfenbrenner, U. *Two Worlds of Childhood: US and USSR.* New York: Russell Sage Foundation, 1970.
Bryan, J. F., and Locke, E. A. "Goal-Setting As a Means of Increasing Motivation." *Journal of Applied Psychology* 51 (1967): 274–277.

Burnstein, E.; Stotland, E.; and Zander, A. F. "Similarity to a Model and Self-Evaluation." *Journal of Abnormal and Social Psychology* 52 (1961): 257–264.

Coleman, J., et. al., *Equality of Educational Opportunity*. U. S. Office of Education. Washington, D. C.: U. S. Government Printing Office, 1966.

Ellis, D. B., and Miller, L. M. "Teacher's Attitudes and Child Behavior Problems." *Journal of Education* 27 (1936): 501–511.

Eron, L. D. "Relationship of TV Viewing Habits and Aggressive Behavior in Children." *Journal of Abnormal and Social Psychology* 67 (1963): 193–196.

Fryer, F. W. *An Evaluation of Level of Aspiration As a Training Procedure.* Englewood Cliffs, N. J.: Prentice-Hall, 1964.

Gaa, J. P. "Goal-Setting Behavior, Achievement in Reading, and Attitude Toward Reading Associated with Individual Goal-setting Conferences." Technical Report No. 142, Wisconsin Research and Development Center for Cognitive Learning, Madison, Wis., 1970.

Gaa, J. P. "The Effect of Individual Goal-Setting Conferences on Achievement, Attitude, and Locus of Control." Paper presented at the Annual Meeting of the American Educational Research Association, New Orleans, 1973.

Gallagher, J. J. "An Analysis of the Research on the Education of Gifted Children." State of Illinois, Office of the Superintendent of Public Instruction, 1960.

Harrison, G. V. "The Instructional Value of Presenting Specific Versus Vague Objectives." California Educational Research Studies, 1967.

Herndon, J. *The Way It Spozed to Be.* New York: Simon and Schuster, 1968.

Hicks, D. J. "Imitation and Retention of Film-mediated Aggressive Peer and Adult Models." *Journal of Personality and Social Psychology* 2 (1965): 97–100.

Holt, J. *How Children Fail.* New York: Pitman, 1964.

Holt, J. *How Children Learn.* New York: Pitman, 1967.

Jencks, Christopher, et. al. *Inequality: A Reassessment of the Effect of Family and Schooling in America.* New York: Basic Books, 1972.

Jones, M. C., and Mussen, P. H. "Self Conceptions, Motivations, and Interpersonal Attitudes of Late and Early Maturing Girls." *Child Development* 29 (1958): 491–501.

Kibler, Robert J.; Barker, Larry; and Miles, David T. *Behavioral Objectives and Instruction.* Boston: Allyn and Bacon, 1970.

Klausmeier, Herbert J., and Ripple, Richard E. *Learning and Human Abilities.* 3rd ed. New York: Harper and Row, 1971.

Kohl, H. R. *The Open Classroom.* New York: Random House, 1963.

Langner, Thomas S., and Michael, Stanley T. *Life Stress and Mental Health,* New York: Free Press, 1963.

Locke, E. A. "The Relationship of Intentions to Level of Performance." *Journal of Applied Psychology* 50 (1966): 60–66.

Locke, E. A. "Motivational Effects of Knowledge of Results: Knowledge or Goal-Setting?" *Journal of Applied Psychology* 51 (1967): 324–329.

Locke, E. A., and Bryan, J. F. "Cognitive Aspects of Psychomotor Performance." *Journal of Applied Psychology* 50 (1966a): 286–291.

Locke, E. A., and Bryan, J. F. "The Effects of Goal-Setting, Rule Learning, and Knowledge of Score on Performance." *American Journal of Psychology* 79 (1966b): 451–457.

Locke, E. A., and Bryan, J. F. "Goals and Intentions As Determinants of Performance Level, Task Choice, and Attitudes." American Institute for Research Report, No. R-67-1 (1967a).

Locke, E. A., and Bryan, J. F. "Performance Goals As Determinants of Level of Performance and Boredom." *Journal of Applied Psychology* 81 (1967b): 398–406.

Locke, E. A., and Bryan, J. F. "Goal-Setting As a Determinant of the Effect of Knowledge of Score on Performance." *American Journal of Psychology* 81 (1968a): 398–406.

Locke, E. A., and Bryan, J. F. "Grade Goals As Determinants of Academic Achievement." *Journal of General Psychology* 29 (1968b): 217–228.

Locke, E. A., and Bryan J. F. "Knowledge of Score and Goal Level As Determinants of Work Rate." *Journal of Applied Psychology* 53 (1969a): 59–65.

Locke, E. A., and Bryan, J. F. "The Directing Function of Goals in Task Performance." *Organizational Behavior and Human Performance* 4 (1969b): 35–40.

Locke, E. A., and Bryan, J. F. "Knowledge of Score and Goal Level As Determinants of Work Rate." *Journal of Applied Psychology* 53 (1969c): 59–65.

Locke, E. A.; Bryan, J. F.; and Kendall, L. M. "Goals and Intentions As Mediators of the Effects of Monetary Incentives on Behavior." *Journal of Applied Psychology* 52 (1968): 104–121.

Locke, E. A.,; Cartledge, N.; and Koeppel, J. "Motivational Effects of Knowledge of Results: A Goal-Setting Phenomenon?" *Psychological Bulletin* 70 (1968): 474–485.

Long, Eugene R. Personal communication.

Maccoby, Eleanor E. "Woman's Intellect." In *The Potential of Woman*, edited by S. M. Farber and R. H. L. Wilson. New York: McGraw-Hill, 1963.

Mace, C. A. "Incentives: Some Experimental Studies." Industrial Health Research Board (Great Britain), Report No. 72, 1935.

Mager, R. F. *Preparing Instructional Objectives*. Palo Alto, Calif.: Fearon Publishers, 1962.

Mager, R. F., and Clark, C. "Explorations in Student-Controlled Instruction." *Psychology Reports* 13 (1963): 71–76.

Maslow, Abraham H. "A Theory of Human Motivation." *Psychological Review* 50 (1943): 370–396.

Maslow, Abraham H. *Toward a Psychology of Being*. 2d ed. New York: Van Nostrand Reinhold, 1968.

Maslow, Abraham H. *Motivation and Personality*. 2d ed. New York: Harper and Row, 1970.

McClelland, D. C.; Atkinson, J. W.; Clark, R. A.; and Lowell, E. H. *The Achievement Motive*. New York: Appleton-Century-Crofts, 1953.

Miles, D. T.; Kibler, R. S.; and Pettigrew, L. E. "The Effects of Study Questions on College Students' Test Performances." *Psychology in the Schools* 4 (1967): 25–26.

Mischel, W., and Gilligan, C. "Delay of Gratification, Motivation for the Prohibited Gratification, and Responses to Temptation." *Journal of Abnormal and Social Psychology* 69 (1964): 411–417.

Mischel, W., and Metzner, R. "Preference for Delayed Reward As a Function of Age, Intelligence, and Length of Delay Interval." *Journal of Abnormal and Social Psychology* 64 (1962): 425–431.

Mussen, P. H., and Jones, M. C. "Self Conceptions, Motivations, and Interpersonal Attitudes of Late and Early Maturing Boys." *Child Development* 28 (1957): 242–256.

Page, E. B. "Teacher Comments and Student Performance: A Seventy-Four Classroom Experiment in School Motivation." *Journal of Educational Psychology* 49 (1958): 173–181.

Payne, David A. *The Specification and Measurement of Learning Outcomes.* Waltham, Mass.: Blaisdell, 1968.

Plowman, L., and Stroud, J. B. "Effect of Informing Pupils of the Correctness of Their Responses to Objective Test Questions." *Journal of Educational Research* 36 (1942): 16–20.

Porat, A. M., and Haas, J. A., "Information Effects on Decision-Making." *Behavioral Science* 14 (1969): 98–104.

Purkey, W. W. *Self Concept and School Achievement.* Englewood Cliffs, N. J.: Prentice-Hall, 1970.

Quilling, M. R.; Fischbach, T.; Rendfrey, K.; and Frayer, D. A.; "Individual Goal-setting Conferences Related to Subject-matter Learning: A Report on the Field Test." Technical Report No. 190, Wisconsin Research and Development Center for Cognitive Learning, Madison, Wis., 1971.

Rosekrans, M. A. "Imitation in Children As a Function of Perceived Similarities to a Social Model of Vicarious Reinforcement." *Journal of Personality and Social Psychology* 7 (1967): 307–315.

Stotland, E.; Zander, A. F.; and Natsoulas, T. "Generalization of Interpersonal Similarity." *Journal of Abnormal and Social Psychology* 61 (1962): 250–256.

Stouffer, G. A. W., Jr. "The Attitudes of Secondary School Teachers Toward Certain Behavior Problems of Children." *School Review* 64 (1956): 358–362.

Sweet, R. C. "Educational Attainment and Attitudes Toward School As a Function of Feedback in the Form of Teachers' Written Comments." Technical Report No. 15, Wisconsin Research and Development Center for Cognitive Learning, Madison, Wis., 1966.

Television Information Office Release SM 15, 1963.

Torrance, E. P. "Explorations in Creative Thinking." *Education* 81 (1960): 216–220.

Vargas, Julie S. *Writing Worthwhile Behavioral Objectives.* New York: Harper and Row, 1972.

Walberg, H. J., and Thomas, S. C. "Open Education: An Operational Definition and Validation in Great Britain and United States." *American Educational Research Journal* 9 (1972): 197–207.

Walters, R. H., and Thomas, E. L. "Enhancement of Punitiveness by Visual and Audiovisual Displays." *Canadian Journal of Psychology* 17 (1963): 244–255.

White, K. "The Effect of Source of Evaluation on the Development of Internal Control Among Young Boys." *Psychology in the Schools* 9 (1972): 56–61.

White, K., and Howard, J. "The Relationship of Achievement Responsibility to Instructional Treatments." *Journal of Experimental Education* 39 (1970): 78–82.

White, Robert W. *The Abnormal Personality.* 3rd ed. New York: Ronald Press, 1964.

Wickman, E. K. *Children's Behavior and Teachers' Attitudes.* New York: Commonwealth Fund, 1928.

7 · Fostering a positive self concept and high self-esteem in the classroom

STANLEY COOPERSMITH
University of California, Davis

RONALD FELDMAN
University of California, Davis

KEY CONCEPTS

Acceptance and trust

Responsive environment

Limits and guidelines

Encouragement

Authoritative

In this chapter we discuss procedures that are designed to foster development of a positive self concept and high self-esteem in young and preadolescent children. The procedures arise from a series of studies one of us (Coopersmith) has been conducting for several years and from a school program, in which we are engaged, that has building self-esteem in the classroom as its primary goal. Another source of information has been the rapidly increasing body of studies on self concept in education and the theory that underlies this research. It is notable that in the past 10 years there have been over 500 studies conducted on self concept and self-esteem in education, and a number of brief books on that topic have already been published. These studies are filling in the gap in self concept research. That is, these studies are spelling out in detail the methods, procedures, and materials whereby a teacher (or parent) can directly and significantly help to produce certain positive and constructive perceptions and feelings in a growing child. Up to very recently this gap in self concept research has resulted in statements about the importance of self concept and self-esteem that do not fill in the details that would enable teachers to achieve that objective. At this point it appears that we can offer a considerable and increasing amount of constructive advice and information on how to promote positive self concepts and self-esteem in the classroom.

ISSUES REGARDING
SELF CONCEPT PROGRAMS IN SCHOOL

There are five issues that have frequently been raised by educators, teachers, and parents regarding self concept programs in the classroom.

These issues reflect an interest in the importance of self-esteem and at the same time some reservations about the consequences of expanding educational objectives to include the "affective domain." The first issue bears on the nature of the self concept and on feelings of self-esteem. What are these constructs, and why do so many psychologists place so heavy an emphasis on their importance in the classroom setting? A second and related issue bears on the consequences of placing emphasis on the self concept and self-esteem at the possible cost of time and effort that could be better spent on increasing the child's skill and knowledge. This issue is basically one of priorities; that is, is raising self-esteem as important in the school as teaching reading, writing, and other academic skills? A third issue is whether teachers and parents (as well as children) are interested in building self concepts and self-esteem or whether this is a concern largely of academic researchers, who are promoting a point of view. This issue is basically that of the school's responsiveness to the community and the question of who shall make the decisions of establishing educational priorities and thus allocate time, money, and space. The fourth issue is a pragmatic concern as to whether the school can overcome the effects of earlier home treatments that may have produced negative self concepts and low self-esteem. Indirectly, this issue asks whether the school can have a favorable influence on the child's self concept in the face of a negative socio-economic status and membership in disadvantaged racial and ethnic groups. The fifth issue is whether any further research or programs are needed to promote self-esteem; methods to achieve that goal have long been recognized and employed. This issue proceeds from the assumption that teachers already know how to improve self concepts and self-esteem via such procedures as giving children good grades, assuring a child that he can succeed, and praising a child profusely.

Taken together these five issues of necessity, appropriateness, public and professional demand, interfering consequences, and the difficulty of raising self-esteem in the schools represent real and sober concerns of educators, teachers, and parents. Before self concept and self-esteem programs in the schools can be recognized and supported, these issues have to be confronted and satisfactorily answered.

The first issue concerning the nature and importance of the self concept and self-esteem requires consideration at both the theoretical and empirical level. At the theoretical level we can indicate that a positive self concept and high self-esteem are as important in school performance as they are in other areas of life such as sports, work, and personal relationships. Athletic coaches know the importance of confidence; sales managers value the man who believes in his ability to sell; and each of us appreciates friendships in which we can reveal ourselves without fear of rejection and from which we gain feelings of support and acceptance. A person's self concept and self-esteem are an important influence in determining how he perceives, feels, and responds to the world, and they do not leave or diminish when he enters the classroom door. Since ability is only one of the factors that enter into academic performance, the attitudes, beliefs, and feelings associated with the self concept and self-esteem have an important influence on how closely a child approaches his potential. On the negative side, a child such as Mary Cairns in the Midview scenario, who thinks poorly of herself, is likely to underestimate her ability and anticipate failure, and she may well stop trying when difficulties arise and then be overwhelmed by her defeats. On the more positive side, a child with a positive self-image and high self-esteem, such as Stanley Robinson in the Midview scenario, acts consistently with that self-image, anticipates success, persists in the face of problems and thereby increases the possibility that he will be successful. Thus the child with a negative self concept and low self-esteem tends to act consistently with that self-image and increases the possibility of failure, whereas the child with a positive self concept and high self-esteem tends to act consistently with an image, beliefs, and feelings that are likely to lead him to success.

Research lends considerable support to the theoretical view that a positive self concept and high self-esteem are likely to result in higher achievement, and more negative beliefs and feelings are likely to be associated with underachievement or failure (for example, Bledsoe, 1964; Bowden, 1957; Brookover, Patterson, and Thomas, 1964). Children with either a positive self concept, high self-esteem, or both exhibit school performance superior to that of children with more negative self concepts and low self-esteem. Other studies indicate that students who are unsure of themselves or who expect to fail are likely to stop trying and give up on school (Quimby, 1967; Shaw and Alves, 1963). Although cause-and-effect factors may be confounded in some of these studies (children may exhibit a positive self concept or high self-esteem because they do well in school rather than because such states lead them to do well in school), one very important study suggests that differences in the level of self-esteem may induce differences in school performance (Wattenburg and Clifford, 1964). In this important study kindergarten children were given an intelligence test and a test on self-esteem before they began learning how to read. Two and one-half years later, when these children were tested for levels of reading achievement, the results indicated that early self-esteem was more closely related to future reading performance than was the child's performance on the intelligence test.

The second issue of whether the schools should divert time and attention from teaching skills and knowledge to help foster positive self concepts and high self-esteem is basically one of the school's priorities and responsibilities. When the issue is phrased as a choice, it seems obvious that skills have priority over esteem—until we ask whether such a choice is really sensible or necessary. As we have already indicated, the child's self concept and self-esteem can have a constructive and positive effect on performance, and they are not something altogether separate and isolated from achievement. When the question is phrased in terms of a choice, or a statement of priorities, between achievement *or* self-esteem, the tendency is to see greater differences between these two goals rather than to recognize that self-esteem is part of performance itself. By fostering positive self concepts and self-esteem in students, the teacher at the same time promotes academic achievement; by providing certain types of academic experiences, the teacher at the same time fosters positive self concepts and self-esteem. Thus the resolution is not a choice of *which* to emphasize but a question of how to develop procedures that increase skills and at the same time promote development of a positive self concept and self-esteem.

The third issue of the desirability and demand for programs intended to build positive self concepts and self-esteem in the school can be answered most directly by referring to Table 7-1. This table is derived from the work of Robert Reasoner, who asked the parents and teachers of children in California schools to rank the educational goals and objectives they set for their school and children. The responses in this table were obtained from teachers at forty-two schools and parents in over two hundred elementary schools throughout California. Since parents from different socioeconomic groups might select different goals for their children, the responses of the parents were divided into three categories: Category 1 includes basically lower middle-class and upper lower-class families; category 2 includes parents in the large range of the middle class; and category 3 includes parents in the upper middle and upper classes. The figures in the table indicate the range and rank of the parents' and teachers' responses when asked to select the first fifteen educational priorities. (The teachers and parents were asked to rank thirty-six goals, but our table focuses on the highest priorities assigned by both groups.) It is noteworthy that building a positive self concept is among the top three goals for teachers and parents of all socioeconomic levels and that objectives involving motivation and decision making are regarded as far more important than spelling, physical education, science, or history. These and other traditional goals are given low priority by both teachers and parents; thus spelling was ranked 16, penmanship 31, physical education 30, science 25, history 26, and geography 28. It is also noteworthy that the

TABLE 7-1 Rankings for Educational Objectives by Parents and Teachers

Rank Position All Schools	Educational Goals	1. (Lower) Rank	Range	2. (Middle) Rank	Range	3. (Upper Middle) Rank	Range	4. Teachers Rank	Range
1	Reading comprehension	1	1–2	3	1–6	1	1–3	7	2–13
2	Self concept	3	2–6	1	1–5	3	2–5	1	1
3	Motivation toward learning	4	4–11	2	1–5	2	1–3	4	2–6
4	Reading skills	2	1–4	4	2–7	4	2–7	11	5–19
5	Listening skills	6	5–8	9	5–9	7	7–9	9	6–12
6	Decision making	7	4–11	6	4–9	6	4–10	6	4–9
7	Math computation	5	4–12	8	7–11	9	9–13	12	9–18
8	Citizenship	8	6–15	5	3–10	11	6–18	3	2–6
9	Social adjustment	9	9–12	7	7–9	16	11–18	5	2–7
10	Personal adjustment	14	9–19	10	5–14	12	6–16	2	1–5
11	Math concepts	12	6–15	13	10–17	8	4–14	17	13–22
12	Math problem solving	13	9–13	12	12–15	13	9–14	14	11–18
13	Thinking skills	16	13–19	11	9–13	5	4–12	8	5–10
14	Use of reading	11	8–15	17	13–17	15	13–15	13	9–18
15	Writing skills	15	11–17	15	13–17	10	7–16	16	14–22

responses of the teachers are very similar to those of the parents in category 2. Although this is not surprising, because most teachers are from middle-class backgrounds, it is noteworthy that teachers, who are in the classroom daily, rate building positive self concepts as one of the leading and most desirable goals of the school. From these data it appears that the parents and teachers regard the building of positive self concepts as one of the most important and desirable objectives of the educational system.

The fourth issue of whether the schools can overcome parental and social influences that shape self concepts and self-esteem can be answered on a factual level. Studies indicate that teachers' attitudes and practices (Engle, Davis, and Meyer, 1968; Gillham, 1967), fellow students serving as models (Fox and Schwartz, 1967), and adult counseling procedures (Dolan, 1964) can all be utilized successfully in the school setting both to foster more positive self concepts and self-esteem and to improve academic performance. Although school-based practices can in themselves promote student growth, there is considerable evidence that parents also have a significant influence in developing self concepts and self-esteem (Coopersmith, 1967; Brookover, Patterson, and Thomas, 1962). We can safely assume that changes in parental child-rearing practices can foster enhancement of the self concept and self-esteem in children. It also seems clear that the most effective program for raising esteem would be a coordinated collaborative effort including the school's and the parents' treatment (Brookover et al., 1965). Since a discussion of such collaborative programs is beyond the scope of this chapter, we shall focus here on school practices that can foster positive self concepts and self-esteem within the boundaries of the classroom.

The fifth issue is whether new methods and programs are needed to raise self-esteem or whether more effective use of available methods would be sufficient. Since this issue avoids a consideration of what actually happens in most traditional classrooms, perhaps a brief examination of those practices will underline the need for different approaches and procedures. In traditional elementary classrooms verbal intelligence has generally been recognized as the major, if not the sole, basis for determining who is capable and likely to succeed. Teachers in these classrooms have generally failed to teach children to recognize, utilize, and value their other skills and abilities. Consequently, many children who are not in the top quarter in verbal intelligence feel that they are incapable and are virtually doomed to failure. Many traditional schools have also favored the use of grades, competition between children, and fear of failure as means of motivating children. The schools have, thus, set up a system for generating negative self concepts and low self-esteem—a system that virtually guarantees that a great many children will feel they are incapable and have not succeeded. It should, therefore, come as no surprise that there is a regular and consistent decline in children's self-esteem between the second and the seventh grades (Morse, 1964). Apparently, the longer today's children are in traditionally structured classrooms, the more likely they are to feel they are failures and ineffective in achieving academically valued goals and skills.

Innovations intended to foster a positive self concept and high self-esteem are being introduced into traditional schools, but many of these innovations have little theoretical or experimental support and tend to be ineffective. For example, telling children that they are successful, encouraging them to persist, or flattering or rewarding them are all unlikely to increase feelings of self-esteem (Brookover, et al., 1965; Weiner et al., 1971). Nor do educational innovations that focus on the open classroom or allowing the child complete expressiveness or exploration necessarily foster a positive self concept or high self-esteem. These well-intentioned procedures often establish conditions that are likely to leave the child feeling uncertain or negative about his judgments, without standards to refer to, and often feeling uncertain of his strengths and skills. For example, although a young child may exercise certain skills in free exploration that are not emphasized in the traditional classroom, he may not focus enough on any one area to arrive at an accurate, positive concept of his abilities. As we shall see, limits, structure, standards are all important aspects of developing high self-esteem, and free exploration, praise, and popularity are not sufficient to achieve that end.

In attempting to confront these issues at the outset, we are striving to deal with some of the psychological and social realities that might cloud the examination and acceptance of programs for the building of positive self concepts and self-esteem in the classroom. To foster the optimal development of these traits requires knowledge of the underlying processes involved in the forming of one's self concept and self-esteem. In the next section of this chapter we will examine the theory and research findings that clarify the processes involved, and in the third and final section we shall describe several of the procedures that have been developed and employed on the basis of that theory.

CONCEPTUAL FRAMEWORK

In this section we present the set of concepts, the terms, and the theory that underlie the procedures for building positive self concepts and self-esteem discussed later in the chapter. The procedures involved in building positive self concepts and self-esteem require a way of thinking about children, learning, and the process of education that is quite different in many ways from that employed in other educational programs. As we shall see, a way of thinking as well as a set of techniques is required if we are to help the child think and feel about himself in a more positive way, become self-rewarding and self-motivating, and break established patterns of failure and withdrawal.

Self concept

The self concept consists of the beliefs, hypotheses, and assumptions that the individual has about himself. It is the person's view of himself as conceived and organized from his inner vantage. The self concept includes the person's ideas of the kind of person he is, the characteristics that he possesses, and his most important and striking traits. The hypotheses, beliefs and assumptions about the self are organized into a self-image, that is, a picture that the individual holds of himself. This image represents the person's view of what he is like and is used to explain himself to himself as well as to others. Thus a child's self concept may include the view that he is a bad child, an ineffective learner, or a capable reader. His self concept may include the view that he is capable or incapable, lovable or unlovable. The self concept includes the assumptions that the person makes about whether he is capable, how he should act toward others, how others should treat him, how to go about getting what he wants, and what goals are appropriate and desirable and fitting for him. Thus, for example, a child who thinks he is lovable expects to be treated by other persons in a manner indicating his charm and good qualities; a child who thinks he is capable is likely to pursue learning and feel comfortable in the classroom. The significant influence of the self concept lies in providing the interpretations of the person's strengths, rights, and salient characteristics. Representing as it does the person's beliefs about the kind of person he is, the self concept serves as a filter for incoming stimuli, an organizer of events and objects, and a guide to appropriate conduct.

A brief look at the terms *self* and *concept* should clarify the importance of the self concept and the processes by which it is formed. Although the term *self* has been used in many ways, our usage refers to the persistent and enduring features of the individual's psychological experiences. Viewed in this light, the self is an abstract object that the person regards as relatively constant over time. Height, weight, and abilities may shift over time, but the person will generally continue to see himself, from his inner perspective, as much the same person. Looking at himself, the person will generally tend to see himself as having certain basic and central features, for example, as being capable, lovable, bright, or good in sports. These perceptions of his central and persistent features may be modified with extended and different disconfirming experiences, but since these perceptions form the stabilizing core of psychological experience, changes are distressing and are strongly resisted. The term *concept* refers to qualities that objects or events share in common. These objects or events may differ in other regards, but they share a particular characteristic. Thus a red ball and a red shirt share the common quality of being red, although they differ in several other ways. People form similar concepts about their own selves and the selves of other people. Thus a teacher who views a child who is exhibiting high performance on word recognition and letter reproduction would say the child is very proficient in verbal skills. The teacher is, in effect, forming a concept regarding the shared and consistent aspects of the child's characteristics in using words. Persons apparently form concepts about themselves in much the same way as they form concepts about others (Hastorf, Schneider, and Polefka,

1970; Wylie, 1961). They observe how they are treated by others, how they behave, how they can deal with tasks and problems, the values that are important to them in making decisions, and form a concept of their underlying and persistent personal characteristics. Thus a child who experiences difficulty in reading from a single book may not conclude that he is a poor reader, but a child who has difficulty with seven or eight readers, observes that he reads slower than other students, and is advised by his teacher that he should spend more time on reading than other subjects is likely to develop, as a part of his self concept, the view that "I am not a very good reader."

The process by which the self concept is formed is similar to concept formation in general. Thus the child begins with some very global and tentative hypotheses about himself quite early in his life and uses these tentative hypotheses as a means for categorizing subsequent experiences. There is, then, an interplay between the concept that the child already has and the information that he gains from his new experiences. With increasing experience the child's self concept becomes more definite and stable, but like other concepts it remains somewhat open to revision and change. The concepts are, after all, tentative hypotheses constructed by the child to organize and otherwise explain the regularities he experiences in his interactions with the environment. The child, like any other explorer of a new territory or idea, may modify his hypotheses when they no longer correspond with the evidence, or he may seek evidence that would clarify the concept he already holds. For example, a child who is uncertain of whether he is physically weaker than his peers may hover on the fringe of a sports activity and observe the actions and strengths of his peers. At some point the child is likely to enter into the play and establish his athletic skills and ability for social play.

Although the teacher can exert considerable influence on the shaping of a child's self concept, ultimately that self concept is constructed by the child himself. The teacher's treatment, beliefs, and expectations are part of the child's experiences and thereby influence the child's developing self concept. The issue here is how the teacher's actions are interpreted by the child. Thus we must give the child a major part in the formation and modification of the concepts that he holds. The teacher can provide experiences and guidance, but the child's interpretation of the teacher's actions and their significance plays an important role in how the child reacts to these experiences. Although teachers can attempt to provide children with success experiences, unless the child believes *he* is responsible for the successes and can attribute them to himself, they do not become part of the self concept (Weiner et al., 1972). Nor do children necessarily accept all kinds of treatment and information to the same extent or in a passive manner. Children sift, reject, seek, and avoid information; they interpret experiences in light of the concepts they have already formed; they do not accept information from adults they do not trust or who have rejected them as readily as they do from adults who they feel have accepted them and are trustworthy.

Teachers can exert significant influence on the forming of the child's self concept by the kind of learning environment they establish in the classroom as well as by their personal attitudes and actions toward the students they teach.

Since the child's concept of his ability is largely built up on the basis of the successes he experiences in the various tasks he undertakes, the teacher can set up a range of tasks that include opportunities for success. He can also help his students to interpret their experiences positively by giving them an awareness of the skills they have developed over an extended period of time. This can be done by comparing performances that were completed several months apart on specific details. He can also help by ascribing the students' successful performance to their own abilities rather than to chance or luck factors. Considerable research indicates that children will work harder at tasks and are thereby more likely to achieve a positive self concept if they believe they (rather than chance or the teacher) are responsible for the successes they achieve (Rotter, 1966; Lefcourt, 1966). In fact, a large-scale national survey indicated that a pupil's belief in his control over his destiny was more important to achievement than any other school factors measured, such as facilities, teachers and curriculum (Coleman, 1966). (For an extended discussion of this research and its implications for the classroom, see Chapter 5 by Solomon and Oberlander.)

The self-referring beliefs that are organized into the self concept are based primarily on two sources. The first of these includes the significant others, for example, parents, teachers, and peers, who are especially important to the child (Mead, 1934). They provide social feedback by their treatment of the child, their responses to his statements, the extent to which they reveal and express themselves, and the manner and extent to which they accept, trust, and support the child. Each person's self concept, to a considerable extent, is a mirror reflection of how he has been (and is) seen by others who are important to him. The role of the significant others is particularly important in the early years, when the child has no other bases for judging the appropriate and suitable ways for him to be treated. In the home the most important significant others are the parents, and to a lesser extent, the siblings; in the school the most significant others are generally the teacher and, depending on the child's age level and personality traits, the peers.

A second source of evidence when the child forms his self concept is the physical feedback that he receives from his explorations of the physical environment. This type of feedback involves information communicated to the child from his own experiences rather than via the opinions and views of other persons. Thus a child who tries to build with blocks and finds he cannot do it because they fall down knows his limits without having to be told that they exist. Many of the activities that children pursue provide direct feedback that enables them to determine directly whether or not they are capable and growing in their skills. Among such activities are bicycle riding, racing, skating, building with blocks, and swimming.

The self concept formed by feedback from the social and physical environment plays an important role in determining how a child responds to himself and other persons. The feedback provides cues that help describe the type of person he is, that define the boundaries of his involvements and commitments, and that underlie the assumptions he makes about how he should treat others and be treated by them. The self concept is, in effect, a guide that the person holds in front of himself and that indicates how much and what he can do and how he can and should be treated. It is the picture of ourselves that we hold in our mind's eye and that serves to tell us what we believe to be appropriate, expected, and realistic for ourselves. There are many facets to the self concept that the person holds, and different facets apply in the home, school, or social play. In this chapter we are primarily concerned with the child's self concept in school. It is this aspect of the self concept that is most directly involved in determining whether the child will be motivated in the classroom, and it is this aspect of his self concept that aids or inhibits him from achieving his potential.

Although our self concept represents inner beliefs and descriptions of ourselves, it is *our* evaluation of that self concept that leads us to like, esteem, and respect that concept to differing degrees. These evaluations and self-judgments are associated with feelings of self-esteem that lead us to be more or less positive, optimistic, and respectful about our traits, capacities, and performance and lead us to be more or less persistent, enterprising and resilient.

Self-esteem

A child's level of self-esteem represents his judgment of the self concept he has formed through his interpretation of the feedback from his physical and social experiences. Self-esteem is the person's evaluation of whether his self concept attains his standards and values. Such evaluations have great significance for the way the person feels and acts, for persons who dislike the concept they hold will tend to feel negative, depressed, sad, and apprehensive, and persons who make favorable evaluations will tend to be more optimistic and exploratory.

The conditions that lead children to make favorable judgments about themselves have been greatly clarified during the past 10 years (Baumrind, 1967; Brookover et al., 1965; Coopersmith, 1967). Among the conditions that appear to be associated with the development of positive self-judgments are acceptance, clearly defined limits, respectful treatment, reasonable yet challenging standards, and psychological defenses to cope with adversity. We shall briefly describe these conditions in this section and illustrate how they can be practiced in the section on classroom practices. The major condition for enhancing self-esteem is the teacher's *acceptance* of the child, while the teacher, at the same time, recognizes the child's strengths, limitations, and problems. By accepting the child, the teacher, as a significant other, indicates to the child that he is worthy of the teacher's attention and respect. This acceptance releases the child to be himself and to work with, utilize, and come to terms with his abilities and limitations. A second condition for producing high self-esteem is the existence of explicit *limits* that are spelled out early and consistently enforced. These limits define acceptable behavior, provide standards of conduct, and establish expectations of the student's role in the classroom. *Respectful treatment* is a third condition for building self-esteem. Such treatment is accorded to children who observe limits and act in accord with the rules and guidelines of the classroom.

The child uses standards and expectations to determine when he succeeds, fails, and is making progress. Within the context of self concept theory these standards, internalized as part of the person, are termed the *ideal self*. Children whose ideal self is higher than their perceived self suffer from feelings of inadequacy and generally have low self-esteem; children whose ideal self is equal to or lower than their perceived self generally have high self-esteem (McCandless, 1967). Children who lack standards cannot develop high self-esteem because they remain uncertain about how to determine their capabilities and performance. Adults who talk of children finding and doing their "own thing" fail to recognize that children need guidelines within which to operate, standards to gauge competence and progress, and assistance in dealing with difficulties that are beyond their immediate present skills. If we look at the backgrounds of children who are self-reliant, exploratory, competent, and self-accepting, we find that their parents make maturity demands, enforce limits firmly, and are responsive to reasonable and valid objections and suggestions (Baumrind, 1967). All of which suggests that the way to help a child to become self-managing, self-motivating, and self-enhancing is to provide standards and support that are real, reasonable and respectful.

These conditions of acceptance, limits, and respectful treatment appear to produce high self-esteem by providing the child with personal concern from people who are important to him, by providing standards that he can use to guide his progress, by defining what is acceptable, and by setting up stable and secure boundaries within which he can safely roam and explore. Children are not born with standards, rules, and definitions; and they apparently require them if they are to make reliable judgments about themselves and come to a meaningful resolution as to their competencies and personal adequacy.

The conditions that result in positive self-images are generally established and maintained by teachers who are themselves relatively confident and secure. They tend to have pretty clear ideas of the actions and goals that are important to them and try to express those goals and values in their lives. As a general rule, these individuals tend to be decisive, aware of what is important and valuable to them, and capable of acting on their beliefs. They appear to have sufficient self-esteem for themselves so that they do not seek further esteem by controlling and dominating the children in their class. In the classroom these teachers tend to focus on producing an environment that increases learning and helps youngsters develop confidence in their abilities, rather than on controlling the actions and growth of their students. Teachers who devalue the child by focusing on his limitations and place continual attention on grading, competition and classroom control cause him to defend himself against the fears and pressures they raise. To defend their self-esteem, children in such situations withdraw their interest and attention, conform passively, attack a routine that induces stress, doubts, and fears, and lose their enthusiasm for learning. Teachers with high self-esteem are more likely to explore alternatives that lead to increased learning and more likely to be flexible and exploratory in their approach to teaching.

Teachers who esteem themselves and focus on the task of student learning tend to have a positive effect on the self-esteem of their students. They apparently do this by serving as models for their children, showing them how to gain skills and express competencies, and also by the style in which they examine questions and make decisions. (For a review of the research in this area and its implications, see Chapter 3 by Good and Brophy.) Teachers who accept themselves are also more likely to accept others, whereas teachers who reject themselves are more likely to reject others. Thus the teacher's attitudes toward himself are an important and basic determinant of whether children will be enhanced or devalued through their contact with him. Teachers who have positive attitudes about themselves and feel confident about their abilities as teachers are better able to relate to others and express their competencies in the classroom. Over a decade of studies by Arthur Combs and his associates have revealed that effective teachers hold quite favorable and realistic attitudes toward themselves and are also quite supportive and firm in their actions (Combs and Soper, 1963; Combs et al., 1969).

Self-reward and motivation

One of the major ideas underlying programs designed to build self concepts and self-esteem in the classroom is that the child should become his own source of reward and motivation. Rather than having the parent or teacher serve as the source of positive and negative incentives, programs to build a positive self concept and self-esteem seek to put the source of reward within the child. Although behavior modification approaches speak of efforts to make the child become his own source of reward, their reasoning and procedures differ markedly from those implied by self-theorists. (For an extended discussion of the behavior modification approach, see Chapter 4 by Wasik.) Self-theorists attempt to have the child set his own standards, explore his own strengths and abilities, and then employ the feedback to form and modify the self concept that already exists. The focus is on having the child use his internal feelings, judgments, and reactions as a source of his actions rather than merely as a respondent to environmental treatment.

The view that self-motivation derives in part from the person's concept of himself requires that the child become aware of his own interests, wants, and desires. The notion of motivation as something apart from the self requires that some external force outside the self be the source of drive and inspiration. A learner will become involved to the extent that he has a sense of control and responsibility for his actions in the classroom (Atkinson, 1966). The most enduring and reliable way of assuring that the child is motivated is to help the child develop an image of himself as someone who is capable of learning and pursuing activities. If he internalizes standards and values that lead him to gain self-esteem from his school activities, the likelihood of a cycling self-reinforcing involvement in learning is all the more certain.

The practices discussed in this chapter fall into three categories. The first area considered concerns acceptance, trust, and the opportunity for choice. These conditions promote internalization but do not convey specific expectations to the child. The second area covered focuses on limits and how they can be formulated, communicated, and enforced. These limits convey to the child specific expectations. The third and final area covered concerns the encouragement process. The teacher's practices that constitute this process assist the child in overcoming the difficulties that arise when his efforts to match his expectations fall short and he is left depressed and with feelings of failure and pessimism.

CLASSROOM PRACTICES

Acceptance, trust, and the opportunity for choice

ACCEPTANCE. The discussions of the various practices considered in this section will all follow the same format. First, the given set of practices will be defined and described; second, the practices will be examined in terms of their function in promoting a positive self concept and high self-esteem; and third, a concrete example of the use and effects of the given practices will be given. The examples sometimes portray the use of a practice and at other times the failure to use a practice; both types of examples are intended to reveal the rationale as well as the procedures involved. The major condition for the child's developing a positive self concept and self-esteem involves acceptance of the child. Acceptance implies liking and showing concern for the child as he is, with his capacities, limitations, strengths, and weaknesses. This acceptance is expressed by interest in the child, concern for his welfare, involvement in his activities and development, support for him in his times of stress, and appreciation of what he is and can do. Acceptance is also expressed by recognition of the child's frailties and difficulties and by the awareness that the child can only do so much and be his particular kind of person at this time of his life. Such acceptance does not mean that the parent or teacher necessarily approves of all the child's qualities, but it does mean that the teacher can see the child for what he is without being affected by his own feelings of dissatisfaction and desire to change the child. *Acceptance,* as we have used the word here, is not necessarily indicated by the amount of time the teacher or parent spends with the child, but by the feelings, attention, and attitudes expressed during that time. In this instance, as in so many human relationships, it is the quality of expression rather than sheer quantity that is critical. Children can sense concern, interest, and appreciation and are not easily fooled by mere words of praise and affection or by insincere demonstrations of physical affection.

The fact that a child is accepted by his teacher as a significant other fosters the child's development of a positive self concept. Believing that he is basically an all right person, the child is less likely to deny the strengths he does possess. Recognizing his particular achievements and potentials for learning, the child is more likely to achieve at his ability level and to elicit the confirming social and physical feedback on the basis of which he maintains and enhances his self-concept.

The teacher's acceptance of the child as he is rather than as the teacher would like him to be fosters the child's development of high self-esteem through two mechanisms. First, the child (if he correctly interprets the teacher's behavior) will be freed from the fear of being rejected if he exhibits or discusses his own weaknesses and imperfections. In fact, accepted for what he is *now,* the child is not hampered by feelings of doubt and rejection and thus has greater emotional support for any attempts he may make at changing. Thus freed to examine his difficulties without fear of rejection, the child is able to see himself more clearly and also use the support that he may have previously interpreted as rejection. Second, the teacher's acceptance conveys to the child the fact that he will not be treated more negatively than other children and that he is accepted for what *he* can do and not in comparison with other children. The teacher, in effect, expects the child to succeed in terms of his abilities and accepts his performance in those terms. Accordingly, the child is more likely to adopt standards appropriate to his abilities and less likely to internalize or project inappropriately high expectations.

Acceptance from others is a basic condition for accepting oneself, and the teacher who forgets this fact in his desire to move the children along is actually hindering the very process he seeks to promote. The following example taken from Katherine Fowler's class at Midview Elementary School describes an interaction where a teacher accepts a child despite her shortcomings:

Mary Cairns, a student in Mrs. Fowler's class, has been given an arithmetic assignment. The assignment, although at the right level of difficulty for the average child in the grade, is too difficult for Mary. Although she tries hard, she misses about one-half of the problems. After grading her paper, Mrs. Fowler says to Mary: "You got lots of answers right, but you also missed some. You understand a lot of things, but there are probably some other things you'd like to ask me about. Is there anything you'd like to ask me?"

In this example Katherine Fowler, the teacher, communicates acceptance of her student, Mary Cairns, by crediting her with accomplishments; at the same time Mrs. Fowler notes her mistakes and offers further assistance. Thus Mrs. Fowler recognizes what Mary is and is not and indicates her continued support for Mary in a time of need. The child does not have only the failure of her mistakes but also the acceptance and support of her teacher as well as her correct answers.

With such treatment she is less likely to adopt standards inappropriate to her abilities, for she has not been rejected by her teacher for failing to achieve a perfect score. Encouraged by Mrs. Fowler's acceptance, Mary Cairns is now better able to recognize and encounter her difficulties and feel motivated to achieve.

TRUST. Trust implies believing and acting on the basis of the belief that the child can make appropriate decisions and achieve and progress on the basis of his decisions. Whereas acceptance implies a liking of the child for what he happens to be, trust implies a faith that the child will learn and progress. Trusting a child involves risk taking on the part of the teacher. The teacher relinquishes some of his control over the child and takes a chance that although the child may not learn and progress as much as the teacher would hope, he will become more aware and appreciative of his own role in learning. In relinquishing part of his control, the teacher invests the child with a greater degree of power over his school life. Seeing himself as responsible for his progress, the child is more likely to attribute his accomplishments to his own capacities and become aware that *his* own efforts and involvement are required if he is to develop. The rationale here is that by relinquishing some of his control, a teacher can promote greater self-control in his students, provided he expresses his trust as trust rather than as a lack of concern for the student's progress. As we shall see, this trust must be exercised within the context of limits appropriate to the child's ability and personality. (For an extended discussion of feelings of control, see Chapter 5 by Solomon and Oberlander.)

Dorothy Cummings has begun a new arts and crafts center in her fifth grade at Midview Elementary School. Dick Williams, one of the students in Mrs. Cummings' class, is making a pot of clay. The pot that he is making is rather lopsided, and Dick has added so little water to the mixture that the pot may fall apart when it dries. Mrs. Cummings suggests to Dick that he add a little water, and Dick follows the suggestion. Then Mrs. Cummings begins to supervise Dick as he shapes his clay—fearful that otherwise the pot will not be aesthetically pleasing.

Mrs. Cummings' suggestion regarding adding water is reasonable and called for. This information fell outside the student's range of knowledge and prevented a minor catastrophe from occurring. On the other hand, Mrs. Cummings' constant supervision of the shaping of the pot indicated a lack of faith on her part in her student's ability to achieve a satisfactory product. Whether or not the lack of faith is justified, as a result of Mrs. Cummings' actions Dick Williams may come to see himself as not being capable of shaping a pot. Two processes are involved here. First, Mrs. Cummings communicated her belief that Dick is incapable directly to him. (Recall how the child's self concept is in part a mirror reflection of how significant others view him.) Second, Mrs. Cummings took the power away from Dick and put it into her own hands. In so doing, she may have led the child to believe that making the pot was her project rather than his. Thus Dick may fail to credit himself with whatever favorable accomplishments result from the efforts and will be likely to believe that he cannot be trusted to work with clay himself. Furthermore, Dick will be unlikely to derive feelings of success from making the pot, because the standards were set by his teacher rather than himself and he was unable to reach them. Thus in the immediate situation he is likely to feel that he failed, and in the future he may judge his works by the teacher's standards rather than his own, thereby setting himself up for further feelings of inadequacy.

OPPORTUNITY FOR CHOICE. Opportunity for choice implies that options are generally available and that the student is trusted to choose freely among these options. The options usually are provided by the teacher, but not infrequently choices may be suggested by the students themselves or built on the students' suggestions. The choices may involve the activity a student pursues, the level at which he pursues it, when he pursues it, and with whom he pursues it. The teacher may set limits by defining the range within which the options fall, the general time schedule, and the due date of activities. For example, the options may all help a student gain better skills but vary in how they approach those skills, for example, through games, workbooks, or tutorial sessions with an older student. By allowing a student an opportunity for choice, the teacher conveys his sense of trust as well as some additional effects. This sense of trust makes it possible for a student to explore his interests and standards for himself and thus more accurately define his self concept, and the possibility for selecting his own choices enables him to believe that he has some control over his actions in the classroom. As a consequence, the student is more likely to see himself as responsible for his choices and also to internalize the teacher's expectation that he is capable of learning and making decisions. Evaluating himself on the basis of self-selected (within bounds) activities and standards, the student is more likely to pursue his school activities and to receive self-esteem from achieving in school. A teacher can give a student the opportunity for choice informally by pointing out two or three courses of action he might pursue. If the teacher wishes to be somewhat more organized about it, he may develop one or more learning centers in his classroom. Learning centers are areas that contain a set of materials (programmed books, games, ordinary reading books, and so on) that a student can use to acquire a given set of skills (for example, learning to recognize the letters of the alphabet). During certain periods the student is free to go to the learning center and to use those materials that are of interest and appropriate to his level of knowledge. However the teacher provides it, the student is given an opportunity to choose. The most extensive program for affording choice to students involves setting up a responsive environment in the classroom. Instead of giving a concrete example of a teacher's behavior in this section, we will describe the responsive environment in some detail.

The responsive environment (Nimnicht, MacAfee, and Meier, 1969), drawing heavily on the Montessori tradition, is based on the notion that the school should be designed to respond to the learner rather than the learner to the school. To this end the responsive environment is notable for five essential features:

1. The student is allowed the opportunity to choose from among several activities. This opportunity allows the student to explore and define his interests and thereby promotes an accurate definition of his self concept and helps the student learn what is important and interesting to him.

2. The activities are self-pacing; the rate of activity and progress is determined by the student. This self-pacing feature guides the student in adopting standards suitable to his particular achievements and potential for learning.

3. The activities provide the student with immediate feedback about the consequences of his actions. This feedback assists the student in creating a positive self concept and in adopting appropriate standards.

4. Teachers respond to the students by giving assistance when they request it. Accordingly, the student again gains a motivating sense of personal power.

5. Although the environment may permit free exploration and pacing, the teacher does establish the limits of that environment, the activities and materials it will contain, and how it will be organized. Thus the teacher determines how many activities shall be available (generally four to six); whether there will be individual, small, or large groups (a choice is usually available); the types of materials that will provide the most information and feedback (varying with the activity); and the limits within which the student can explore (generally broad and clear). The teacher, in effect, plans the environment to achieve the objectives he would like to accomplish. For example, if preparation for reading is a major goal, he sets up an environment of materials to promote that goal, for example, letter blocks, books, typewriter, and chalk.

Examining a typical day in a classroom that is set up according to the principles of a responsive environment provides some concrete idea of the activities and program found in this type of classroom. Observing the students as they enter, we find that they are free to choose from among such different activities as looking at books, listening to records, building with blocks, solving puzzles, playing with manipulative toys, or painting. They may stay with an activity as long as they like and move on to another activity as often as they wish. The teacher and assistant are available as resources. They respond to the students rather than initiating interactions in which students respond to them. Student-initiated conversation and activities are encouraged, with the teacher providing supportive service by reading, playing, and participating in their activities. There are large-group activities each day such as planned lessons, singing, or listening to the teacher read a story, but the student does not have to join in any of these activities. If he prefers to pursue some other activity in the classroom, he can work by himself as long as he does not disturb the group.

This discussion of the responsive environment is intended to give you an understanding of an ongoing program specifically designed to promote positive self concepts and high self-esteem in the classroom. The program focuses on the feedback students receive from learning materials and attempts to make the student more aware and responsive to his own part in the learning processes. The program does not directly focus on the significance of limits and the teacher's expectations—two topics we shall now consider.

Limits, guidelines, and authoritative enforcement practices

The practices discussed in this section are intended to provide the student in the classroom with a structure—a framework designed to promote learning and within which he can explore and define his interests and abilities. As long as the student lives within the conditions of the framework, he receives acceptance, trust, and opportunities to choose among alternatives. In this section we describe some of the major features of the structure and discuss the effects of a structure designed to promote the development of a positive self concept and feelings of high self-esteem.

LIMITS. Limits indicate a teacher's expectations to the student. As such, limits indicate what the teacher wants the student to refrain from doing and also the accomplishments he expects the student to achieve. The student is given clear and rational statements of behaviors that are not permissible in the context of a learning environment, and the teacher enforces these limits in a firm and consistent manner.

In indicating his expectation that a child should achieve and learn in school, a teacher is requiring that the child play a certain role in the school setting. This role is the one of a student and carries with it the implicit demand (Orne, 1962) that the child see himself as a student who has the obligation of using his school time to gain skills and knowledge.

In conveying these demands a teacher, as the most significant other in the school setting, should demonstrate faith that the student has the ability to achieve. Teachers who believe that their students will fail are more than likely to have a negative impact on the students' performance and are apt to do more harm than good in the classroom. Teachers with negative expectations are poor significant others and are likely to have an adverse effect on the child's self concept and self-esteem. The teacher's demands cause the child to define himself as a student; the teacher's faith promotes a child's believing that he is a student who is able to achieve. Two very important research studies document the influence of teachers' demands (Brookover, Erickson, and Joiner, 1967) and of teachers' beliefs about students' ability levels (Rosenthal and Jacobson, 1968) on promoting school achievement in children. A teacher's limits (demands and beliefs) are very much interrelated with the specific guidelines he promulgates. An example illustrating the effects of both factors will be given following the discussion of guidelines. (Good and Brophy also discuss this topic in Chapter 3.)

GUIDELINES. To be effective in communicating his beliefs, the teacher should focus on the specific actions that are required or excluded rather than on general statements. Since children tend to function and test adults at very concrete levels of behavior, specific guidelines are most useful and meaningful to the child in making decisions and evaluating his own performance.

To maximize the probability that a child will actually use the limits as guidelines, the teacher should base the limits on realistic and reasonable grounds and set a relatively small number of limits. By basing the limits on realistic and reasonable grounds, the teacher ensures that the limits make sense *to him*; accordingly, he is more likely to be able to convey the significance of the limits to the children. By setting a relatively small number of limits, the teacher increases the likelihood that the limits can be maintained without making enforcement into a burdensome and tension-building way of life for the teacher and child. Since children are inclined to test limits, it is almost inevitable that the limits set will be clarified and elaborated over the course of time. Since limit testing is ever present, it is vital that teachers establish limits that are based on the realities of the classroom rather than on abstract considerations and remote possibilities. General, vague limits are likely to be heavily tested and will generally end up redefined, overly defended, or abandoned. Such limits are likely to reflect the teacher's anxieties or need for control rather than situational realities, requirements for increasing learning, or considerations of the child's development.

The teacher's setting of limits in a form that can serve as guidelines to students promotes the development of a positive self concept and of high self-esteem by providing the students with standards for judging conduct, avoiding censure, and establishing expectations and roles for achieving success. The effect of not setting limits and giving guidelines is illustrated in the following example taken from the rather unstructured environment of Knightcrest Middle School. (Authoritarian school practices are as detrimental to the developing self concept and feelings of self-esteem as is the extremely unstructured school. Because of space limitations we give an example only of the latter type of school.)

Marvin Blake is a student in the experimental Knightcrest Middle School, where the children are accepted, trusted, and given opportunities for choice by their teachers. Mrs. Holmes, the master teacher and team leader for the mathematics–science team at Knightcrest Middle School, believes very strongly that teachers should not set limits or communicate guidelines, because such adult-imposed restraints will impede rather than promote the development of a positive self concept and feelings of high self-esteem in the children. In this school teachers do not monitor or evaluate the progress of the children, and they give assistance and offer their opinion only after such guidance has been requested by a student.

Marvin Blake has been working this particular day in a mathematics–science learning center that contains materials on astronomy. He is enjoying a game that teaches some principles of astronomy, but feels frustrated because some of the mathematical concepts required are at a level of difficulty slightly beyond his current level of achievement. Knowing that either Mrs. Holmes or Miss Carter will respond to his request for guidance, Marvin says to Miss Carter, "I can't understand this. Help me with it."

Miss Carter, in giving guidance to Marvin, carefully avoids setting limits or communicating specific guidelines, for she knows that a primary objective of Mrs. Holmes', her team leader, and indeed Knightcrest Middle School, is to teach students to be self-directing, and she sees constraints as constituting an undue imposition of the adult world. Thus she gives Marvin some information about the required mathematical concepts, so that the game will be easier for him, but she lets Marvin decide whether or not to pursue the activity at any level of difficulty. Marvin resumes the activity for a few minutes and then decides to go outside to play.

Contrary to Miss Carter's beliefs and the philosophy of Knightcrest Middle School, her actions are likely to have a detrimental influence on Marvin's developing self concept. Having failed to monitor or otherwise evaluate his progress, Miss Carter is uncertain as to the level of his achievement and learning potential, and thus Marvin is uncertain also. Because Marvin has not been given feedback, focus, and direction, he is unable to credit himself for the resources he possesses and does not have an extended opportunity to define himself as a learner. Not having been required to adopt the role of student (let alone being given specific guidelines), Marvin quits various tasks when they become difficult and lose the immediate appeal of novelty and pleasure. (Note the comments of his former teachers.) Consequently, his achievements do not match his potential; he receives insufficient nonsocial feedback confirming his abilities and fails to credit himself with the skills that he possesses. Thus both social and nonsocial feedback in Knightcrest Middle School lead to Marvin's adoption of a negative self concept.

Miss Carter's actions also have a detracting influence on Marvin's experiencing feelings of high self-esteem. Not having received guidelines (whether from the teacher or from himself as the result of teacher–pupil conferences) regarding appropriate levels of achievement, Marvin fails to develop stable standards for evaluating his own performance. Lacking these standards, he does not have a basis for determining whether he is succeeding or failing and is left with uncertainty regarding his competencies and performance.

AUTHORITATIVE ENFORCEMENT PRACTICES. If limits and guidelines are to have significance, they must be enforced by the teacher. Research indicates that the most productive enforcement practices, whether in the home (Baumrind, 1967; Coopersmith, 1967) or in the school (Lippitt and White, 1943), are authoritative and democratic rather than authoritarian. The broad limits and guidelines are established and enforced by the adults, as described in the preceding section, and these structuring constraints are explained to the children and sometimes modified in response to the suggestions and needs that the children communicate. The practices that are effective in evoking high levels of performance avoid the use of physical punishment and emphasize the use of rewards. In such environments, as in a larger democracy, each child is entitled to a "Bill of Rights" for living within the rules of the group. Thus children who abide by the broad, realistically based limits and guidelines are accorded acceptance, trust, and opportunities for choice. The teacher acts in a decisive firm manner but does not seek to maintain tight control over all the actions of his students; nor does he act in an arbitrary impulsive manner. The following example illustrates the firm yet flexible use of authoritative enforcement practices.

Jimmy Barber, a student in Mr. Bellamy's sixth grade class at Bridges Elementary School, has chosen (from an array provided by Mr. Bellamy) an arithmetic assignment to complete by an agreed-upon reasonable deadline. Trusting Jimmy, Mr. Bellamy does not prod him to stick to the task. Jimmy goofs off and fails to complete his task on time. To comply with the school's function and demand that the child be a student who learns, Mr. Bellamy tells Jimmy that he must complete the assignment by five o'clock in the afternoon and that he may do so by staying in during recess and staying after school. Jimmy claims that he goofed off because he was stuck on how to do the problems, and Mr. Bellamy was busy helping other children. Mr. Bellamy hears Jimmy, assesses and decides to believe his story, gives him the needed assistance, and requires that the assignment be completed before noon of the next day. Mr. Bellamy's actions indicate a considered and reasonable appraisal of Jimmy's performance and a firm insistence that he be responsible for his performance.

In enforcing the limits and guidelines, Mr. Bellamy causes Jimmy to credit himself with the capacities that he possesses and to adopt standards suitable for his self evaluation. And by using authoritative rather than authoritarian enforcement practices, Mr. Bellamy conveys acceptance and trust, and maintains a supportive relationship with Jimmy.

The encouragement process

Most children from time to time encounter difficult situations and may require some guidance and support in order to negotiate these situations successfully. In such situations the children may benefit from certain types of teacher-given encouragement. This section of our chapter focuses on the encouragement process and how this process dovetails with and complements the practices previously described (Dinkmeyer and Dreikurs, 1963).

The encouragement process involves several interrelated aspects, three of which will be considered here in some detail. By fostering an optimistic outlook, a teacher can inspire a child with hope, courage, and spirit and stimulate him to do his best. In so doing, the teacher can assist a child in breaking a pattern of inactivity that is based on fears and expectations of failure or rejection. An optimistic outlook gains substance and significance if a teacher indicates realistic avenues for success specifically attuned to the child's present capacities for performance. By giving this information, the teacher focuses the child's attention on fruitful, concrete approaches to life situations and difficulties. A teacher, however, does a child a disservice unless he invests the child with the responsibility for his own growth. By placing the responsibility on the child rather than on himself, the teacher guides the child toward becoming a self-reliant individual, who is capable of making decisions, persisting in their execution, and assuming control and direction over his life and learning.

FOSTERING AN OPTIMISTIC OUTLOOK. The sense of cheering faith that accompanies an optimistic outlook increases the likelihood that a child will attempt to master difficulties and succeed at these attempts. As a consequence, he will develop or else solidify an already developed positive self concept. The goal of fostering an optimistic outlook involves several processes and certain pitfalls. As the following discussion indicates, effective encouragement requires an appreciation of the child's unique strengths and interests and an acceptance of him as a person as well as a learner.

First, fostering of optimism involves indicating to the child that he will be accepted and respected whether he succeeds or fails. Such non-contingent acceptance affords encouragement because the child can try to deal with his tasks and problems with relative freedom from the fear that his performance may lead to personal rejection. Not fearing possible rejection from his teacher, the child can focus more fully on the task at hand. He will also learn that he can achieve esteem by succeeding at a level appropriate to his abilities rather than the level appropriate for his classmates.

Second, a teacher can foster optimism by dwelling on a child's strengths rather than on his deficiencies. By noticing and recognizing the child's strengths, the teacher helps the child to credit himself with the abilities that he really possesses. This focus on strengths helps the child recognize that although his work may not be good or excellent in certain areas, he does have notable abilities in other skill areas.

These first two processes prepare a child in a general way for encountering difficulties. Through their use a teacher can give a child reassurance and thereby assist him to do his schoolwork with greater confidence that he will achieve some degree of success. This assistance is more directly expressed by reassurances that, in effect, say to the child: "I believe that you will succeed." This specific belief is conveyed by such supportive statements as "You're going to do fine" and "You're smart enough to do that." In voicing his reassurance, however, a teacher may unwittingly discourage rather than encourage a child. Thus an overzealous teacher may evidence support for the child before the child shows interest and desire to master some given difficulty. As a consequence, the child may interpret the teacher's words not as reassurance but either as a demand that he attempt to master the difficulty or as an implicit threat that he will be rejected if he fails in the task. A second and often related pitfall involves giving a child reassurance when the task is indeed too great for him to master. Such unrealistic reassurance can cause a child to place unreasonable demands on himself, to fail in terms of the teacher's expectations and his own standards, and to come to distrust the teacher as a future source of reassurance. (In the next section we describe practices for assisting a child in developing the abilities necessary to surmount a task currently beyond his capacity to master.)

A teacher can also foster a child's optimism and willingness to encounter a specific difficulty by utilizing the child's personal interests. This process entails employing the child's present enthusiasm rather than trying to develop new ones. Thus in giving reassurance to a child, a teacher might point out how the child can approach the difficulty using techniques and strategies of immediate personal appeal to him and through further study of topics in which he is already interested. By putting parts of the child's self at the center of his schooling, the teacher is indicating support and acceptance of the child and an appreciation of his capacities. The teacher is putting the child's self at a starting and central point of his school program.

Teachers can supplement reassurance given before a child attempts a task by giving the child praise after he has attempted a task. Praise is communicated by such statements as "That's good" and "You got a lot done today." These statements communicate the teacher's interest and support and in addition give the child social feedback confirming his accomplishments. In giving praise, a teacher should recognize a child's efforts as well as his real successes. A child may need to learn how to focus and use his energies before he can learn how to use those energies effectively. As in the case of reassurance, the giving of praise can involve serious pitfalls. If praise is given too frequently when a child exerts effort but fails to succeed, the praise may be interpreted by the child as saying: "You need help, and I am going to be nice to you." A child may reach the same interpretation if his real successes are almost always followed by praise. In such cases he may devalue the relevance and sincerity of the teacher's praise and assume it is a token gesture unrelated to performance. An additional pitfall involves the fact that praise directs the child's attention to the judgments that others place on his achievements. This latter pitfall can be reduced if the praise is accorded only when the child achieves or makes an effort to achieve (a) his own goals or (b) goals that are part of the regular classroom program but are consistent with his abilities and interests.

Although it is useful for teachers to develop general strategies for encouraging children, teachers should employ different individual prescriptions for each given child. A study by Page (1958) revealed that teachers' comments are most effective when the comments are very specific to the child and his individual performance. Such individualization makes the teacher more credible and also helps develop the warm, trusting type of teacher–child relationship that often is critical to the child's starting to take even small steps forward.

The example that follows illustrates some of the processes involved in fostering an optimistic outlook. In the example Katherine Fowler, a teacher at Midview Elementary School, attempts procedures that are designed to increase the likelihood that Sheila Smith will recognize and credit herself with her normal and special abilities.

Sheila Smith underachieves in reading (language IQ of 73rd percentile with a reading achievement at the 55th percentile) largely because of an inaccurate belief that she is deficient in phonic skills. Mrs. Fowler has indicated that she wants Sheila to master some new phonic skills—a demand consistent with Sheila's abilities and present performance. Mrs. Fowler gives Sheila a set of materials from which to choose, and Sheila picks some learning games that relate to her personal interests. Going through some of the early exercises with Sheila, Mrs. Fowler praises and otherwise notes some of the many successes Sheila achieves. Then she indicates to Sheila that she should proceed on her own, reassuring her by saying: "It's not very hard. You can do it." It is worth noting that all the materials that Mrs. Fowler presented to Sheila required skills that she already possessed. Sheila, however, did not credit herself with the possession of these skills and would probably have been reluctant to try using them on her own. Giving Sheila an excuse to consult her and at the same time indicating that her acceptance is noncontingent, Mrs. Fowler says: "If something is hard, come to me and we'll figure it out together." To supplement this unscheduled type of interaction, Mrs. Fowler on occasion approaches Sheila to see how she has been doing. She also schedules conferences with Sheila during which she gives praise as Sheila recounts her efforts and especially when she demonstrates new phonic skills. During these conferences Mrs. Fowler also discusses the progress Sheila has made and reviews the assignments (stored in a folder) that Sheila has prepared and completed.

INDICATING REALISTIC AVENUES FOR SUCCESS. The processes considered in the preceding section help children to recognize, and to act on the basis of, skills that they have already mastered. Those processes help children bring a full array of strengths and interests to bear on mastering a given difficulty. In this section we consider another set of procedures, which are designed to help children in planning an effective approach to difficulties whose mastery requires skills that they do not yet possess. The procedure may be used to encourage other efforts, but they are particularly useful in helping children move into new and different areas of achievement.

A realistic plan differs from a mere fantasy in that it specifies concrete and appropriate actions by which children can achieve the goals that have been set. These component actions are concrete in that they represent specific and detailed intermediate steps that can lead to achievement of the goal. The actions are appropriate and likely to have encouraging consequences when they relate closely to the child's capacities, achievements, and interests. Although reassurance and praise can offer a child temporary encouragement, a realistic plan can sustain genuine achievement of new competencies, long-term growth, and thus the enhancement rather than mere maintenance of a positive self concept.

By making a clear statement of small, graduated steps, a teacher (or child) can break a large task into a sequence of smaller, discrete units that are relatively easy for the child to master. As a result, the child achieves frequent successes and can experience a reassuring sense of genuine progress as he pursues longer-term goals. This procedure of setting up assignments and tasks with graded intermediate steps builds a motivational bridge that a child can follow and cross.

After a child has successfully mastered a new skill, teachers can communicate their knowledge of the results to the child rapidly, clearly, and in detail. For example, a teacher can keep a child's written materials in a folder and review the materials with the child occasionally to indicate that the child has made progress in mastering a new skill.

Grading is the most widely used method for communicating knowledge of results to a child. Frequently, this evaluation procedure involves comparing a child on an A-B-C-D-F basis with his classmates or in terms of some absolute criterion. Grading carried out in this fashion can cause discouragement to all children except those at the very top of the heap. In contrast, grading a child in terms of his own past performance can motivate him to achieve by rewarding him for *his* progress. In addition, such individually tailored indications of results serve as social feedback, confirming the fact that the child has attained successes. By supplementing or replacing letter or plus-minus grades with occasional conferences or written reports indicating the specific progress that the child has made, the teacher provides detailed indications of progress, which are far more useful and encouraging than general letter grades.

INVESTING THE CHILD WITH RESPONSIBILITY FOR HIS OWN GROWTH. A teacher's well-intentioned efforts at encouragement can be ineffective or even harmful if he fails to give the child some responsibility for his own growth. A teacher can take several precautions to help him give greater control and responsibility to the children in his room. Three of these measures are described in the following discussion.

As a first precautionary measure, a teacher can discriminate between *his* need and the child's need for progress at a given rate in school. A child's progress may have slowed down because of his fears of failure or of parental, peer, or teacher rejection rather than because of simple laziness. If a fearful child is prodded because of the teacher's impatience, the child may see the teacher as a threat and a source of pain rather than as a support and source of hope. Some teachers, goaded by their own impatience and need for student success, advocate a "sink or swim" approach to a child's progress. Such an approach can backfire by causing a child to resist the teacher's suggestion and is more likely to result in a waterlogged child than an expert swimmer.

As a second precaution, a teacher can discriminate between *his* need to help and the child's need for assistance. A teacher's need to help may cause him to offer more prodding, assistance, and encouragement than the child requires for mastering difficulties at hand. If cast too frequently in a passive role, a child may not credit himself with the ability to overcome difficulties using his own resources. He may come to view himself as an academic cripple, who needs the crutch of his teacher if he is to make any progress. As a third precaution, a teacher can help the child to develop skills and increase his competencies and thereby give him more power to learn and appreciate *his* strengths rather than those of his teacher.

In the long run the central goal of encouragement is to help the child to become his own source of encouragement, motivation, and reward. This goal can best be accomplished by improving the specific skills that assure the child that he is indeed capable of learning and achievement. In this regard, reading is probably the most important skill to impart, because reading is the key to so much of the child's learning in other areas.

Individualized contract-based instruction procedures are a particularly suitable vehicle for teaching children competencies while at the same time causing them to assume responsibility for their own growth. In practicing this method, teachers meet with children in one-to-one conferences and discuss suitable individual goals and realistic plans for accomplishing each child's goals. Children are given the option for setting up contracts with different demands that receive different grades. Thus a child may read 50 pages of a certain book and receive a C, 100 pages for a B, or 150 pages for an A. Within the limits and structure set by the teacher, the child chooses goals and develops plans. These choices are indicated in a contract negotiated by the child. The child carries out the contract, and then may meet with the teacher to evaluate the appropriateness of his goals and plans and to assess the progress he has made. Utilizing this feedback, the child is asked to negotiate another contract utilizing the information and skills he has gained.

To help the child achieve and improve skills in any area, the teacher must start at the level at which the child presently performs, utilize his interests as a source of energy and involvement, focus on his strengths, and reward his efforts as well as his attainments. Time and patience on the part of the teacher and the child are particularly important requirements in the early stages of the child's gaining new skills, because the discouraged child often drops out emotionally from striving to deal with his academic work. At such points the teacher may have to be satisfied with small indications of progress, because that is all he is likely to receive. In general, it takes at least a few months before a previously discouraged child moves at a steady and notable pace again. In the sense that the teacher gains patience and long-term rewards, the proper application of the encouragement process can be a growth experience for the teacher as well as the student.

In the following example Mr. Bellamy, a sixth grade teacher at Bridges Elementary School, effectively gives a child encouragement by indicating a realistic avenue for success. At the same time, he invests the child with the responsibility for his growth:

During the spring of the school year, Rick Washington, previously fearful of learning to read, approaches Mr. Bellamy, saying; "Mr. Bellamy, I wish that I could read more words." Mr. Bellamy says, re-assuringly, "I know some really good books. They are interesting and just right for you." The books, in fact, have been written by Mr. Bellamy during this school year, and each contains a small number of high-interest words. By mastering these high-interest words, a child can read the entire book.

To prepare Rick, Mr. Bellamy drills him on the high-interest words. Then he allows Rick to read the book to him. Occasionally, he praises Rick by commenting on the accuracy of his reading. By completing the book (and mastering the first step in a concrete and appropriate plan), Rick achieves an early success experience based on very tangible non-social feedback. Mr. Bellamy's praise provides supplementary social feedback. Thus Rick receives an encouraging indication of progress, achieves this feedback as a consequence of his efforts, and in addition, develops competencies that can prepare him for future mastery experiences.

As the preceding paragraphs reveal, effective encouragement requires more than simple praise and reassurance. Individualization, graduated steps, recognition of effort, utilizing the child's interests, and building of specific skills are all part of the teacher's repertoire in helping a child to move onward. Praise, contingent on success and effort exerted voluntarily by the child, and social feedback that helps the child recognize and appreciate his capacities are major conditions that help a child develop an appreciation of his strengths.

SUMMARY

In this chapter we have examined the significance of the self concept and of self-esteem for the educational process and indicated some of the methods by which teachers and parents can help build self-esteem. The question of the relevance of these traits in the classroom is most directly answered with the recognition that the self concept and self-esteem are significantly involved in students' motivation and that several studies have indicated that they are a major factor underlying academic achievement. The chapter provides a theoretical framework and considers how the child's self concept and self-esteem are formed, defended, and altered. The teacher is given some theoretically based procedures on how to help the child by helping him develop skills and competencies that focus on academic skills. These procedures promote, in the area of academic performance, a self concept that is constructive and motivating in that it emphasizes the child's idiosyncratic strengths and leads him to believe in his power and competency as a learner. These procedures also promote positive feelings of self-esteem by providing the child with acceptable bases for judging himself to be successful and increasing in personal competencies. The procedures increase the likelihood that the child will be self-directing, self-motivating, and self-rewarding. The procedures are intended to give the child an increased awareness of his interests, feelings, and abilities, his individuality, and his particular assets. By focusing on gaining increased competencies and utilizing his strengths, the child is equipped not only with a positive self concept and high self-esteem but also with the skills for maintaining and enhancing his self-referring beliefs and feelings.

From the available evidence it appears that many of the previously accepted ideas and procedures on how to promote the development of a positive self concept and high self-esteem—for example, freedom without limits, praise, and pressuring a child to encounter difficulties—are not effective. However, certain procedures appear to be capable of fostering positive and constructive developments in this regard. These general procedures supplement each other and may not be sufficient to enhance the child's self concept and self-esteem when employed separately. Among the procedures are acceptance of the child; appreciation of his strengths and acceptance of his weaknesses; trust in his ability to direct, motivate, and reward himself; giving him an opportunity to choose among alternatives, both in the content of the materials and in the level for which he strives; providing a responsive environment in which he responds directly to materials and people rather than through the teacher; and providing a clear and definite set of responsible, realistic limits. These limits serve as definitions and expectations, and provide an environment in which the child can explore his own interests and ideas without fear of arbitrary rejection or punishment.

Teachers can also employ various aspects of the encouragement process to give a child support in difficult situations and enable him to move to new levels and new areas of interest and challenge. These procedures seek to give the child greater control over himself and, in doing so, help the child to recognize that he is responsible for his strengths, to deal with his problems, and slowly and realistically to confront his difficulties. For the child to have a positive self concept as a learner and high self-esteem by virtue of academic success, he must be actively engaged in making decisions, gaining competencies, and defining his interests, standards, and successes.

SUGGESTED ACTIVITIES

1. Select one child whose performance is below average in basic skill subjects. Through observation and conversation attempt to determine in which areas of performance this child has talents and strengths.
2. Rate the classrooms you are observing in terms of:
   a. The number of options provided to the students.
   b. The teacher's acceptance of his students.
   c. The use of materials that provide feedback directly to the child.
3. In your own teaching, attempt to set up records and materials that will provide indications of small specific indices of increased competence gained by one of your students.
4. Employ the steps spelled out in the encouragement process with a student in your classroom.
5. Select one child with high self-esteem and another with low self-esteem and observe their behaviors in the classroom over a period of five days.

REFERENCES

Atkinson, J. W., and Feather, N. T., eds. *A Theory of Achievement Motivation*. New York: Wiley, 1966.

Bandura, A. "Vicarious Processes: A Case of No-trial Learning." In *Advances in Social Psychology*, vol. 2, edited by L. Berkowitz. New York: Academic Press, 1965.

Bandura, A.; Grusec, J. E.; and Menlove, F. L. "Some Social Determinants of Self-monitoring Reinforcing Systems." *Journal of Personality and Social Psychology* 5 (1967): 449–455.

Baumrind, D. "Child Care Practices Anteceding Three Patterns of Preschool Behavior." *Genetic Psychology Monographs* 75 (1967): 43–88.

Bledsoe, J. C. "Self-concepts of Children and Their Intelligence, Achievement, Interests and Anxiety." *Journal of Individual Psychology* 20 (1964): 55–58.

Bowdin, F. B. "The Relationship Between Immature Self-concept and Educational Disabilities." Doctoral thesis, Michigan State University, 1957.

Brookover, W. B.; Erickson, E. L.; and Joiner, L. M. *Self-concept of Ability and School Achievement. III: Relationship of Self-concept to Achievement in High School.* U. S. Office of Education, Cooperative Research Project No. 2831. East Lansing: Office of Research and Publications, Michigan State University, 1967.

Brookover, W. B.; Patterson, A.; and Thomas, S. *Self-concept of Ability and School Achievement.* U. S. Office of Education, Cooperative Research Project No. 845. East Lansing: Office of Research and Publications, Michigan State University, 1962.

Brookover, W. B.; Patterson, A.; and Thomas, S. "Self-concept of Ability and School Achievement." *Sociology of Education* 37 (1964): 271–278.

Brookover, W. B.; LePere, J. M.; Hamachek, D. E.; Thomas, S.; and Erikson, E. L. *Self-concept of Ability and School Achievement, II: Improving Academic Achievement Through Students' Self-Concept Enhancement.* U. S. Office of Education, Cooperative Research Project No. 2831. East Lansing: Office of Research and Publications, Michigan State University, 1965.

Colman, J. S.; Campbell, E. Q.; Hobson, C. J.; McPortland, J.; Mood, A. M.; Weinfeld, F. D.; and York, R. L. *Equality of Education Opportunity.* U. S. Office of Education. Washington, D.C.: Department of Health, Education, and Welfare (1966).

Combs, A. W., and Soper, D. *The Relationship of Child Perceptions to Achievement and Behavior in the Early School Years.* U. S. Office of Education, Cooperative Research Project No. 814. Washington, D.C.: Department of Health, Education, and Welfare (1963).

Combs, A. W., et al. *Florida Studies in the Helping Professions.* University of Florida Social Science Monograph No. 37, 1969.

Coopersmith, S. *The Antecedents of Self-esteem.* San Francisco: Freeman, 1967.

Dinkmeyer, D., and Dreikurs, R. *Encouraging Children to Learn: The Encouragement Process.* Englewood Cliffs, N. J.: Prentice-Hall, 1963.

Dolan, K. G. "Effects of Individual Counseling on Selected Test Scores for Delayed Readers." *Personnel and Guidance Journal* 42 (1964): 914–917.

Engle, K. B.; Davis, D. A.; and Meyer, G. "Interpersonal Effects on Underachievers." *Journal of Educational Psychology* 61 (1968): 208–210.

Fox, D. J., and Schwartz, P. M. Effective Interaction Between Older and Younger Pupils in an Elementary School Peace Corps Project. Final Report, City University of New York, City College, School of Education, 1967.

Gillham, I. "Self-concept and Reading." *The Reading Teacher* 21 (1967): 270–273.

Hastorf, A.; Schneider, D.; and Polefka, J. *Person Perception* Reading, Mass.: Addison Wesley, 1970.

Hoffman, M. "Moral Development." In *Carmichael's Manual of Child Psychology*. 3rd ed., vol. 2, edited by Paul H. Mussen, New York: Wiley, 1970.

Keister, M. E. "The Behavior of Young Children in Failure: An Experimental Attempt to Discover and to Modify Undesirable Responses of Preschool Children to Failure." *University of Iowa Studies in Child Welfare* 4 (1938): 27–82.

Keister, M. E., and Updegraff, R. "A Study of Children's Reactions to Failure and an Experimental Attempt to Modify Them." *Child Development* 8 (1937): 241–248.

Lefcourt, H. M. "Internal Versus External Control of Reinforcement: A Review." *Psychological Bulletin* 65 (1966): 206–220.

Lewin, K. "Decisions and Social Change." In *Readings in Social Psychology*, edited by T. M. Newcourt and E. L. Hartley. New York: Holt, Rinehart, and Winston, 1947.

Lippitt, R., and White, R. K. "The Social Climate of Children's Groups." In *Child Behavior and Development*, edited by J. S. Kounin and H. F. Wright. New York: McGraw-Hill, 1943.

Ludwig, D. J., and Maehr, M. L. "Changes in Self-concept and Stated Behavioral Preferences." *Child Development* 38 (1967): 453–467.

McCandless, B. *Children: Behavior and Development*. 2d ed. New York: Holt, Rinehart, and Winston, 1967.

Mead, G. H. *Mind, Self and Society from the Standpoint of a Social Behaviorist*, edited by C. W. Morris. Chicago: University of Chicago Press, 1934.

Morse, W. C. "Self-concept in the School Setting." *Childhood Education* 41 (1964): 195–198.

Nimnicht, G.; MacAfee, O.; and Meier, J. *The New Nursery School*. New York: General Learning Corp., 1969.

Orne, M. T. "On the Social Psychology of the Psychological Experiment with Particular Reference to Demand Characteristics and Their Implications." *American Psychologist* 17 (1962): 776–783.

Page, E. "Teacher Comments and Student Performance: A Seventy-four Classroom Experiment in School Motivation." *Journal of Educational Psychology* 49 (1958): 173–181.

Quimby, V. "Differences in the Self–Ideal Relationship of an Achieved Group and an Underachieved Group." *California Journal of Educational Research* 18 (1967): 23–31.

Rosenthal, R., and Jacobsen, L. *Pygmalion in the Classroom: Teacher Expectation and Pupils' Intellectual Development*. New York: Holt, Rinehart, and Winston, 1968.

Rotter, J. B. "Generalized Expectancies for Internal Versus External Control of Reinforcement." *Psychological Monographs*, 80 (1, Whole No. 609), 1966.

Shaw, M., and Alves, G. "The Self-concept of Bright Academic Underachievers: II." *Personnel and Guidance Journal* 42 (1963): 401–403.

Wattenberg, W. W., and Clifford, C. "Relation of Self-concepts to Beginning Achievement in Reading." *Child Development* 35 (1964): 461–467.

Weiner, B., et al. *Perceiving the Causals of Success and Failure*. New York: General Learning Press, 1971.

Weiner, B., et al. "Causal Ascriptions and Achievement Behavior: The Conceptual Analysis of Effort." *Journal of Personality and Social Psychology* 21 (1972): 239–248.

Wylie, R. C. *The Self-concept: A Critical Survey of Pertinent Research Literature*. Lincoln: University of Nebraska Press, 1961.

8 · Intelligence in the classroom: Individualized curriculum based on intelligence test patterns

MARY N. MEEKER
Loyola University of Los Angeles

KEY CONCEPTS

Intelligence

IQ

Theory of human intelligence

Model of human intelligence

IQ or intelligence tests

Diagnostic patterns of intellectual abilities

Diagnostic-based individualized instruction

Recently, a staff of education professors decided to revise their teacher-training procedures. They felt that students who wanted to become teachers should have classroom experiences with children as early as their sophomore year. It was reasoned that this would make the education of teachers more relevant and would act as a stimulant for involving and motivating future teachers. The staff was not prepared for, nor had they foreseen, the consequences of their "higher education innovation," for when the student teachers (sophomores, juniors, and seniors) were exposed to real-life teaching situations, many of them found that though they knew well the subject matter they hoped to teach, they did not know children very well. They learned not only that students were children but, in fact, many found that they did not even like children.

And so what would have been a future shock (that teachers teach children, not subject matter) became a present shock. Consequently, as a result of this innovation approximately one-third of the would-be future teachers changed their majors. The children who would have been students of these teachers were spared a binding experience with teachers who would have been unhappy and would have probably adversely affected them. At the undergraduate level, the decision not to enter teaching and to change one's major is relatively inexpensive and nondisruptive, but after four or five years of schooling such a change is expensive and can be quite disruptive.

Perhaps teachers are born, not made—who knows? But in teaching, one thing is certain: The learner's intelligence and other developmental characteristics are of paramount importance in the learning situation.

Yet the process of schooling continues to proceed as though (1) the curriculum of the classroom is subject matter and nothing more and (2) that subject matter can be transmitted to any student merely by using the correct methodology.

So a second shock awaits the new teacher. He soon realizes that curriculum is not now, nor has it ever been, organized or developed in accordance with any child's individual ability to learn. The curriculum has not been based on a theory or model of human intelligence.

The future teacher, in his undergraduate course in developmental psychology, has learned the various ages and stages of growth, but he probably has not learned that some of his students also have other individual differences that are much more likely to affect their ability to learn. For example, most subject matter content is presented visually, but many students will not be visual learners—they will be auditory learners or tactile learners. Consequently, their not learning visually presented material is a result of a preference for a very individual mode of learning rather than a low level of intelligence. (See Chapter 9 by Sigel and Coop for other differences in styles of learning.) And how is the teacher to know this? Rarely will it be demonstrated to the student teacher that even when students have identical or similar IQ scores, each has his own unique patterns of intellectual abilities. And even though the future teacher has had a course on "individualization," the essence of individualizing will again have been oriented toward subject matter. That is, the teacher has learned that to individualize the curriculum the pace is either slowed down or speeded up; the content is broken down into different size units, depending on the ability of the learner to consume it. It is written down for some learners and presented verbally for others. Certain student responses are rewarded, and others are not. However, it is likely that the individual child's unique intellectual pattern for learning is unknown to the teacher. In some schools teachers will have access to group IQ scores and will have discussed IQ ranges and expectations. In most schools, however, the individual's pattern of intelligence has neither been diagnosed nor related in any way to procedures designed to produce efficient learning for that individual.

Not all of the problems a teacher faces stem from inadequate or insufficient training. Some of the problems facing the teacher stem directly from the organizational structure of the school. These problems are likely to be so deeply rooted in the school systems as to be outside the teacher's control. (See Chapter 2 by Schlechty for a further discussion of these problems.) But within a teacher's domain, and included in those matters over which he does have direct control and responsibility, is knowledge of the intellectual, social, emotional, physiological-neurological conditions of students. These areas of personality are as important to the teacher as knowledge of subject matter. He must know these characteristics of his students if he is to individualize instruction and be accountable ultimately for his students' learning. The thing that must matter most to the teacher is information about how the individual student is equipped as a learner. A teacher's mastery of his subject is a necessary but not sufficient part of his preparation for teaching.

This chapter will describe theoretical information concerned specifically with the body of knowledge relating to intelligence. The reader is cautioned that intelligence is only one aspect of the child; knowledge about physiological and emotional differences is equally important, for these characteristics of students also affect learning.

TRADITIONAL USE OF IQ SCORES

Conventional thought is that an IQ is a global number and that certain IQ scores indicate certain intellectual limits. This pervasive assumption stems from the school of thought that there is a g factor of general intelligence, and that somehow all other aspects of intellectual functioning are specific abilities stemming from but not part of the general factor of intelligence. We could diagram it in the model shown in Figure 8-1.

This traditional concept of general intelligence has been one of the invidious and pervasive troublemakers for children who need specific types of curricula if their own individual patterns of intellectual abilities are to be utilized to facilitate their learning. Traditionally, the training of teachers has resulted in the belief that any IQ score that appears in a student's cumulative folder has predictive validity for expected achievement. The teacher most likely has not been trained to ask questions such as:

1. Is the score derived from a group test? Which test?
2. On whom was the test validated?
3. Eighty-one percent predictive correlation validity sounds good, but what does it mean?

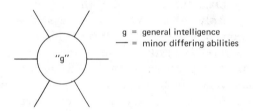

g = general intelligence
— = minor differing abilities

Figure 8-1

4. What kind of population made up the norm or distribution?
5. Were Mexicans, Puerto Ricans, blacks, Indians, poor, rich, retarded, and gifted included in the sample?
6. Was the test normed in the East? West? South? North? Nationwide?

Group IQ tests give notably erratic scores over time. Different IQ tests contain different questions, and individual children will make different scores on different tests. With the "old" way of thinking, this circumstance probably doesn't matter too much if the child stays within a certain range, say 100–115 (high average), because he is expected to do slightly better than average work. But what if he doesn't? What about those who do much better or much worse? Again, without questioning the score and its projected meaning, we have basic assumptions or coined words to describe these children. They are overachievers or underachievers. The latter label may be understandable and may even be defensible, but the former, an overachiever, is indefensible—if he's done it, he's done it. Then a major retort from teachers becomes, "Well, the IQ score is wrong." Never is this comment heard more frequently than when a child is tested and found to place in a gifted score range. If he is not doing well in school, the teacher quickly maintains, "The test is wrong! Look at his spelling!" Or when a child is referred for testing for a program for the gifted and his score is average, even though he makes straight As, it's easy for the teacher to say, "The test is wrong."

It seems that teachers find it difficult to accept the possibility that the intelligence test may be correct in what it measures (validity), and it is *their* understanding of the meaning of the student's individual pattern of intelligence that is incorrect.

There is an obvious reason why teachers don't understand and utilize the individual's pattern of intellectual abilities. Most intelligence tests are not based on a theory or model of human intelligence and thus do not provide the user with information about patterns of intellectual abilities. In fact, the first IQ test in the early 1900s (Simon and Binet) had only one goal—to develop test questions that would, if incorrectly answered, identify "those children who could not learn traditional subject matter in school"—the forerunners of our current educable mental retardates.

Today, however, we need intelligence tests that do more than serve as screening devices. There is a great need for theoretically based IQ tests that will provide the teacher with diagnostic information on which he or she can make instructional decisions for a given child. The present *Stanford-Binet* IQ test measures many different aspects of intellectual functioning and has the potential of providing teachers with much of this diagnostic information. The Wechsler scales also have this potential. The diagnostic potentiality of these IQ scales will be explained later in this chapter. But before that is discussed there is a need to describe how intelligence test scores tend to be distributed and to explain the significance of this for predicting achievement. The reader must remember that predicting academic achievement is by far the most common use of IQ scales and that these predictions are usually based on a single IQ score.

The unitary or single IQ score has been an expensive commodity, with years of research and much money being spent in attempting to predict overall achievement. What the teacher must know if he is to teach a child well, if he is to individualize for a child, and if he is to be held accountable is not how well the child's general achievement can be predicted but rather how the child's unique pattern of intelligence, his unique abilities to learn, can be utilized to better teach him.

Intelligence tests are constructed so that they will yield a normal distribution of scores. This means that the average score is established as 100, and that the largest number of persons obtain scores around this average score of 100 near the middle of the distribution. Also, the further a score is from the average, the smaller the number of individuals who make that score. Specifically, based on the statistics of the normal distribution for large groups of individuals, such as the population of the United States, our expectations would be that 14 percent of all persons would obtain IQ scores between 70 and 85; 68 percent would obtain IQ scores between 85 and 115; and about 14 percent would obtain scores between 115 and 130 (superior students). An additional 2 percent would obtain scores over 130 and would be considered potentially gifted, with another 2 percent receiving IQs below 70 and being considered retarded.

Due to accidents, inutero, perinatal birth damage, cultural and environmental factors, nutritional deficits, and drug damage, the theoretically expected lower 2 percent is increased to an estimated 3–5 percent or more. Thus the population of children in low socioeconomic areas, where nutrition and pre- and postnatal care are inadequate, drug ingestion is a way of life, poverty and lack of education are the rule, there is low familial intelligence, there is little or no inducement to learn, and a different language is spoken by preference, will yield a distribution of intelligence scores shifted to the lower extreme. For these groups there will be an average IQ score, not of 100, but of approximately 87. This cultural differential of thirteen points found so frequently in disadvantaged children (Canadian Indians, Samoans, poor blacks, poor whites, bilinguals, and so on) may be called the thirteen-point disadvantaged differential. Figure 8-2 shows how the distribution for these disadvantaged populations differs from the normal distribution. The statistics for the disadvantaged population are such that the distribution of the expected normal curve tends to be flattened.

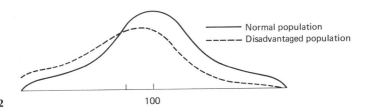

Normal population
Disadvantaged population

Figure 8–2   100

This has the effect of making it easier to predict academic achievement, because the number of persons at the lower end of the distribution, where it is easier to predict achievement, is increased and the number in the middle of the distribution, where it is most difficult to predict achievement, is decreased.

It is as though statisticians and test makers consider a high predictive validity correlation as the criterion of truth. In the past such use of test results may have been acceptable, but today's teacher needs to know more. That is, the teacher soon learns that the score in the cumulative folder does not account for performance across the various courses of study as validly as is imputed by the correlation. He is left empty and frustrated, because the credibility is so deceiving.

Can a diagnostically useful pattern of abilities be derived from the IQ test? Can the test be related to a model of intelligence so as to give meaning to such a profile? If the answer to these questions is Yes, then with the investment of a little more time and training, a more useful outcome could be realized from IQ testing. As it stands now, the situation is comparable to purchasing the finest automobile made today without being given a manual to explain how to properly drive and maintain it. The IQ test is like the car, expensive to make and expensive to get, but limited in use if there is no manual for the utilization and maintenance of it.

Let me repeat that at the present time most children are routinely given *group* IQ tests of mental ability in order to determine where they should be placed and/or what is to be expected of them in the way of learning. Most of these tests yield a general (global) IQ score. For these group-administered IQ tests there is not yet a solution to the questions posed above, although we hope to have one available eventually. However, if the individually administered *Stanford-Binet* or *WISC IQ* test is used, there is currently available a method whereby diagnostic patterns of intellectual abilities based on a model of intelligence can be derived. The model of intelligence used is the structure of intellect (SOI) developed by Guilford (1956). The teacher, counselor, or psychologist can use a procedure designed by Meeker (1965) and based on the SOI model to develop from this test a profile of a child's individual intellectual pattern as it is reflected and measured at the time of testing.

Important here is the fact that the individual's profile reflects intra-individual differences, the real basis of individualized instruction. Intelligence test scores alone show only interindividual differences, and it may be much more useful to look at intraindividual differences, because these cut across subject areas. This could help to reduce the disappointment experienced by teachers when they realize that the child's IQ score is predictive of his performance in some subject areas but not in others.

GUILFORD'S STRUCTURE OF INTELLECT (THE SOI) AS A THEORY OF HUMAN INTELLIGENCE

In 1962 the present author made the first analysis of individual items in individually administered IQ tests in order to analyze the items into their components as defined within Guilford's structure of intellect, thus grounding the intelligence test in a theory of intelligence. Grounding an IQ test in a model of intelligence, it was reasoned, would make possible the identification of intraindividual differences and thus allow remediation of intellectual weaknesses and enhancement of intellectual strengths. Guilford's theory offers the best available possibility for identification of specific, well-defined, measurable, and rather separate intelligence dimensions. Guilford and his associates over a period of 20 years have identified over 90 of the 120 predicted factors (specific intellectual abilities) in intelligence in their model of acculturated abilities, that is, skills coming out of our culture and milieu of expected abilities.

Guilford's theory and model have been well discussed in many journals since 1957, and can be studied in detail in his book *The Nature of Human Intelligence* (1967) and in Meeker's *The Structure of Intellect: Its Interpretation and Uses* (1969a).

At this point it seems appropriate to look at a diagrammatic representation of Guilford's structure of intellect theory of human intelligence. (See Figure 8-3.) An understanding of the major dimensions and subcategories of the SOI is requisite to the discussion of the model's application, which is presented in a later section. These dimensions and subcategories are given in the following outline:

I. Operations: Major kinds of intellectual activities or processes; things the organism does with the raw materials of information, information being defined as "that which the organism discriminates."

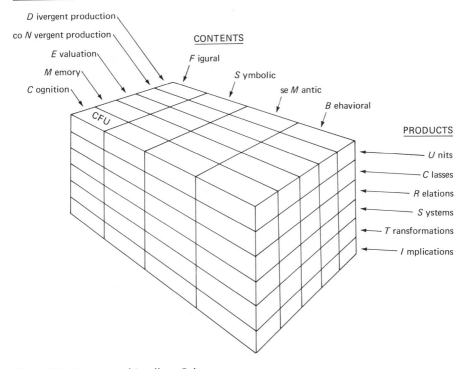

Figure 8–3. Structure of Intellect Cube

A. Cognition (C): Immediate discovery, awareness, rediscovery, or recognition of information in various forms; comprehension or understanding.

B. Memory (M): Retention or storage, with some degree of availability, of information in the same form it was committed to storage and in response to the same cues in connection with which it was learned.

C. Evaluation (E): Reaching decisions or making judgments concerning criterion satisfaction (correctness, suitability, adequacy, desirability, and so on) of information.

D. Convergent production (N): Generation of information from given information, where the emphasis is on achieving unique or conventionally accepted best outcomes. It is likely the given information (cue) fully determines the response.

E. Divergent production (D): Generation of information from given information, where the emphasis is on a variety and quality of output from the same source. Likely to involve what has been called transfer. This operation is most clearly involved in aptitudes of creative potential.

II. Contents: Broad classes or types of information discriminable by the organism.

A. Figural (F): If the contents are figural, they may be shown as shapes, such as trees, forms, or concrete objects, and most of them would be cognized, or comprehended, as visual or kinesthetic forms or totalities.

B. Symbolic (S): If the stimulus material is cognized in the form of a numeral, a single letter, a note of music, or a code symbol, this kind of stimulus, which is distinguishable from a figural one, is called a symbol.

C. Semantics (M): Semantics refers to words and ideas where an abstract meaning is so associated in the individual's repertoire of knowledge that its external referent calls up the internally associated stored word. As one reads the word *tree*, it has meaning and is semantic.

D. Behavioral (B): Perhaps behavioral contents are the most intriguing from the psychologist's point of view. Behavior is both a manifestation of a response and a stimulus. Only a few of the behavioral cell abilities have been identified, and thus they present a new dimension yet to be clarified and yet to be factored within the SOI model.

III. Products: The organization that information takes in the organism's processing of it.

A. Units (U): Figures, for example, can be processed singly, in which case it is a unit that is being perceived; that is, one figure, one symbol, or a single word or idea is a unit.

B. Classes (C): There is a hierarchy implied in the products dimension, for in a sense each product subsumes the preceding one. For example, classes follow units. It is valid to suppose that before one can make classifications or perform a classifying task, one would have to perceive the units to be classified.

C. Relations (R): Following classes, reading down the right side of the model shown in Figure 8-3, is the relations dimension. The individual is asked to process relations or connections between the contents involved—relations between figures, between symbols as in deciphering a code, or between words or ideas (semantics).

D. Systems (S): The next dimension down (Figure 8-3) is that of systems. Systems may be composed of figures, symbols, or semantics. A system can be mathematical, as in arithmetic, where one must comprehend the idea of a sequence of arithmetic operations necessary for solution.

E. Transformations (T): Transformation, the next kind of product, labels a more abstract ability. If a task requires that redefinitions or modifications of the existing information be made into other information, the person is in some way transforming the original material. This kind of ability may demand visual, auditory, abstract, or motor flexibility and has been found to characterize people who have been termed creative.

F. Implications (I): The final and most abstract ability category in the model is implications. The ability to foresee consequences involved in figural problems can be demonstrated visually, vocally, or by motor expression. Maze tracing, a task most commonly found in IQ tests, tests the ability to see implications in figural material.

Thus as you read this material, you are cognizing words and meanings, this process being the cognition (C) of semantics (M), or CM. If you can turn away from this page and repeat all the definitions you have just read, you have demonstrated short-term memory for semantics, MM. If you evaluate the meanings (semantics) of the words, the process is evaluation of semantics, EM; if you reproduce them in order, the process is convergent production of semantics, NM; or if you creatively develop many ways to use the material, the process is divergent production of semantics, DM.

How these inputs are organized relates to the products dimension of the model. Any of the content inputs, F, S, M, or B, can become products singly and labeled a unit, U. They can be classified, C; they may reflect relationships among the inputs, R; they may form a system, S; they can be transformed, T; or the product may be implied, I. For example, simple vocabulary demands the ability called Cognition of seMantic Units, CMU. Whether a child can judge a correct use for a classification would depend on his ability to Evaluate seMantic Classes, EMC. Of course, one could cognize a class, reproduce it, recall it, or reorganize it constructively and originally.

As a model, the SOI has long held the interest of many psychologists, but they did not envision its utility. As the demand for information applicable to classroom learning increased, educational psychologists began to investigate the usefulness of at least one of Guilford's five major operations, divergent production (Torrance, 1970a; Gallagher, 1970; Getzels and Jackson, 1962; Williams, F., 1965).

Divergent production has been defined loosely as creativity, or creative intelligence. Since many psychologists believe that the creativity aspect of this operation is an ability that needs to be developed in young children, several divergent production tests have been developed for testing children. Concurrently, educators, recognizing the need to give special educational services to gifted children, began testing gifted children with these tests. It was at that time that this author,

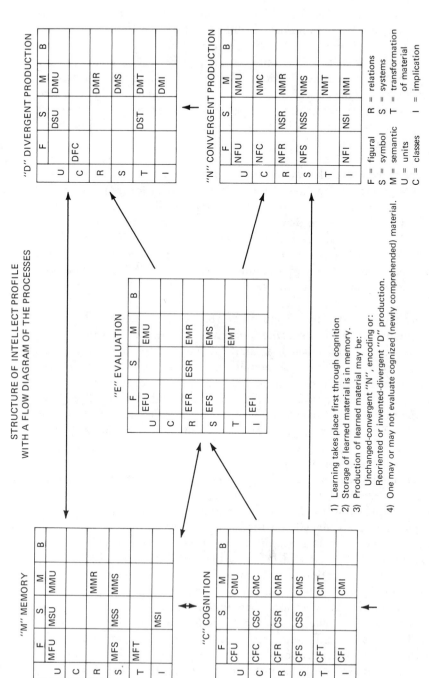

STRUCTURE OF INTELLECT PROFILE
WITH A FLOW DIAGRAM OF THE PROCESSES

"D" DIVERGENT PRODUCTION

	F	S	M	B
U	DFC	DSU	DMU	
C			DMR	
R			DMS	
S			DMT	
T		DST		
I			DMI	

"N" CONVERGENT PRODUCTION

	F	S	M	B
U	NFU	NSU	NMU	
C	NFC		NMC	
R	NFR	NSR	NMR	
S	NFS	NSS	NMS	
T			NMT	
I	NFI	NSI	NMI	

"E" EVALUATION

	F	S	M	B
U	EFU	ESU	EMU	
C				
R	EFR	ESR	EMR	
S	EFS		EMS	
T			EMT	
I	EFI			

"M" MEMORY

	F	S	M	B
U	MFU	MSU	MMU	
C				
R			MMR	
S	MFS	MSS	MMS	
T	MFT			
I		MSI		

"C" COGNITION

	F	S	M	B
U	CFU	CSU	CMU	
C	CFC	CSC	CMC	
R	CFR	CSR	CMR	
S	CFS	CSS	CMS	
T	CFT		CMT	
I	CFI		CMI	

F = figural   R = relations
S = symbol   S = systems
M = semantic   T = transformation
U = units   of material
C = classes   I = implication

1) Learning takes place first through cognition
2) Storage of learned material is in memory.
3) Production of learned material may be:
   Unchanged-convergent "N", encoding or:
   Reoriented or invented-divergent "D" production.
4) One may or may not evaluate cognized (newly comprehended) material.

Figure 8-4

having been a student of Guilford's, saw the need for going beyond an IQ score and for identifying different kinds of giftedness in intelligence. Flow charts were developed to analyze test items for their component parts. Thus by analyzing an item, one can determine (1) the mental operation required, (2) the kind of content dealt with, and (3) the type of product produced. Each of these components is then represented by the appropriate symbol and combined to form a trigraph. The trigraph is a combination of three symbols, one indicating the mental *operation*, another referring to the *content*, and the other depicting the *product*. This procedure has made intelligence test data much more adaptable for computer and personal use.

It was considered necessary, however, to make a transformation of the model of the SOI, which was depicted as a three-dimensional matrix. The model of cubes was taken apart and two-dimensionalized so as to provide a profile of the actual responses for any child (see Figure 8-4), regardless of his IQ score. This resultant profile would allow the psychologist and the teacher to note any intellectual patterns of strengths or weaknesses in operations, contents, or products as they occurred in the *Stanford-Binet* test.

You will note that each of the blocks represents a particular mental *operation*, that each of the columns in a block represents a kind of *content*, and that each of the rows in a block represents a *product*. When a given child responds to any test item in the *Stanford-Binet* test, it is possible to select the appropriate block for the mental operation, the appropriate column for the kind of content, and the appropriate row for the resulting product. If the child responds correctly to the item, a plus is recorded in the proper cell (or the point where the column and row identifying the content and product intersect) in the identified block. If the item is missed, a minus is recorded in the identified cell. When this kind of analysis is done for a complete test, it is possible to add up and compare the number of correct answers and the number of wrong answers for *each* operation, for *each* content, and for *each* product.

The structure of intellect (SOI) profile (see Figure 8-4) can also be explained in terms of how information processing is accomplished. Follow the arrows beginning in the lower left corner. The organism first cognizes or comprehends (C) a stimulus. He may then store the information in memory (M) or evaluate (E) it and decide to forget it (or to store it), or he may be expected to reproduce the correct solution, convergent production (N), without ever evaluating or storing the material.

The two-dimensional convergent production (N) square, which appears in the lower right-hand corner of Figure 8-4, is called the "school block of abilities," because in teaching we so frequently tend to expect exact regurgitation rather than the use of evaluation or other abilities. Seldom do we teach cognition alone before expecting convergent production. Simple comprehending or stimulation without testing is rare in the schoolroom. That cognition occurs is taken for granted. A good description of cognition is that it is like TV viewing, where the individual is stimulated and interested but does not have to pay the price for his interest by being tested. Equally rare is the teacher who teaches evaluation skills; yet evaluation skills may be more important for everyday living than the other abilities.

APPLICATIONS OF SOI TO EDUCATION

When the SOI model began to be used to analyze IQ test responses, the evidence showed unmistakably and graphically that children of the same age with similar IQ scores have very different patterns of abilities. Furthermore, some abilities were seemingly much more necessary for success in school learning than others.

That a student fails twenty memory items out of twenty-two on the *Binet*, even though his IQ score is above 100, may not be important in traditional test theory, but to the teacher and parent this evidence is quite helpful in understanding why he is unable to learn. Furthermore, such evidence provides the foundation for the specification of a remediation program. The failing of twenty out of the twenty-two memory items on the *Binet* typifies the pattern found in children who do not learn academic material and who are categorized as educationally handicapped. When their *Stanford-Binet* test scores are analyzed into SOI profiles, this pattern is found regardless of whether the student is in Canada, any state in the United States, or American Samoa, and regardless of his IQ score.

Consider the school psychologist and the teacher who have this information about the student in question. They are now able to specify the exact intellectual abilities that need developing. With such diagnostic information, an individually prescribed program to remedy the problem for the child can be developed. The educational psychologist can turn away from the medical-clinical model of test interpretation, which is typically psychoanalytic; he can take Freud out of the schoolroom and put him back in the clinic from whence he originally came.

The psychologist can now say to the teacher: Give this child this kind of memory training, and we can expect to observe improvement in these abilities and a consequent improvement in school learning. Workbooks have been designed for just this purpose, and the teacher can individualize teaching for the child's intellectual differences, using whatever subject matter he sees fit, for these abilities cut across subject matter (Meeker and Sexton, 1971).

A recent investigation has added to the theoretical base for the use of the SOI model for remedying intellectual disabilities. Ball (1973), having studied SOI abilities in 3-, 4-, and 5-year-olds, was interested in learning whether the disabilities were stable over time. She found that the abilities were not stable. A child strong in cognition at age four might not still possess this strength when tested a year later. It was found that environmental variables played an important role in the stability of abilities.

Recent research has also demonstrated the utility of the SOI pattern analysis for improving classroom instruction. A sample of the findings of the most recent studies is described here. Children who do not learn to read by the end of the first grade and who are not mentally defective generally show deficits in the evaluation of figural units (EFU), in memory for figural units (MFU), and in the cognition of figural units (CFU). These deficits tend to exist for both auditory and visual tasks (Feldman, 1971).

A study by Hess (1972) used four classes of incoming first graders in four schools. Two were control groups and received the typical "good" first grade reading program. Two other classes received SOI workbook tasks in the areas diagnosed as individual weaknesses plus work in those abilities identified by Feldman (1971) as underlying reading. The teachers were given in-service training, so they would learn the model and how to organize their material accordingly. At the end of 4½ months the control group with the "good" traditional reading program showed no gains on standard reading tests. The experimental group, which did not receive reading instruction but received training to develop the specified SOI abilities, made significantly higher scores on the standard reading tests.

SPECIFIC PATTERNS OF ABILITIES ON THE STRUCTURE OF INTELLECT MODEL

Following are some structure of intellect profiles that typify different learning problems.

Profile No. 1, shown in Figure 8-5, is from a seventeen-year-old male student. Note the poor evaluation abilities; the student answered only four of sixteen evaluation items correctly. Yet his cognition is very high, his score on this being 27/31. His memory for semantics is also weak, as he missed all five such items. The suggested program designed to improve this boy's cognitive ability consisted of individually prescribed tasks for each specific weakness to be pursued three times

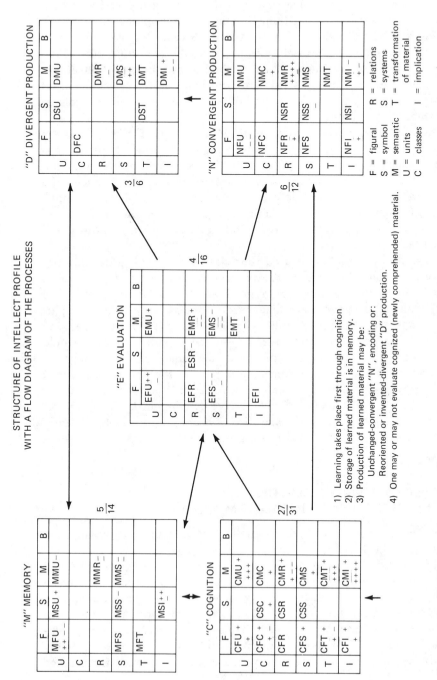

Figure 8–5. Profile No. 1

a week for 20 minutes a day. After two years of this work, he went into regular classes and was graduated from high school. Parenthetically, he had no further difficulties in school. With his past history he would have probably been a dropout had there been no intervention.

Profile No. 2, shown in Figure 8-6, is of a gifted girl in the primary grades who was having learning problems that were so severe her family wanted to place her in a private school. They blamed the school for making her a failure. Note the symbolic weakness reflected in the fact that she missed all nine test items dealing with symbolic content, giving her a profile score of 0/9 in the symbolic content category. Her educational program became totally remedial for symbolic tasks.

CASE HISTORY: WILLIAM BAKER, JR.

William Baker, Jr., whose profile is given in Figure 8-7, typifies perfectly the educationally handicapped student. He has an average IQ score (91) and after 6 years in school still does not read.

Bill remained in the first grade two years, and even then was promoted to the second grade over the "better judgment" of his first grade teacher, who believed he was "still not doing first grade work." While generally described as slightly below average in mathematics performance, William has exhibited persistent reading problems, of which even he is painfully aware. Although enrolled in a remedial reading class for several months in the third grade, his performance apparently did not improve noticeably. A year later his fourth grade teacher summed up the situation: "William has not acquired basic reading skills —he has difficulty reading even the simplest passages and cannot follow the class in reading assignments." This same teacher, it should be pointed out, also recommended that William would be "better off" in a special education class. (Note failures in memory, where he missed eleven out of twelve items).

Behaviorally, Bill is not considered to be a discipline problem. (Note good evaluation skills, 8/13). When working with small groups of classmates, he appears alert, good-humored, and interested as the group plans its activities. (Note high cognition, 8/13). In the small group he verbalizes freely and seems to be at ease; his behavior toward group members, as well as their behavior toward him, is generally that of respect.

Bill is above average in psychomotor skills and is well coordinated. These psychomotor traits, coupled with his easygoing and at times enthusiastic manner, rank him near the top of his peers in physical education activities.

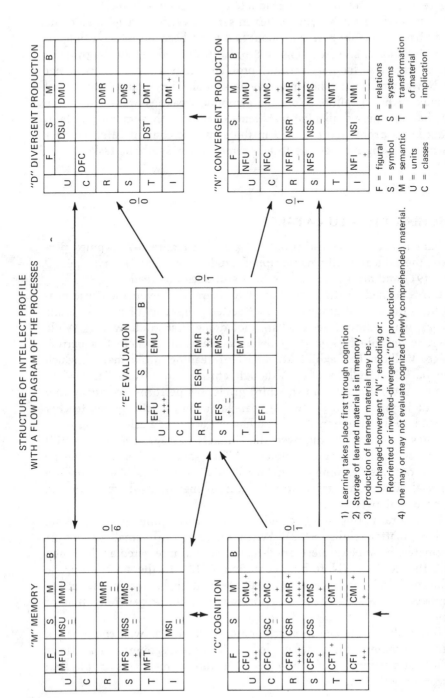

STRUCTURE OF INTELLECT PROFILE
WITH A FLOW DIAGRAM OF THE PROCESSES

"D" DIVERGENT PRODUCTION

	F	S	M	B
U	DFC	DSU	DMU	
C			DMR −	
R			DMS +++	
S		DST	DMT	
T			DMI + − −	
I				

0|0

"N" CONVERGENT PRODUCTION

	F	S	M	B
U	NFU − −	NSU	NMU +	
C	NFC −	NSS	NMC +	
R	NFR −	NSR	NMR +++	
S	NFS	NSS −	NMS	
T			NMT	
I	NFI +	NSI	NMI	

0|1

F = figural   R = relations
S = symbol   S = systems
M = semantic   T = transformation
U = units   of material
C = classes   I = implication

"E" EVALUATION

	F	S	M	B
U	EFU +++	ESU	EMU	
C				
R	EFR	ESR −	EMR +++	
S	EFS + − −	EMS − − −		
T			EMT − −	
I	EFI			

0|1

1) Learning takes place first through cognition
2) Storage of learned material is in memory.
3) Production of learned material may be:
    Unchanged-convergent "N", encoding or:
    Reoriented or invented-divergent "D" production.
4) One may or may not evaluate cognized (newly comprehended) material.

"M" MEMORY

	F	S	M	B
U	MFU −	MSU − −	MMU −	
C				
R	MFS + −	MSS − −	MMR − − MMS + −	
S	MFT			
T		MSI − −		
I				

0|6

"C" COGNITION

	F	S	M	B
U	CFU + −	CSU	CMU + +++	
C	CFC −	CSC	CMC +	
R	CFR +++	CSR	CMR + +++	
S	CFS	CSS	CMS +	
T	CFT + − −		CMT − − − −	
I	CFI + +++		CMI + + − −	

0|1

Figure 8–6. Profile No. 2

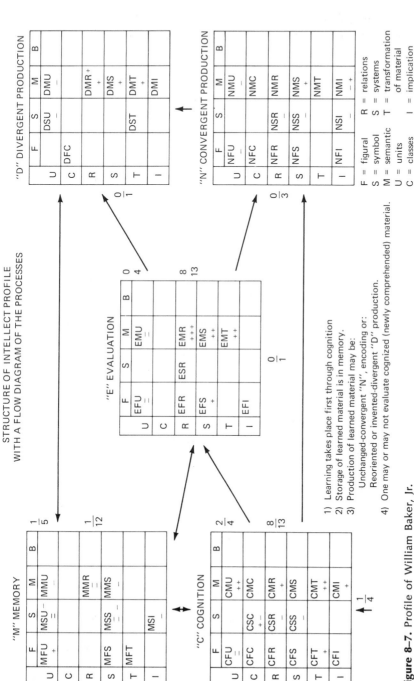

STRUCTURE OF INTELLECT PROFILE
WITH A FLOW DIAGRAM OF THE PROCESSES

"D" DIVERGENT PRODUCTION

	F	S	M	B
U		DSU −	DMU −	
C	DFC			
R			DMR+ +	
S			DMS +	
T		DST	DMT +	
I			DMI −	

$\frac{0}{1}$

"N" CONVERGENT PRODUCTION

	F	S	M	B
U	NFU −	NSR −	NMU −	
C	NFC −		NMC −	
R	NFR −	NSR	NMR −	
S	NFS −	NSS −	NMS +	
T			NMT −	
I	NFI −	NSI −	NMI − +	

$\frac{0}{3}$

"E" EVALUATION

	F	S	M	B
U	EFU − −	ESR	EMU − −	
C				
R	EFR −	EFR	EMR +++	
S	EFS +	ESR	EMS + +	
T			EMT + +	
I	EFI			

$\frac{0}{1}$
$\frac{0}{4}$
$\frac{8}{13}$

"M" MEMORY

	F	S	M	B
U	MFU +	MSU − −	MMU −	
C				
R			MMR − −	
S	MFS −	MSS − −	MMS −	
T	MFT			
I		MSI −		

$\frac{1}{5}$
$\frac{1}{12}$

"C" COGNITION

	F	S	M	B
U	CFU − −	CSC	CMU + +	
C	CFC −	CSC + −	CMC −	
R	CFR +	CSR −	CMR +	
S	CFS −	CSS −	CMS −	
T	CFT −		CMT + +	
I	CFI −		CMI +	

$\frac{2}{4}$
$\frac{8}{13}$
$\frac{1}{4}$

1) Learning takes place first through cognition
2) Storage of learned material is in memory.
3) Production of learned material may be:
   Unchanged-convergent "N", encoding or:
   Reoriented or invented-divergent "D" production.
4) One may or may not evaluate cognized (newly comprehended) material.

F = figural	R = relations
S = symbol	S = systems
M = semantic	T = transformation
U = units	of material
C = classes	I = implication

Figure 8–7. Profile of William Baker, Jr.

The *Sequential Test of Educational Progress*, administered during the last quarter of fifth grade, credited Bill with a math level at the 9th percentile (note low symbolic responses, 1/16) and a reading level at the 1st percentile (note poor units, 3/17, and memory, 1/12).

CASE HISTORY: SHEILA SMITH

Sheila Smith, whose profile is shown in Figure 8–8, is an 11-year-old student in Mrs. Fowler's class. Sheila is somewhat of a tomboy and is very interested in how things work. (Note high relations.) Her non-language IQ on the *California Test of Mental Maturity* was 126, and her language IQ was 120. She is at the 90th percentile in math achievement and at the 55th percentile in reading.

Her first grade teacher noted that Sheila entered school at the age of five and "does not apply herself with diligence, because she is still immature." Mrs. Barker, her second grade teacher, suggested that Sheila did "not work up to her potential" and spent "too much time fooling around with the things on her desk." In the third grade Sheila was described as "an intelligent, eager student, but she would have better results if she worked slower and more carefully. She is a real talker." Her fourth grade teacher observed that Sheila "is quite good at arithmetic [high symbolic] but has very little interest in reading [low cognition]. She frequently fails to ask for help with her work when she needs it and consequently has to redo it [low systems]."

On the basis of this profile, therapy for emotional growth would be recommended after a thorough check for learning disabilities. (Note high memory and low cognition, mixed units strength, and low divergent production.) Though her teacher thinks she is "creative," the relations strength is deceivingly representing creativity. Low cognition and poor units coupled with hyperactivity often indicate minimal brain damage (MBD), and her teacher, Mrs. Fowler, should use this information together with other observations of Sheila's behavior in considering the need to refer Sheila for a more extensive psychological examination by the school psychologist.

USE OF PROFILES FOR REMEDIATION

The importance of a model or theory of intelligence in which to anchor education is obvious. Educational practice has never been based on a theory of human intelligence. The defined abilities in Guilford's model offer great utility for this purpose. The model is a very positive one, with one of its principal assumptions being that abilities can be

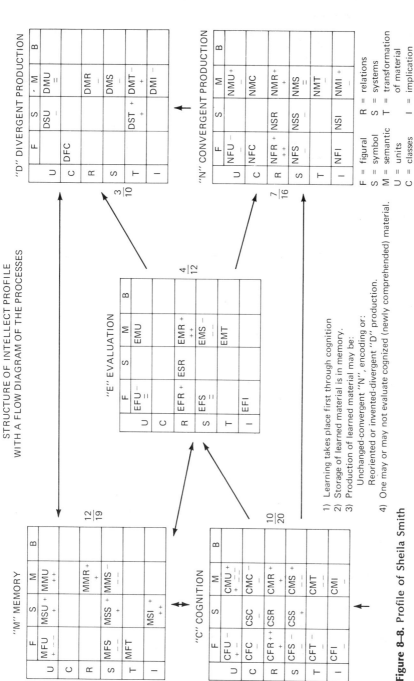

Figure 8–8. Profile of Sheila Smith

changed (Christensen, 1963). Furthermore, in this model the important instruments of change are teachers. The teacher, knowing the precise measured abilities of any given student, can actually develop intellectual tasks that will remedy the individual student's deficiencies or enhance his skills, because the definitions of the tasks in the model lend themselves to precise teaching objectives. For example, a teacher of the children whose profiles you have just studied can now quite readily identify individual strengths and weaknesses and provide a curriculum that will enhance the development of specific abilities. Further training can prepare the teacher to develop his own materials for these purposes. For specific examples of these types of materials, see Meeker and Sexton's *Structure of Intellect Abilities Workbook* (1971).

CONCLUSION

There is a current movement to eliminate all intelligence testing, because some children do not do as well as others on intelligence tests and because the test results are misused in practice. It is understandable that some people want to throw out intelligence testing, especially since judgments are usually based on an interpretation of global scores. This kind of thinking has led to self-fulfilling prophecies and phenomena such as that described in Rosenthal and Jacobson's *Pygmalion in the Classroom* (1968). (Also see Chapter 3 by Good and Brophy.) But educators should be careful not to do away with IQ tests just because global scores have been misused and misunderstood in the past. Recent efforts to use the theory of intelligence described in this chapter in the conducting of diagnostically based teaching have indicated that this concept of intelligence can be useful in helping children to learn more effectively.

The concept itself is new. To suggest the use of intelligence testing as a diagnostic procedure and further to suggest the development of a curriculum based on a diagnosis of any one student's intellectual pattern is a step forward in education. As yet such a step has not been widely taken beyond special education efforts. This movement signals growth and points to positive new directions in our profession—directions that are centered on the child rather than subject matter.

Since teaching can never be reduced to a fixed set of rules and formulas, any procedure necessarily has to be applied with sensitivity and care, appropriateness and rationality. The model presented in this chapter is a means of analyzing perplexing problems when ordinary methods do not produce sufficient results for students. Although the structure of intellect model is primarily useful in the development of intellectual skills, these same skills are related to the personality and motivation of the student, and so, indirectly, many peripheral learnings in other aspects of the child's functioning are accomplished. This is serendipity, but it does point out that there is an interrelationship between intelligence, personality, environment, and physical-neurological functioning. Good teaching in any of these areas brings a good return to the teacher and his student in all related areas.

SOME SUGGESTED ACTIVITIES

1. Observe in a classroom situation and analyze the teacher's questions in terms of the mental operations that are a part of Guilford's SOI model. After having observed for an entire class period, compute the percentage of questions that require each of the five mental operations (memory, cognition, convergent production, divergent production, and evaluation). This same procedure can be repeated, analyzing the teacher's questions in terms of the content and product categories. See if you can identify specific patterns for a particular teacher.

2. Analyze a classroom achievement test in terms of the mental operations from Guilford's model. After this has been done for the entire test, compute the percentage of test items in each category. This procedure can be repeated, analyzing the same items in terms of Guilford's content categories and in terms of Guilford's products. See if you can identify a specific pattern for a particular teacher's test.

3. Develop at least three training tasks for each of the mental operations in Guilford's SOI model. The tasks should lead to the development of the mental operations for which they are designed. This same procedure can be repeated by preparing training exercises designed to facilitate the development of specific content and product abilities.

REFERENCES

Ball, Rachel. "A Longitudinal Study of Intellectual Patterns in Disadvantaged Blacks and Whites." *Journal of School Psychology*, 1973 (in press).

Ball, Rachel, and Stott, Leland. *Factor Analyses of Infant Mental Scales.* Detroit: Merrill Palmer, 1964.

Bruch, Catherine. "Reducing the IQ Differential for Blacks on the Binet SOI Factors." Unpublished paper, University of Georgia, n.d.

Bruch, Catherine. "An Analysis of Characteristics and Classroom Behaviors of Effectively Creative Teachers." Unpublished doctoral dissertation, University of California at Los Angeles, 1965.

Buchanan, L., and Baer, C. "A Developmental Approach to Cognitive Processes of Adolescents." Unpublished thesis, Wayne State University, 1971.

Christensen, P. R. *The Function Sharing Approach to Research on Joint Man-Machine Intelligence.*" Santa Monica, California: Systems Development Corporation, 1963.

Feldman, B. "Deficit Skills of Children Who Do Not Learn to Read." Unpublished doctoral dissertation, University of Southern California, 1971.

Fraser, D. "Mental Abilities of British Columbia Indian Children." Unpublished thesis, University of British Columbia, 1968.

Gallagher, J. J. "Peer Acceptance of Highly Gifted Children in Elementary Schools." In *Readings in Educational Psychology*, edited by Victor H. Noll and Rachael P. Noll. New York: Macmillan, 1962.

Gallagher, J. J. *Teaching the Gifted Child.* Boston: Allyn and Bacon, 1970.

Getzels, J. W., and Jackson, P. W. *Creativity and Intelligence: Explorations with Gifted Students,* New York: Wiley, 1962.

Guilford, J. P. "The Structure of Intellect." *Psychological Bulletin* 52 (1956): 267–293.

Guilford, J. P. *The Nature of Human Intelligence.* New York: McGraw-Hill, 1967.

Hebb, D. O. *The Organization of Behavior.* New York: Wiley, 1949.

Hess, J. "Final Report, ESEA, Title III, Glendora California Public Schools." Glendora, California, 1972.

Karradenes, M. "A Comparison of the Differences in Intelligence, Achievement, and Learning Abilities Between Anglo and Mexican Children." Unpublished doctoral dissertation, University of Virginia, 1971.

McGuire, Lenore. "The Influence of the Unique Aspects of Blindness on the Development of Blind Children." Unpublished doctoral dissertation, University of Southern California, 1968.

Meeker, Mary N. "A Procedure for Relating Stanford-Binet Behavior Samplings to Guilford's Structure of the Intellect." *Journal of School Psychology,* 3 (3) (1965): 26–36.

Meeker, Mary N. "Differential Syndromes of Giftedness." *Journal of Special Education* (Winter 1968).

Meeker, Mary N. *The Structure of Intellect: Its Intrepretation and Uses.* Columbus: Charles Merrill, 1969a.

Meeker, Mary N. "A 2-Year Follow-up of High School Problems." *Educational Therapy II,* Seattle: Special Child Publications, 1969b.

Meeker, Mary N., and Sexton, K. M., CSJ, *Structure of Intellect Abilities Workbook.* Los Angeles: Loyola University of Los Angeles, 1971 (limited edition).

Meeker, R. J., and Weiler, D. *Education and Urban Society,* vol. 3, no. 2. Beverly Hills: Sage Publications, 1971.

Merrifield, P. R.; Gardner, S. F.; and Cox, Anna B. "Aptitudes and Personality Measures Related to Creativity in Seventh-Grade Children." *Reports from the Psychological Laboratory* No. 28. Los Angeles: University of Southern California, 1964.

Meyers, C. E.; Dingman, H. F.; Orpet, R. E.; Sitkei, E. G.; and Watts, C. A. "Four Ability Factor Hypotheses at Three Preliterate Levels in Normal and Retarded Children." *Monograph of the Society for Research in Child Development* 29 (5) (1948): 80.

Orpett, R. E., and Meyers, C. E. "A Study of Eight Structure-of-Intellect Hypotheses in Six-Year-Old Children." Report, NIMH Grant No. MHO8666-01, University of Southern California, 1965.

Rogers, C. E. "Towards a Theory of Creativity." In *Creativity and Its Cultivation,* edited by H. H. Anderson. New York: Harper and Row, 1959.

Rogers, C. E. *On Becoming a Person.* Boston: Houghton-Mifflin, 1961.

Rosenthal, R., and Jacobson, L. *Pygmalion in the Classroom.* New York: Holt, Rinehart, and Winston, 1968.

Steele, J. "Does the Binet Yield Patterns of Guilford Operations?" Chicago: University of Illinois Center for Instructional Research, n. d.

Stormer, C. "Dimensions of the Intellect Unmeasured by the Binet." Chicago: University of Illinois, n. d.

Torrance, E. P. "Must Pre-Primary Educational Stimulation Be Incompatible with Creative Development?" In *Creativity at Home and in School,* edited by F. E. Williams, St. Paul: Macalester Creativity Project, Macalester College, 1968.

Torrance, E. P. *Encouraging Creativity in the Classroom,* Dubuque, Ia.: William C. Brown, 1970a.

Torrance, E. P. "Stimulation, Enjoyment, and Originality in Dyadic Creativity." *Experimental Publication System,* Issue No. 7 (1970b), Ms. No. 246-34.

Williams, B. "Comparison of Profiles of EMRs on Binet Retesting for Placement Outside of Special Education Classes," Tracy, Calif.: Tracy School District, n. d.

Williams, Frank E. "Creativity—An Innovation in the Classroom." In *Productive Thinking in Education,* edited by Mary Jane Aschner and Charles E. Bish. Washington, D. C.: The National Education Association, 1965.

Williams, M. "Kindergarten Boys." Unpublished thesis, University of Southern California, 1969.

Wilson, M. P. "The Relation of Sense of Humor to Creativity, Intelligence, and Achievement." Unpublished doctoral dissertation, University of Southern California, 1970.

9 · Cognitive style and classroom practice

IRVING E. SIGEL
Educational Testing Service, Princeton, N. J.

RICHARD H. COOP
University of North Carolina at Chapel Hill

KEY CONCEPTS

analytic style
relational-contextual style
categorical-inferential style
field independence
field dependence
reflectivity
impulsivity

Imagine for a moment that you are sitting in the back of Mrs. Fowler's classroom at Midview School, observing her life sciences class. She is presenting a lecture on the bone structure of the human body to a class of sixth grade students. Mrs. Fowler has a beautifully illustrated chart showing a human figure that has had the outer skin layers removed to depict the underlying bone structure. As she points to the section of the chart that shows the connective tissue between two bones, you begin to wonder what it would be like if you could somehow see inside the thinking processes of each student in this classroom as he sits listening (or pretending to listen) to the teacher. Suppose, for a moment, that we were given the ability to see what each student is looking at or thinking about at this instant. We might find that Mary Cairns is focusing on two little knobs that project from the tips of each of the bones and remind her of spurs on cowboy boots. Stanley Robinson might be trying to relate the graphic artist's use of various colors and shadings to give the chart an illustration of depth. Sheila Smith is having some difficulty separating the tissue that the teacher is pointing out from some of the surrounding muscle fibers that are also included in the drawing. She wishes that the artist had made a clearer distinction between the various tissues and the surrounding muscle fibers. William Baker quickly glances at the chart, but does not immediately see what the teacher is trying to point out and turns his attention to the aquarium on the other side of the room.

Each of the students in this class is being presented with the same stimulus materials by their teacher. All the students have the capability of hearing what the teacher is saying and seeing the area of the chart that Mrs. Fowler is pointing to. Yet each student is attending to different aspects of the stimulus situation, and each is categorizing these different perceptions in a manner that is different from the other students in this class. Although different mental activities are going on within each of the students, the teacher is probably assuming that each student is looking at the same section of the chart and that each is categorizing and, in fact, learning the information she is presenting to them in a similar manner. She proceeds with her lecture on that assumption—namely, that all the students have, in fact, processed the same information and that the information they have processed is the information she intends them to process.

Psychologists and educators have long known and studied the individual differences among students in a given classroom. They have looked at a number of personality and cognitive, or intellectual, factors that might explain these variations found in any group of learners. One of the most intriguing concepts studied in this area has been an information-processing variable called *cognitive style,* a term used to refer to the consistency of patterning that individuals show in responding to various types of situations. It refers to intellectual approaches (for example, categorization of stimuli) and/or to strategies in solving problems (for example, analysis of environmental events). It is a broad concept encompassing a variety of seemingly different behaviors, attitudes, and dispositions. We shall have occasion to discuss this issue in more detail later. This concept reflects an attempt by psychologists to bridge the gap between the individual's personality factors and his cognitive performance. Cognitive style is an integrated concept in that its definition implicitly bridges the personality-cognitive dimensions of the individual.

The term *cognitive style* has been used by a number of psychological investigators to denote the different ways in which children and adults perceive and categorize their environment in particular situations. However, each psychologist has a different meaning in mind when he defines his construct of cognitive style. The definition of style is most frequently expressed by the type of tasks that the researcher uses to elicit the responses on which he classifies his subjects. Therefore, there is some general confusion on the part of many readers when they are examining cognitive style. It is necessary, therefore, to specify which investigator you are using as a reference when using the cognitive style concept. Perhaps an examination of the most frequently used measures of cognitive style will help to clarify this issue. We will present examples of some of these measuring instruments as we discuss the specific style categories in more detail.

FOUR CONCEPTS OF COGNITIVE STYLE

In this chapter we shall confine our discussion to the cognitive styles proposed by four different investigators: Kagan, Moss, and Sigel; Witkin; Gardner; and Broverman. The work of these investigators would seem to hold the most promise for the educational setting at this time. The Kagan, Moss, and Sigel (1963) group defines cognitive style as a "term that refers to stable individual preferences in mode of perceptual organization and conceptual categorization of the external environment" (p. 74). The Kagan group defines three specific stylistic modes as follows: *descriptive-analytic, relational,* and *categorical-inferential.* These modes of perceiving and categorizing are based on subjects' responses to pictorial stimuli such as those presented in Figure 9-1.

A *descriptive-analytic* response reflects the tendency to classify items on the basis of objective, observable characteristics that are *part* of the total stimulus situation. For example, the individual looking at Figure 9-1 might classify figures D and F together because both women have on black shoes. This response is characterized by a splitting of the stimulus situation into discrete parts and attending to these pieces as a basis for categorizing the total stimulus, in essence breaking a unitary stimulus into discrete parts. If you recall the example of Mary Cairns' thought patterns given in our hypothetical classroom situation,

Figure 9–1. Sigel Conceptual Style Test

Directions: Choose two of the three pictures that you think go together, belong together, or are alike in some way. Write the letters of these two pictures, and then tell why you feel these two go together or are alike in some way. There are no right or wrong answers, so just put what you think is best.

you will note that she is focusing on a fraction of the total stimulus situation, the knobs on the bones, and is categorizing this particular situation in terms of these pieces rather than the total situation. This breaking up of the environment into pieces and attending to discrete parts is a behavior indicative of the descriptive-analytic response.

Relational-contextual responses occur when items are grouped together on the basis of functional, temporal, or spatial contiguity. These responses many times reflect a certain story line or theme that integrates the various items characterized together in a relational manner. For example, in Figure 9-1 items E and F may be paired because the maid (F) has the responsibility to clean the house (E). In relational responses no one stimulus can serve as an independent example of the concept— each stimulus must relate to the other stimuli in order to be included as a member of the concept. Stanley Robinson's attempt to integrate the use of colors and shading in the biology chart could be an indication of a relational response based on function.

The *inferential-categorical* classification is illustrated by an individual who chooses to form his categories on the basis of inferences made about the objects he groups together. No one objective characteristic is singled out by the person as the basis of classification. For example, in Figure 9-1, D and F may be paired together because they are both women. Any stimulus object in the group can be an independent example of the classification chosen by the person. Suppose, for illustrative purposes, that the same life sciences class that is presently studying bone structure later attempts to classify certain plants or animals in their respective phyla. We can expect the students to make a large number of inferential categorical responses in this process. For example, man can be classified, on the basis of a number of characteristics, into such categories as vertebrate, mammal, and omnivore. Correspondingly, in English classes words are categorized as certain parts of speech such as nouns and verbs, and the verbs are further divided into categories of transitive and intransitive.

As Kagan pursued his work with these three dimensions of cognitive style, he noticed that many people tended to take a long time to reflect over various stimulus situations before giving a response, and other persons tended to give a very quick response to the tasks presented them. Kagan was intrigued by the difference in rate of response time to tasks having a high degree of response uncertainty (that is, where there are two or more answers that are highly plausible). He developed a test, the Matching Familiar Figures Test (MFF), to obtain measures of response time and errors made by the subjects. Based on this test Kagan proposed a new stylistic dimension called *conceptual tempo.* Conceptual tempo refers to the speed with which an individual responds to a task of high response uncertainty and the number of errors made in the responses. Rapid respondees who make many errors are called *impulsive,* and slower respondees who tend to make few errors are called *reflective.* Kagan found that generally individuals producing descriptive-analytic responses on the Conceptual Styles Test tended to be reflective individuals (long response time and few errors) when they were given the conceptual tempo task. We might hypothesize from William Baker's behavior in the life sciences class that he could have tendencies toward impulsivity (short response time and many errors) *if* his behavior in this one instance is typical of his overall pattern of responding to stimuli. This is a good place to consider the question of the generality of William Baker's behavior. Does the behavior he shows in life sciences class have to be consistent with his behavior in all his classes, or is there something particular about life sciences? You might ask yourself if your own behavior is consistent from class to class. For example, do you make more errors in one subject than another?

A basic distinction should be made at this point in regard to the conceptual tempo-cognitive style concepts. The conceptual tempo test (MFF) requires an *ability* on the part of the student to delay his response time and to make few errors in choosing among similar alternatives. Cognitive style, however, tends to measure a personal *preference* on the part of different individuals in the manner in which they choose to perceive and categorize their environment.

A second major concept of cognitive style is presented by Witkin, Dyk, Faterson, Goodenough, and Hays (1962). Witkin describes a cognitive style based on an *analytic-global* continuum. He determines the extent to which individuals are able to overcome the effects of distracting background elements (the field) when they are attempting to

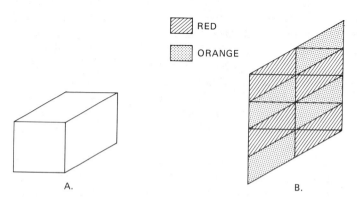

Directions: Find the simple geometric figure (A) in the more complex figure (B).

Figure 9–2. Sample of Simple and Complex Figures of the Embedded Figures Test

differentiate relevant aspects of a particular situation. Figure 9-2 presents an example of one of the tasks Witkin uses to test for the cognitive style of his subjects. This is not unlike the puzzles you may have tried to solve as a child, when line drawings of a squirrel, a rabbit, and a dog were "hidden" in a tree, and you were asked to trace or find these animals. The more independent the person is from the distracting elements, the more analytic he is said to be. Conversely, the more dependent or incapable the individual is of being freed from the distracting elements, the more global. People who are able to operate in an analytic manner are said to be *field-independent,* and people who operate in the more global manner are called *field-dependent.* Look back at the beginning of this chapter at Sheila Smith's thoughts. Do you think Sheila might be field-independent (analytic) or field-dependent (global) in her response patterns? If you think she might be field-independent, you probably need to reread this paragraph.

It is possible that you are a bit confused at this point with the word *analytic* being used as a description of one type of cognitive style by the Kagan group and quite a different cognitive style by Witkin et. al. Witkin does not believe that the two "analytic" modes are the same process at all, and an unpublished study by Coop and Hovenden (1967) indicates that, in fact, there is very little empirical relationship between the two measures purported to test these constructs. Frehner (1971) also found no relationship between the Embedded Figures Test used by Witkin and the Sigel Conceptual Style Test when he sampled sixth grade children. Frehner did find, however, that each of these measures relates, to about the same degree, to a number of school achievement tasks.

A third school of thought in the area of cognitive style is the work of Gardner and his colleagues (Gardner, Holzman, Klein, Linton, and Spence, 1959; Gardner, Jackson and Messick, 1960). Gardner perceives cognitive style from a psychoanalytic framework. His notion of cognitive style encompasses a number of different principles all of which function to assist the individual in adapting to a complex environment. Although Gardner and his colleagues propose six control principles that in their totality describe an individual's style, we shall focus on those most germane to education. These are *leveling-sharpening, equivalence range, focal attention,* and *constricted versus flexible control.*

Let us use the classroom scenes described in the opening of this chapter as our point of departure. You will recall, the teacher is presenting an illustrated chart, which at first glance is an organized whole. Gradually, parts become differentiated; and for some it can be viewed as a total of discrete but related elements, and for others it tends to be viewed as a blend with little distinctiveness. For Gardner the process involved in differentiating the chart into discrete elements is sharpening, and the nondifferentiating is *leveling*. The individuals who are sharpeners are better able to hold particular events in mind as a basis for comparison.

Equivalence range, another control principle, is fundamental in classification. It refers to those judgments by which different objects or events are organized within the same category heading. In our illustration with the human body, the brain, nerve centers, and nerve fibers, although different in appearance, can be considered as equivalent because they share certain common functions. Thus differences are overlooked in the process of accentuating the similarities, or in Gardner's terms, when items are judged as equivalent.

Individuals vary in the quantity as well as the quality of information they receive from any complex stimulus. Some children will study Mrs. Fowler's chart literally from head to toe and side to side, and others will fix on a particular area. This type of behavior Gardner calls *focusing*, which essentially is a measure of attention and the degree and range to which this attention is deployed.

Mrs. Fowler's chart is complex, containing a large amount of information and is therefore potentially distracting. For some students, attending to the nervous system and following the route of various nerve fibers may pose difficulties, because they cannot separate the fibers from the embedded context of muscle, bone, and so on. For some children, disengaging the nerve fibers from their surrounding is difficult, because these children are constricted and not flexible enough to disregard the background; for others, such disengagement is easy. Gardner refers to this behavior as *constricted versus flexible control*.

As can be seen, these principles encompass a wide variety of organizing behaviors, which can play a prominent role in the child's adjustment to the broad environment in general and to school in particular. Of course, the way these principles are patterned for the child may influence the quality of his adaptation to the environment.

A fourth perspective of cognitive style is that of Broverman, who conceptualizes cognitive styles as expressions of different "response probabilities or response strengths in certain types or classes of behaviors" (Broverman, 1960b, p. 167). That is to say that individuals have developed ways of responding to particular types of situations and that the chance of a particular response being employed depends on the nature of the task and the intensity with which a particular response is held. For example, when an individual is presented with a novel, difficult, and concentration-demanding task (for example, verbal reasoning or problem solving), a particular class of response patterns may be elicited. The type of response elicited in problems that are familiar and do not demand concentration calls forth different styles. For the novel, problem-solving type of situations, Broverman reports a *conceptual versus perceptual motor dominance* style, and for the automatic habitual type of situation, *strong versus weak automatization* is proposed.

Of interest in Broverman's approach is his distinction between styles relative to task. Other concepts of cognitive style do not take the nature of the task into account. Broverman, by conceptualizing styles in relation to the type of task, suggests that style responses vary as a function of types of task. For education this becomes relevant. When novel tasks are introduced, those who are conceptually oriented will approach tasks on a different level than those who are dominated by the concrete, observable aspects of a situation. For example, imagine Mrs. Fowler's asking the students to discuss the relationship between the nervous system and the skeletal musculature. This relationship can be discussed in terms of principles of relationships or by describing specific parts with little cognizance of the general principles. Broverman's automatization style would be relevant for the part of the task involving already learned names, for example, but when the students attempt to discover unique relationships between these two broad systems, a conceptual dominance might prevail.

REVIEW OF RESEARCH ON COGNITIVE STYLE

Research involving each of these different notions of cognitive style has provided an extensive body of literature indicating relationships between cognitive style and intellectual achievement and personality variables. (For a review of the many results dealing with theoretical and methodological issues, see Kagan and Kogan, 1970).

Research involving Witkin's notion of cognitive style has indicated that field-independent individuals tend to be analytic in intellectual approach, somewhat distant from others, emotionally independent, high achievers, and active and controlling their environments rather than being controlled by them. Field-dependent individuals tend to be the opposite. Thus it would appear that the field independents are the preferred group, because their behavior fits the achieving society's objectives. (The reader should note the relationship between these findings and the locus of control construct discussed in Chapter 5 by Solomon and Oberlander.)

A recent paper by Ramirez III (1972) has proposed that curricula be arranged for Mexican-American children compatible with the field-dependence approach, because this is compatible with the cognitive style of Mexican-Americans. Although at this writing no data are available on this project, it seems to raise more questions than answers. What would be the consequences of such an emphasis? If negative results occurred, would they be reversible? What cognitive limitations would fostering such approaches create?

The variables studied by Witkin have also been studied by Kagan and his colleagues (Kagan, Moss, and Sigel, 1963; Kagan, Rosman, Day, Albert, and Phillips, 1964), Sigel (1963), and Broverman (1960). For Kagan et. al. descriptive-analytic styles are also related to personality, social, and intellectual characteristics. These can be summarized as follows: Sex differences were found, with boys employing more descriptive-analytic responses than girls, and girls using more relational-contextual ones. No sex differences were found in the use of inferential-categorical responses. Further, people who were high on descriptive-analytic responses tended to score higher on nonverbal IQ tests, learning of concepts, and memory for details. Although there were no differences in frequency of particular styles among 4- and 5-year-old boys and girls, the correlates of the styles varied. The boys' analytic responses were related to cautiousness, learning skills, achievement orientation, independence and activity; for girls the reverse held true for most variables; for example, they were found to be low on cautiousness, independence, and activity.

Kagan and his colleagues (Kagan, Moss, and Sigel, 1963; Kagan et al., 1964) also report that analytic children showed longer decision time. It was this type of result that led Kagan to propose the reflective-impulsive dimension as a style variable. A number of studies have been reported examining the relationship between the reflective-impulsive dimension and personality, intellectual, and academic variables. First, there is some evidence to support the contention that the person's reflective-impulsive style is consistent across situations (Kagan and Kogan, 1970). Data have been reported showing that reflective children make fewer errors than impulsive children in recall, reading, and reasoning (Kagan and Kogan, 1970).

Sigel's (1961a) results tend to confirm those of Kagan's in regard to personality factors relating to cognitive style. However, the personality factors related to particular styles of categorization vary with sex and social class. Boys, for example, who are analytic tend to be cautious, independent, achievement-minded, nonimpulsive, and masculine; girls employing an analytic style of categorization are quick responders (but accurate), tend to daydream, and are generally inattentive (Sigel, Jarman, and Hanesian, 1967).

No sex differences, however, were found with categorical-inferential styles. Persons high on categorical-inferential responses tended to score higher on the *Binet* IQ test. These results were interpreted as an indication that categorical-inferential behavior may well be a product of conventional socialization experiences in boys and girls (Sigel, Jarman, and Hanesian, 1967).

When using objects familiar to children, such as fruits, doll furniture, or toy cars, in a free sorting task (subjects were allowed to sort the objects into groups any way they chose) with children from lower socioeconomic levels, Sigel found they differed in style from children from higher socioeconomic levels. Lower-class children used more relational-contextual categories (Sigel, Anderson, and Shapiro, 1966). When descriptive categories were used, these children tended to use descriptions that were not structured, but rather were vague and obvious (for example, attributes such as straight edges or color), whereas middle-class children used structural attributes (for example, given a group of fruits, stems might be the criterial attribute).

Class differences are reported by other investigations, all of which tend to suggest that middle-class groups are more analytic, reflective, and field-independent (Kagan and Kogan, 1970; Frehner, 1971; Sigel, 1971; Sigel and Olmstead, 1970).

One interesting and relevant finding, which is somewhat discrepant from the findings reported by Kagan, was reported by Serafica and Sigel (1970). These researchers found that the style distinguishing good and poor readers was categorical-inferential. These authors examined a group of children diagnosed as poor readers, who were in remedial reading classes, and compared their cognitive style scores to a group of children reading at a level commensurate with their grade level. It was found that the only style approach that distinguished the readers from the nonreaders was the categorical-inferential one. The readers tended to produce more categorical-inferential responses than did the nonreaders. The authors interpret this result as suggestive of the importance of the role of interpretive-conceptual processes in reading, as compared to the emphasis on discrimination of particular details.

Let us now turn to Witkin and his co-workers in order to establish the relevance of field independence–field dependence to the academic scene. Much has already been reported by Witkin and his colleagues about the relationship between field independence and personality, perceptual, and cognitive variables. One of the most intriguing and relevant findings for our purposes is the finding, reviewed by Kagan and Kogan, that

> both the test taking and the looking behavior of the children suggested that field dependents were more disrupted by an unfavorable emotional climate than were field independents. The dependent group appears to be more externally directed in the sense that their cognitive affective behavior is differentially influenced by the positive or negative social cues emitted by others [Kagan and Kogan, 1970, p. 1331].

A logical extension of these ideas suggests that style can influence those classes of behavior that require differentiation of figure from ground, of part from whole. Although not every relationship between field independence and field dependence and psycho-educational variables has been investigated, the classroom teacher should be alert to behaviors of students in this area in order to sharpen his or her diagnosis of the child's perceptual abilities as well as a means of enhancing understanding of the child's cognitive performances.

DEVELOPMENTAL LEVELS OF COGNITIVE STYLE

Little attention has been paid in this discussion to the developmental stages of these styles. There are data to reveal an array of not too surprising results. Field independence tends to increase with age up to age seventeen, with no further change from seventeen to twenty-four. "Within this general developmental trend children show marked relative stability in extent of field dependence, even over 14 years. At each age, individual consistency in performance across tests of field independence is found" (Witkin, Goodenough, and Kays, 1967, p. 291). For Kagan et. al. (1964) reflectivity increases with time, which is not too surprising. Sigel et al. report that analytic and categorical-inferential responses increase with age and relational contextual responses tend to remain relatively stable (Sigel, Jarman, and Hanesian, 1967).

Gardner and Moriarty (1968) repeated a study originally done with adults with a group of sixty children age nine to thirteen. Using many of the same measures employed in the Gardner et. al. study (1959) with adults, Gardner and Moriarty found that the relationships among control principles that emerged was similar to those for adults. Gardner and Moriarty discuss the issue of cognitive controls from the psychoanalytic perspective, invoking the concept of patterning of psychological defense mechanisms. They see controls as contributing to the adaptation of children. The control aids the child in coordinating environmental demands and his own motivations. In essence, from a psychoanalytic perspective, these controls are mechanisms that act as intermediaries between motivational forces and reality demands. In this sense cognitive controls serve as a defense mechanism. Gardner and Moriarty conclude that the defense and cognitive control organizations are

> apparently more fully and clearly developed at preadolescence than has often been assumed. Defense organization in particular is rather sharply discernible in terms of its recognizability, the degree of differentiation of specific defensive functions, and the interrelations among specific defenses. . . . the notion that defense organization at preadolescence is universally global or amorphous can apparently be disposed of rather completely [Gardner and Moriarty, 1968, p. 299].

Gardner and Moriarty's emphasis on the personality aspects provides an interesting and provocative perspective—pointing out not only the complexity of these relationships but also the significant role personality variables play. Although it may appear that these writers minimize the cognitive aspects, the reader might consider the place of such personality variables as defense mechanisms in influencing the quality of cognitive behaviors—for example, judgments and classification. Thus although there are some changes with age, these changes do not alter the relative importance of particular style preferences among adults. These age changes are not surprising in view of the obvious fact that children change in their competence to think conceptually and to be more controlled and analytic.

IMPLICATIONS OF COGNITIVE STYLE FOR EDUCATION

The research reported has presented some of the empirical evidence regarding a contemporary concept employed to categorize and explain individual differences in cognitive behavior. Although each of the writers reviewed invokes the term *cognitive style*, each has somewhat different concepts, uses somewhat different measures, and examines somewhat different problems.

Irrespective of the investigator, however, it seems clear that individual differences in cognitive functioning exist, and most important, these differences are *not* attributable to differences in intelligence, but rather are manifestations of personality. The significance of this perspective for education will be the focus of this section. Before proceeding, let us point out that the relationship between cognitive style and education is relevant for all participants in the educational enterprise, be they children or adults. Children vary in styles as a function of developmental level, in addition to the usual socioeconomic, cultural, and sex variables; adults, irrespective of their role or responsibilities, manifest variations in cognitive styles. The significance of particular styles relative to particular roles in the educational enterprise is an important question that needs considerable study. The cognitive style variable, then, is probably germane in influencing a host of relevant interpersonal interactions—teacher–child, administrator–teacher, curriculum supervisor–teacher, and so on. No doubt you will see other points of impact in education.

Cognitive styles have been found to relate to intellectual and perceptual performance (Coop and Sigel, 1970). Some examples are as follows: Children who are reflective make fewer errors in reading (Kagan et. al., 1964); production of relational-contextual responses relates to reading (Annesley, 1971) and to creativity (Wallach and Kogan,

1965); and leveling-sharpening relates to memory and attention (Kagan and Kogan, 1970). The previous section exemplifies these relationships, especially if one considers that education involves a host of motivational and experiential factors influencing learning and socialization in school.

If one accepts these findings, then it is apparent that the cognitive style factor has to be taken into consideration in the educational process. It may be the key to why some children make considerable progress and others do not; it may reveal why children having comparable IQ scores vary in interest and performance levels on the same type of material; in general, herein resides one major area that can help the teacher understand the dynamics of a child's performance.

Given these possibilities the teacher has to consider cognitive styles when evaluating behavior and performance in academic and nonacademic areas. Becoming sensitive to the child's style can influence teaching strategy. For example, if children are having difficulty in grasping material, it could be due to the child's style or a discrepancy between the teacher's style and that of the child. Consider children whose conceptual tempo is impulsive. It is quite likely that they may be having difficulty in developing accurate reading habits. How a teacher relates to this situation may be crucial to the child's success. The teacher who is aware of tempo as a psychological variable and who understands it as a style is likely to respond differently from the teacher who sees the tempo as a negative attitude or intentionally malicious behavior. Further, the strategy the teacher uses will probably derive from his or her conceptualization of the problem. To aid the child, the teacher has to have some idea of the feasibility of devising strategies to accomplish the ultimate objective—to facilitate the child's learning how to read in the face of his stylistic predispositions. Consequently, one of the basic questions the teacher has to answer is: Are cognitive styles modifiable? There are in fact two issues here: First, are styles modifiable? Second, what are the implications involved in such a modification? Let us address ourselves to these two issues in the subsequent section.

Modifiability of cognitive style

To answer the question of modifiability requires a further consideration of the origins and psychodynamics of cognitive style. If cognitive style is an acquired predisposition, then modification requires constructing learning experiences to alter cognitive styles in the predicted or desired direction. Unfortunately, more research has focused on change in style as a function of increasing age than as a consequent of deliberate efforts at modifying the existing approach (Kagan and Kogan, 1970). (For some ideas on modifying behavior generally, see Chapter 4 by Wasik.)

Efforts have been expended to influence style, especially when conceptualized according to Kagan or Sigel's definition. Although the results are equivocal at this writing, indications are that instructions to alter one's tempo and to use different strategies for problem solving can be successful (Yando and Kagan, 1968). Baird and Bee (1969) attempted to increase the frequency of analytic and nonanalytic responses by social reinforcement. Their analytic training produced significant increases in analytic responses for all subjects. Nonanalytic training did not produce significant decrease in analytic responding, and random reward produced a significant increase in analytic responding for analytic subjects only. The authors concluded that a learning model is appropriate for the acquisition of cognitive styles, but the developmental level of the responses interacts with the training procedure in a complex manner. Another study reported by Sigel and Olmstead (1970) showed that training kindergarten, black children to attend to the various attributes of objects influenced their classification styles. Children increased in the frequency of analytic responses and categorical-inferential responses, and decreased in the frequency of relational-contextual responses.

Long-term effects of indirect influence on style have been described by Scott and Sigel (1965) and Scott (1964, 1966, 1970, 1972). When children involved in an inquiry science program were encouraged to ask questions, to form hypotheses, and to make inferences, they were found to shift more in stylistic responses than children in conventional science programs. Some of the innovative programs at Knightcrest Middle School may have components similar to this inquiry approach. Further, acquisition of an analytic approach seems to persist from fourth grade to high school.

Several studies indicate that predisposition for reflectivity-impulsivity can be modified (Kagan, Pearson, and Welch, 1966; Briggs, 1966; Debus, 1968; Yando and Kagan, 1968). These studies tend to support the notion that it is possible to inhibit impulsive children and also to increase reflectivity by directing them to use alternative strategies and to slow down.

Since lower-class children show greater tendency toward impulsivity than middle-class children and since lower-class children manifest more learning problems, increasing reflectivity among lower-class children should enhance their learning. Consequently, effecting this change may be a very important educational objective. The previous efforts at modifying impulsivity, as we mentioned, have used direct manipulation of response time by instructing or requiring children to wait before responding (Schwebel, 1966; Kagan, Pearson, and Welch, 1966; Baird and Bee, 1969). Heider (1971), in discussing these studies, concludes that "one motivational factor underlying individual difference in conceptual tempo (reflectivity-impulsivity) is anxiety over accuracy of intellectual performance" (pp. 1276–1277). This is not the interpretation that Heider would offer for performance among lower-class children, however. Rather she suggests that lack of accuracy and speed among lower-class children results from inappropriate strategies of information processing. "Class difference in habitual strategies of information processing might origi· nate in differing motivation concerning intellectual performance, but once established may not readily be changed by manipulation of motivation." (Heider, 1971, p. 1277).

Consequently, she set out to modify impulsivity in a group of Caucasian, 7- and 9-year-old boys within a normal IQ range. Using instructions that contained an explanation of appropriate task strategy, she found that errors were reduced and response time increased for lower-class boys only. Heider concludes that direct instructions in methods of information processing may be effective in influencing impulsivity among lower-class children. It may be important for Mr. Bellamy to look at some of these studies in connection with Julia Clark about whom he says, "If Julia would just stop and think before she answers, she would do much better."

The results of these studies raise an interesting issue: Should training programs be differentiated on the basis of social class? For example, should Katherine Fowler attempt to create separate programs for Stanley Robinson and Mary Cairns, who are in the same classroom but come from widely divergent social classes? How can this be accomplished in an integrated program? What are the implications for school organization? Are classes to be organized on the basis of social class? If not, what will be the effects of such training programs on middle-class children, who seem to generally be more reflective? Of course, even though middle-class children are relatively more reflective than lower-class children, there is variability among middle-class children on this dimension. Consequently, it is conceivable that such programs would enhance reflectivity for some middle-class individuals. Of course, all these are speculations, which can only be answered by further research.

In any event, it seems clear that conceptual tempo is modifiable. Chances are that individual differences in modifiability exist. One source of this difference may be the degree to which cognitive style serves to facilitate the individual's coping with his anxiety.

Although little is known about the psychodynamics and origins of cognitive style, a notable exception is a study of relationships between child rearing and cognitive style (Witkin et. al. 1962) Witkin suggests that the cognitive styles of field independence and field dependence are in part a function of child-rearing practices. Mothers of field-independent children provide more differentiating experiences and create distance between themselves and the children more frequently than mothers of field-dependent children. Similar studies have yet to be done using the other style constructs. Consequently, little can be said about their origins.

What these studies point to is the possibility that styles of approach can be modified. Questions still remain regarding the conditions under which modification can be done and the requirements for such achievement. If certain styles are preferences and they are deeply ingrained habits, then we are speaking about alteration of habit patterns. The source of these habits, however, is still open to question. They may well be habits that are analogous to defense mechanisms, where children employ certain styles in the service of coping with anxiety or some other adaptation procedure. If this is the case, simple alteration through the type of studies described may be ineffective. Other procedures may be required that deal with the child's anxiety level, while altering his coping strategies. This might be particularly important for the teacher working with students such as Linda Grey at Knightcrest Middle School. Some of the teachers' comments in Linda's cumulative record would indicate that she may be somewhat anxious in certain situations related to the classroom. If, however, the styles are functions of learning—that is, experience—acquired because of a particular set of circumstances, then it may well be that shifting the circumstances may alter the behavior.

The ethics of inducing change is the second issue. Kagan and Kogan (1970) raise this question in regard to efforts aimed at creating field independence in children. They do not raise the issue regarding increasing reflectivity, but it seems that the issue is the same. To consider modification of style an ethical problem may appear to the reader rather far-fetched and not comparable to the induction of attitudes and beliefs, for example, regarding religion or moral issues. The data reveal that styles do influence quality and even quantity of learning, and styles are strategies used in problem solving. In essence, cognitive style tends to determine whether the individual is an effective learner, information processor, and knowledge utilizer. And education has as its business enhancing the individual's opportunity to become these things. Consequently, modifiability of cognitive style would appear to be inherent in the educational process. A good example of this is provided by the studies reported by Scott (1964, 1966, 1970, 1972). Although his intent as a teacher was to teach science, he also contributed to the child's development of an analytic approach, in part as a function of the teaching program he selected. True, he did not know he would accomplish this at the time he elected to participate in the Suchman inquiry program; yet the side effects occurred. How often does this happen in education? We can only conjecture the differential effects that the open classroom curriculum of Knightcrest and the traditional programs of Midview will have on the cognitive functioning of the students in these schools. It is doubtful if the teachers or administrators are aware of these stylistic variables. Scott only discovered this effect because of his research—and research is not too common among classroom teachers or curriculum supervisors. (See Chapter 7 by Coopersmith and Feldman regarding other side effects.)

Education always involves modifications, and if cognitive styles may be modified in the course of education, it can be argued that such changes are usually serendipitous and not deliberate or planned. They occur in the service of other objectives. But to set out deliberately to change cognitive style is another issue. If education is in the business of contributing to the development of effective learners, then it has to be in the business of modifying cognitive styles. The basic question is: To what degree and under what conditions can or should educators attempt changes in style? Are educators in the business of inducing personality changes? For example, should Mr. Bellamy try to change the cognitive style of his students? If so, how far should he go in attempting to modify the thought processes and, indirectly, the life-styles of his students? These questions are beyond the scope of this review, but they are relevant.

Let us turn now to an examination of the other implications of cognitive styles for the educational enterprise.

Diagnosis of child performance

First, the basic proposition is that performance level and quality are in part attributable to the interaction between the child's cognitive style and particular types of material. Implicit in this assertion is the idea that on various tasks, such as learning and formal and informal tests, "an individual's style dictates the cues he will use, but not necessarily determines the level on which he performs. The style of categorization sets the direction but not the levels" (Sigel, 1963, p. 45). The cues selected by the child, however, may be discrepant from those expected by the teacher, and consequently, the child's performance may be negatively evaluated. For example, the child may respond only to part-whole dimensions in a classification task (for example, he may say dogs and cats are alike because they have legs or they have eyes or they can bite), or the child may learn details quickly but have some difficulty making inferences. It must be kept in mind that the responses are not necessarily wrong, but reflect a preferential choice.

To be sure, errors can occur as a function of style. Errors in computation and/or recording may be due to lack of attention to detail or to not scanning the problem adequately—symptoms of impulsivity rather than reflectivity. The errors can be attributed in part to the child's orientation to respond quickly rather than reflectively (Sigel, 1963). Marvin Blake of Knightcrest Middle School might be a case in point. His third grade teacher has noted that "Marvin is very impulsive and seems to lack self-restraint." His teachers should keep in mind the possibility that Marvin has an impulsive style while working with him and seek further data that support or disconfirm this hypothesis.

Cognitive style influences acquisition of new materials as well as utilization of already acquired knowledge. Kagan et. al. (1964) have shown that children's learning of concepts is related to style. Thus we can conclude that the child's cognitive style is significantly involved in information processing in general.

Given this knowledge, how is a teacher to use it? The options are many, ranging from employment of time requirements on the tasks to careful observation and analysis of children's classroom behavior. Given current knowledge, the latter course is probably the most practical. The teacher can diagnose the child's style by first settling on a concept that has demonstrated maximal educational utility. Second, observational analysis of children's behavior can prove very productive, especially as expressed in oral and written work. If the teacher has truly internalized the concept of style, it is not an unreasonable expectation for him to apply it. Of course, such an approach requires one additional safeguard. Recall that cognitive style cannot be dealt with independently of material. Thus the particular preference may be more readily apparent in some contexts than others. For example, Scott found cognitive style a very relevant variable in his science program, where he used an inquiring approach. In that type of situation a teacher can readily identify the student's style on the basis of the questions he asks.

Relationship of styles to teachers' behavior

A second area of interest is that teachers too have their own stylistic pattern of responding to and categorizing information. Some exploratory studies with student teachers have indicated that teachers' memory of children and the organization of their knowledge about children varies with their cognitive style (Sigel, 1961b). A group of students preparing to be teachers were presented with a case study of a child and were then asked to repeat this case study from memory on three successive occasions. Over the 3-day period the type of story content remembered and its organization varied with the cognitive style of the student teachers. Those who were descriptive-analytic remembered more details in sequential order. This is in contrast to those who were relational in their approach; they tended to respond in a more global condensed way, omitting the details, and they tended to reorganize the sequence of the story. (The reader might wish to review some of the factors about teachers' expectancies presented in Chapter 3 by Good and Brophy in connection with this material.) The research points out that teachers as much as any individual are selective in what they remember, what they attend to, and how they use the information. The cognitive style of the teacher becomes a relevant variable influencing professional behavior. Look at the teachers' comments in the cumulative records of Marvin Blake and Linda Grey at Knightcrest and William Baker of Midview School, and see if you can pick out different stylistic preferences of the teachers who wrote these reports.

Another way in which the teaching function varies with the teacher's style lies in the kinds of emphasis the teacher places on the materials to be learned. Although not much research has been done in the area, it is reasonable to believe that teachers who tend to be more global would tend to emphasize that approach in their teaching in contrast to teachers who have preferences for an analytic approach. Thus one has reason to consider teaching styles in relation to cognitive style dimensions. Consider this question in reflecting on your own experiences with various teachers and think through the differences among them on these stylistic bases.

Another related question in the educational domain is the interaction between the teacher and the child in terms of each of their cognitive styles. Certainly, an attempt to match the teacher and child in terms of their styles would pose certain kinds of problems, but at the same time the possibility raises some interesting questions. The question is: Is it easier for teachers to work with children whose styles are compatible with theirs or with students whose styles are discrepant? If it is argued that one way that children develop cognitively is through increased confrontation with the environment and if this kind of intellectual conflict facilitates growth, then there would be more virtue to discrepancies between teachers' and students' styles. This, of course, would have to be contingent on the teachers and children being able to tolerate these differences. Just for the moment, however, it would be well to conjecture on the implications of this situation in examining teacher–child interaction. Conversely, one might ask the question about the compatibility of styles. Here we are faced with a more complex and serious question. If the child's style and the teacher's style are highly compatible, but their styles tend to be somewhat dysfunctional, are we in effect, shortchanging the child? Suppose, for example, that Mary Cairns is field-dependent and Mrs. Fowler is also field-dependent. Does that mean that there are more reinforcements or reward values for Mary's nonanalytic, global approach and very little inclination or encouragement for her to be analytic. The significance of this question rests in the assumption that global approaches tend to be dysfunctional for certain classes of problems. If the results reported by Scott and Sigel (1965) are generalizable, then the more varied and flexible the style option that individuals have, the more successful they are in problem-solving behavior. It would, therefore, be advantageous for the children to have more options. In consideration of this problem, therefore, it seems reasonable to think of what the educational objectives are and the necessary cognitive styles for meeting these objectives. We come back, then, to a value question and also to the question of origins of cognitive style. The latter we have already discussed. The value question remains one that still needs to be faced. It is not appropriate in this chapter to attempt to provide the answers to that question. It is appropriate to raise the question, and hopefully you can work this out in the course of your deliberating on how to apply cognitive style data and knowledge to practical educational situations.

SPECIFIC APPLICATION
OF COGNITIVE STYLE DATA TO THE CLASSROOM

Let us now turn to a more precise application of the cognitive style material and set this up in the way of an exercise. The first consideration is to define those areas in which cognitive styles can be relevant. (We are not now concerned with any particular style, but the concept in general.) The first consideration is diagnostic-prescriptive, and the second is in curriculum organization.

Diagnostic–prescriptive applications

Since cognitive styles are evident in a variety of tasks, it becomes important to examine the performance of the student in relation to his cognitive style. Observing the type of errors students make on formal tests is a readily available method for the teacher to do this. Thus in reviewing the test data available for your students, you should look for variations in test patterns and acquire some understanding of what the children have had difficulty with. For example, it may be discovered that some students fail to make fine discriminations between discrete parts of a factual problem. Such failures are many times written off as careless errors. But it may be that they are not carelessness at all; rather they may reflect the student's basic orientation toward the problem stimuli. In other words, in making a diagnosis, one must discover what the child's predominant orientation is. In this example, one source of variation in performance can be identified.

The next question, then, is: How can cognitive style be modified?

Here the educator is faced with a very practical problem. How do you modify cognitive style within the context of the educational setting? One method has been used that provides content at the same time that it allows style modifications to be made. Let us assume that some of the Midview sixth graders are studying housing problems in social studies, and Mrs. Fowler presents to the students the concept of domicile, using three diverse examples—an apartment, a cave, and a clapboard house. The object of the lessons is for the students to understand and compare how people live and why they live the way they do. First, the students could be asked to describe each of these types of housing. Then they could be asked to select any two and compare them. Such a comparison could be the statement that a cave and a house are alike because they have a roof or because they keep out the rain. Or a house and an apartment could be compared because they both have windows and both have rooms and so on. Now the kinds of comparisons that are made could be further elaborated and discussed in terms of further justification, and this could then be a second type of examination. Evaluating these responses on the basis of their rationale and their significance could provide children with the opportunity to assess the degree to which particular responses provide different information. Mrs. Fowler, attending to children who tend to give more global responses, might try to elicit more specific responses on the next go-around with another set of materials. In this way, Mrs. Fowler, by keeping a mental record of the kinds of responses the students give, can begin to encourage and elicit other types of responses. More important, she can indicate how each type of response is valid and how each contributes different kinds of information. In this way, the students begin to learn, in the context of learning about different domiciles, that various types of responses can be relevant depending on particular situations. For the teacher such an approach can reveal the range of information the various students possess and how they can use it. A variety of teaching strategies can be developed with this format, ranging from the inquiry approach to asking the students to elaborate their responses, justify their responses, and/or extend their responses (Sigel and Olmsted, 1970).

CURRICULUM ORGANIZATION

Up to this point the emphasis has been on the student, the teacher, and their match in the classroom. Yet it should not be overlooked that the educational enterprise is dedicated to learning, to acquiring new information, and to the utilization of this new learning. In view of these objectives, should the curriculum itself be considered in the context of cognitive style?

The answer is a qualified Yes, qualified in terms of the cognitive style concept that is used. For example, from Broverman's perspective, educators might be concerned with distinguishing between those tasks that lend themselves to routinization and those that are more conceptual.

The issue of course is what is to be learned? If strategies are to be learned, there are at least two levels at which curriculum can be considered; one is emphasis on the learning of strategies to solve particular classes of problems, for example, science, mathematics, social studies. (See Scott, 1964, 1966, 1970, 1972 for longitudinal studies in physical science.) There is also evidence that acquisition of concepts is related to style when analytic concepts are learned by children with analytic style preferences (Kagan et. al., 1964). Curriculum can be organized on a descriptive level (for example, factual information), and on an inferential level (for example, organizing factual data into generalizations). In effect, if curriculum is information and if cognitive styles are modes of processing information, the relationship is between the materials to be processed and the modes or strategies for processing certain classes of material. It seems reasonable to conjecture that such organizational strategies could be of value, particularly by facilitating the articulation between the learner's characteristics and material to be learned.

This strategy, however, must be exploratory, because the evidence for such a relationship is more theoretical than empirical. Hervey (1966), for example, in studying the relationship of the individual's cognitive style and his school behavior found no significant relationship. Using the Kagan, Moss, and Sigel model, she presented college students with cognitive style tests and a paper-and-pencil instrument assessing school behavior, defined as the . . . "individual's preferences for ways of organizing tasks to be performed and his preferences for certain tasks over others" (Hervey, 1966, p. 58). No relationship was found between these two classes of events. However, a relationship was found between cognitive style and academic ability. The lack of relationship, however, does not necessarily invalidate the logical inference that how curriculum is organized can be related to cognitive style. Rather, it indicates that research is needed here as for so many aspects of this complex field.

It would behoove the curriculum experts to consider the importance of the kinds of material to be used and the sense modalities to be emphasized, and to identify the relationship between cognitive style and the organization of curriculum. Finally, it is also important to seek the relationship between curriculum objectives and cognitive style. If, for example, the intent is to emphasize the discovery of principles or generalizations, some cognitive styles are more appropriate than others; if facts are emphasized, other stylistic approaches are more relevant. It is interesting to note that Scott (1972) found the ability to shift strategy and, in that case, style was predictive of success in solving physical science problems. This is an area where the cooperative efforts of the teacher, the educational psychologist, and the curriculum constructor would be most profitable and exciting.

SUMMARY AND CONCLUSIONS

The review of the literature here, although incomplete, points out the diversity in concepts, methods, and interpretations. Nevertheless, commonalities do exist and have been pointed out as well as the differences. It would perhaps appear, then, that such diversity of form, substance, and method precludes the usefulness of the concept of cognitive style. Quite the contrary. Is it not remarkable that, in spite of the variety of findings, empirical relationships relevant to education are found for each theoretical perspective? The fact that academic achievement can be explained by more than IQ or motivational variables begins to teach us more about the nature of man in the learning environment. (For a discussion of intelligence, see Chapter 8 by Meeker. For a discussion of motivation, see Chapter 6 by Waller and Gaa.)

For the teacher the knowledge described in this chapter is but the beginning. Now an additional perspective can be brought to bear in the course of developing an understanding of the dynamics of the learning process.

True, there is much more empirical knowledge to be obtained before our knowledge base is firm and consolidated. For now, we are involved in the process of ever expanding our awareness of a class of variables interacting in the classroom that influences the course of learning, of teaching, and of education in general. Such awareness is a first step in moving from a simple to a complex basis of understanding the educational process.

SOME SUGGESTED ACTIVITIES

1. Look at the cumulative records of at least fifteen students who have had a number of different teachers in their academic careers. (You may have to obtain permission to do this if you are student teaching.) Note the comments the individual teachers have made about

these students; and see if you can find specific instances where you feel that the teacher's cognitive style influenced either the remarks he or she made about a student or the way the remarks were recorded on the cumulative record.

2. Observe in a classroom situation where there is some interaction between the students and the teacher. See if you can detect any patterns occurring in which the teacher consistently (either consciously or unconsciously) rewards students who give a response that is related to a specific cognitive style. For instance, you might find some teachers who consistently praise descriptive-analytic responses but ignore other types of responses (relational and categorical) and other teachers who praise or reward relational responses but fail to reward the other two categories of responses. What is the reaction of the students whose responses are rewarded? What is the reaction of the students whose responses are not rewarded?

3. Observe in a classroom or a video tape of classroom behavior for an extended period of time. See if you can record instances where impulsive or quick responses on the part of the students are required or rewarded. Also note any instances where the teacher forces the students to reflect on his thoughts before answering a question or making a response. Look for any individual differences among the various students when they are exposed to these two different classroom situations.

4. Obtain a sample of instructional materials (books, charts, film strips, slides, and so on) that are designed for use with students in the grade level you will be (or are currently) teaching. Try to determine if these materials are developed or constructed in such a manner that they are consonant with a particular cognitive style and dissonant with other styles. Discuss some of the possible effects that these materials might have on learners who have cognitive styles that differ drastically from that for which the materials are constructed.

REFERENCES

Annesley, F. R. "Cognitive Style as a Variable in the Reading Achievement and Intelligence of Boys." Unpublished doctoral dissertation, Temple University, 1971.

Baird, R. R., and Bee, H. L. "Modification of Conceptual Style Preference by Differential Reinforcement." Child Development 40 (1969): 903–910.

Briggs, C. "Training and Generalization of Reflective and Impulsive Styles in School-age Children." Unpublished doctoral dissertation, University of Minnesota, 1966.

Broverman, D. M. "Cognitive Style and Intra-individual Variation in Abilities." Journal of Personality 28 (1960): 240–256.

Broverman, D. M. "Dimensions of Cognitive Style." *Journal of Personality* 28 (1960b): 167–185.

Coop, R. H., and Hovenden, W. E. "A Correlational Study of the Analytic Dimension of Cognitive Style." Unpublished study, Indiana University, 1967.

Coop, R. H., and Sigel, I. E. "Cognitive Style: Implications for Learning and Instruction." *Psychology in the Schools* 8 (1971): 152–161.

Debus, R. L. "Effects of Brief Observation of Model Behavior on Conceptual Tempo of Impulsive Children." Unpublished manuscript, University of Sydney, Australia, 1968.

Frehner, V. "Cognitive Style As a Determinant of Educational Achievement Among Sixth Grade Elementary School Students." Unpublished doctoral dissertation, Utah State University, 1971.

Gardner, R. W.; Holzman, P. S.; Klein, G. S.; Linton, Harriet; and Spence, D. P. "Cognitive Control: A Study of Individual Consistencies in Cognitive Behavior." *Psychological Issues* 1 (4, Monograph 4), 1959.

Gardner, R. W.; Jackson, D. N., and Messick, S. J. "Personality Organization in Cognitive Controls and Intellectual Abilities." *Psychological Issues* 2 (4, Monograph 8), 1960.

Gardner, R. W., and Moriarity, Ahar. *Personality Development at Preadolescence.* Seattle: University of Washington Press, 1968.

Heider, Eleanor R. "Information Processing and the Modification of an Impulsive Conceptual Tempo." *Child Development* 42 (1971): 1276–1281.

Hervey, Sarah D. "Cognitive Style and Preferences in School Tasks." Michigan State University: unpublished doctoral dissertation, 1966.

Kagan, J., and Kogan, N. "Individual Variation in Cognitive Processes." In *Carmichael's Manual of Child Psychology,* edited by P. Mussen. New York: Wiley, 1970.

Kagan, J.; Moss, H. A.; and Sigel, I. E. "Psychological Significance of Styles of Conceptualization." In *Basic Cognitive Processes in Children,* edited by J. C. Wright and J. Kagan. *Monographs of the Society for Research in Child Development* 28 (2, Serial No. 86), 1963, pp. 73–112.

Kagan, J.; Pearson, J.; and Welch, L. "Modifiability of an Impulsive Tempo." *Journal of Educational Psychology* 57 (1966): 357–365.

Kagan, J.; Rosman, B. L.; Day, D.; Albert, J.; and Phillips, W. "Information Processing in the Child: Significance of Analytic and Reflective Attitudes." *Psychological Monographs* 78 (1, Whole No. 578), 1964.

Ramirez, III, M. "Implications of Cultural Democracy and Cognitive Styles for Evaluative Research." Paper presented at American Educational Research Association, April, 1972.

Schwebel, A. J. "Effects of Impulsivity on Performance of Verbal Tasks in Middle and Lower Class Children." *American Journal of Orthopsychiatry* 36 (1966): 12–21.

Scott, N. "Science Concept Achievement and Cognitive Functions." *Journal Research in Science Teaching* 2 (1964): 7–16.

Scott, N. "Strategy of Inquiry and Styles of Categorization." *Journal Research in Science Teaching* 4 (1966): 143–154.

Scott, N. "Strategy of Inquiry and Styles of Categorization: A Three Year Exploratory Study." *Journal Research in Science Teaching* 7 (1970): 95–102.

Scott, N. "Cognitive Style and Inquiry Strategy: A Five Year Study." Paper presented at American Educational Research Association, 1972.

Scott, N., and Sigel, I. E. "Effects of Inquiry Training in Physical Science on

Creativity and Cognitive Styles of Elementary School Children." Research report for U. S. Office of Education, 1965.

Serafica, F. C., and Sigel, I. E. "Styles of Categorization and Reading Disability." *Journal of Reading Behavior* 2 (2) (1970): 105–115.

Sigel, I. E. "Cognitive Style and Personality Dynamics." Interim progress report for National Institute of Mental Health, M-2983 (1961a).

Sigel, I. E. "Cognitive Style and Memory for Case History Material." Unpublished manuscript, Merrill-Palmer Institute, Detroit, Michigan, 1961b.

Sigel, I. E. "How Intelligence Tests Limit Understanding of Intelligence." *Merrill-Palmer Quarterly* 9 (1963): 39–56.

Sigel, I. E. "The Development of Classificatory Skills in Young Children: A Training Program." *Young Children* 26 (1971): 170–184.

Sigel, I. E.; Anderson, L. M.; and Shapiro, H. "Categorization Behavior of Lower and Middle Class Negro Pre-school Children: Differences in Dealing with Representation of Familiar Objects." *Journal of Negro Education* 35 (1966): 218–229.

Sigel, I. E.; Jarman, P. D.; and Hanesian, H. "Styles of Categorization and Their Intellectual and Personality Correlates in Young Children." *Human Development* 10 (1967): 1–17.

Sigel, I. E., and Olmstead, Patricia P. "Modification of Cognitive Skills Among Lower Class Black Children." In *Disadvantaged Child*, vol. 3, edited by J. Hellmuth, New York: Bruner, Mazel, 1970.

Wallach, M. A., and Kogan, N. *Modes of Thinking in Young Children*. New York: Holt, Rinehart, and Winston, 1965.

Witkin, H. A.; Dyk, R. B.; Faterson, H. D.; Goodenough, D. R.; and Kays, S. A. *Psychological Differentiation*. New York: Wiley, 1962.

Witkin, H. A.; Goodenough, D. R.; and Kays, S. A. "Stability of Cognitive Style from Childhood to Young Adulthood." *Journal of Personality and Social Psychology* 1 (1967): 291–300.

Yando, R. M., and Kagan, J. "The Effect of Teacher Tempo on the Child." *Child Development* 39 (1968): 27–34.

Biographical notes

Richard H. Coop is currently an associate professor of educational psychology at the University of North Carolina at Chapel Hill and is the coordinator of the undergraduate educational psychology program. His special area of research is cognitive development and its application to the classroom. Dr. Coop has been a high school science and biology teacher and has coached at both the junior and senior high school level. In 1972 he was given the *Peabody Excellence in Teaching Award* by the graduate students in the School of Education at the University of North Carolina. He is also a Danforth Associate. Dr. Coop received his B.S. and M.A. degrees from Western Kentucky University and his Ed.D. degree from Indiana University.

Kinnard White is professor of educational psychology at the University of North Carolina at Chapel Hill. His research interest is in the area of mental health and schooling. He has also done considerable work on the evaluation of school programs and practices. Dr. White holds a B.S. from Florida State University and an M.S. and Ph.D from Indiana University.

Phillip Schlechty is associate professor of education at the University of North Carolina at Chapel Hill. Dr. Schlechty's special area of expertise is in educational sociology, and he is particularly interested in studying the interaction between psychological and sociological variables in the classroom. He has developed a series of training programs for secondary social studies teachers. These programs, which have been funded by the National Science Foundation, train teachers in the teaching of sociology and in the application of sociological principles to an analysis of school settings. Dr. Schlechty holds a B.S., M.A., and Ph.D. from Ohio State University.

Thomas Good received his A.B. in 1965 in political science at the University of Illinois. Subsequently, he was awarded an M.A. (1967) and Ph.D. (1968) in educational psychology from Indiana University. For 3 years (1968–1971) Dr. Good was associated with the University of Texas at Austin, where he served as an assistant professor of educational psychology and as a research scientist in the Research and Development Center for Teacher Education. For a year he also served as staff development coordinator for the Early Childhood program of the Southwest Educational Development Laboratory in Austin. Presently, he is at the University of Missouri at Columbia, where he is an associate professor of curriculum and instruction. He is also on research appointment at the Center for Research in Social Behavior at the University of Missouri.

Jere Brophy received his B.S. (Honors Program) in 1962 in psychology at Loyola University in Chicago. He later received an M.A. and Ph.D. (1967) from the Committee on Human Development at the University of Chicago, where he majored in both human development and clinical psychology. In 1967–1968 he was research associate (assistant professor) in the Committee on Human Development of the University of Chicago, in which capacity he served as project director of the follow-up phase of the Study of the Cognitive Environments of Urban Preschool Children. Since 1968 Dr. Brophy has been at the University of Texas at Austin, where he is presently associate professor of educational psychology, a research scientist in the Research and Development Center for Teacher Education, and the staff development coordinator for the Early Childhood Program of the Southwest Educational Development Laboratory (SEDL) in Austin. His research interests cover a broad range of topics in the areas of child development and education, although his primary interest is in child rearing and education, especially the education of young children.

Barbara H. Wasik is currently an associate professor of school psychology and the assistant dean of the Graduate School at the University of North Carolina at Chapel Hill. She is also a member of the research faculty at the Frank Porter Graham Child Development Center and serves as a member of the Governor's Advisory Committee on Youth Development. Most recently, she has been involved as a consultant to Janus House, a residential facility for delinquent boys, and has instituted a successful behavior modification program for use with these delinquents. Dr. Wasik earned a B.A. degree in psychology from the University of Georgia and M.A. and Ph.D. degrees from Florida State University. She was also a postdoctoral research fellow at Duke University.

Daniel Solomon is currently a social psychologist in the Division of Psychological Services of the Montgomery County, Maryland, Public Schools. He is a researcher, and has worked previously at the Institute for Juvenile Research and the Center for the Study of Liberal Education for Adults, both in Chicago. He has conducted numerous studies investigating social psychological processes in education. He received his social psychological training at the University of Michigan, where he received a Ph.D. in 1960.

Mark I. Oberlander is a psychological research worker and a practicing clinical psychologist with a 1967 Ph.D. from the University of Chicago. He has conducted several studies in the areas of personality development and creativity. He recently conducted a study in Israel to assess the effect of different educational environments on the development of creativity in children.

Patricia Waller is an associate professor of public health and a research associate at the Highway Safety Research Center at the University of North Carolina at Chapel Hill. She has taught psychology in the School of Education and clinical psychology in the psychology department. She is currently conducting research on behavioral aspects of highway safety. Dr. Waller earned her B.A. and M.A. from the University of Miami and her Ph.D. from the University of North Carolina.

John Gaa, assistant professor of educational psychology at the University of North Carolina at Chapel Hill, is developing and researching methods for motivating students in the classroom. He is presently investigating the effects of goal setting on the academic performances of students. Dr. Gaa is a member of the Board of Directors of Janus House, a residential facility for juvenile delinquent boys. He has also taught at the Michigan Catholic Conference Job Training Center. In 1973, he received the *Peabody Excellence in Teaching Award*. Dr. Gaa earned his B.S. degree from Michigan State University and his M.S. and Ph.D. degrees from the University of Wisconsin.

Stanley Coopersmith has been involved in studying the factors involved in forming and changing self-esteem for over a decade. He is currently engaged in a program to build self-esteem in the classroom at the Bancroft School, Walnut Creek, California. He regularly conducts workshops and training programs for teacher and parent groups interested in raising esteem. He has consulted widely with government agencies, and his book *The Antecedents of Self-Esteem* summarizes current knowledge on the subject. Since receiving his doctorate from Cornell University he has taught at Wesleyan University and the University of California, Davis.

Ronald Feldman received his doctorate in psychology from Stanford University, and is now a lecturer in the Department of Psychology at the University of California, Davis. After receiving his degree, Dr. Feldman worked as a teacher and resource person in nursery schools and thereby gained direct teaching experience to complement his research and theoretical training.

Mary N. Meeker is an associate professor at Loyola University of Los Angeles and is the director of training for school psychology and psychometry. She has served as a consultant to many different state departments of education in the United States as well as to educational programs in Canada, South Africa, Belgium, and Norway. Her special expertise is in the area of identification of intellectual patterns among exceptional children. Her first degree in psychology was earned at the University of Texas, and her master's and doctorate degrees were awarded by the University of Southern California.

Irving E. Sigel is a past president (1971–1972) of the Developmental Division of the American Psychological Association. Dr. Sigel is one of the foremost American psychologists in the area of cognitive development, and he has written numerous articles relating cognitive functioning to the educational process. In addition to his research work, Dr. Sigel has recently served as a principal for a preschool program for disadvantaged children in Buffalo, New York. He is also a recognized American authority on the developmental psychology of Jean Piaget. Dr. Sigel has been a professor of psychology at the State University of New York at Buffalo. He has also taught at Michigan State University, Wayne State University, and the Merrill-Palmer Institute at Detroit. He also served as director of research at Merrill-Palmer. Dr. Sigel is currently leading a research section on cognitive development at the Educational Testing Service in Princeton, N.J. He was awarded his B.A. degree from Clark University and M.A. and Ph.D. degrees from the University of Chicago.

Index